The Cultural Analysis of Kinship

The Cultural Analysis of Kinship

The Legacy of David M. Schneider

Edited by
RICHARD FEINBERG AND
MARTIN OTTENHEIMER

University of Illinois Press
URBANA AND CHICAGO

Library of Congress Cataloging-in-Publication Data
The cultural analysis of kinship : the legacy of David M. Schneider /
edited by Richard Feinberg and Martin Ottenheimer.
p.   cm.
Includes bibliographical references and index.
ISBN 0-252-02673-x (cloth : alk. paper)
1. Kinship—Philosophy. 2. Cultural relativism. 3. Schneider, David
Murray, 1918–1995. I. Feinberg, Richard. II. Ottenheimer, Martin.
GN487.C83   2001
306.83—dc21   2001000389

Contents

Acknowledgments

We are indebted to many people for making this book possible. In particular, the editors would like to thank the contributors to the two panels from which the volume has emerged. Their insight, patience, and good humor made a potentially onerous job into a gratifying experience for both of us. In addition to those colleagues whose work appears in this volume, Michael Salovesh and Loki Pandey participated in the sessions, made important observations, and offered invaluable encouragement.

We are grateful to the manuscript reviewers—Mac Marshall, Andrew Strathern, and Pamela Stewart—for their careful readings and constructive criticisms. The Central States Anthropological Society and the American Anthropological Association provided venues in which we were able to gather and discuss the difficult and complex issues addressed herein. Elizabeth Dulany of the University of Illinois Press supported the project and helped guide us through the publication process. Our wives, Nancy Grim and Harriet Ottenheimer, also deserve much credit for their inspiration and encouragement during the creation of this book.

Finally, without David Schneider this book would not have come into existence. While most contributors may disagree with specific aspects of Schneider's symbolic anthropology and his treatment of kinship as a cultural system, he raised important questions and forced us to rethink some of the central issues in our discpline.

The Cultural Analysis of Kinship

Introduction:
Schneider's Cultural Analysis of Kinship and Its Implications for Anthropological Relativism

RICHARD FEINBERG

Cultural Relativism and the Study of Kinship

FEW ACADEMIC BATTLEGROUNDS have been so littered with the ink-stained corpses of their scholarly protagonists as those surrounding kinship and cultural relativism. Few scholars have staked out a position in such stark terms, then fought and died amid such academic controversy as did David Schneider. This collection is a critical appraisal of Schneider's work: his contribution to symbolic anthropology, and to the study of kinship.

Kinship has occupied a central position in anthropological discourse for well over a century. Lewis Henry Morgan, often spoken of appropriately as the father of American anthropology, called attention to the subject in his pioneering ethnographic contribution, *League of the Iroquois* (1969 [1851]: 83–87). His *Systems of Consanguinity and Affinity of the Human Family* (1871) was the first systematic, cross-cultural analysis of kinship nomenclature.[1] Over the next hundred years, virtually every major figure in American, British, and French anthropology felt compelled to consider kinship, sometimes briefly, but more often at considerable length. Such discussion can be found in writings of J. F. McLennan (1970 [1865]), Sir E. B. Tylor (1871, 1889), Émile Durkheim and Marcel Mauss (1967), W. H. R. Rivers (1900, 1906, 1907, 1910, 1914, 1915), A. R. Radcliffe-Brown (1950, 1965 [1952]), and Bronislaw Malinowski (1913, 1929, 1930). Claude Lévi-Strauss's *Elementary Structures of Kinship* (1969 [1949]), in its first half century as a modern anthropological classic, generated debates among such luminaries as George Homans (Homans and

Schneider 1955), Rodney Needham (1962), Edmund Leach (1961, 1970), and Robin Fox (1967). Major figures in the British functionalist and structural-functionalist schools, including Meyer Fortes (1945, 1949, 1950, 1969), E. E. Evans-Pritchard (1940, 1951), and Sir Raymond Firth (1936, 1957, 1964) made their reputations largely through kinship studies—the first two in Africa, the last in Polynesia. In American anthropological history, the kinship debate is most closely associated with Alfred Kroeber (1909, 1917, 1936, 1938), Robert Lowie (e.g., 1920, 1929, 1930, 1932, 1948), George Peter Murdock (e.g., 1940, 1947, 1949, 1960), and perhaps Fred Eggan (1937, 1950, 1972). During the 1950s and 1960s, when American anthropology experienced a brief infatuation with componential analysis, such leading scholars as Floyd Lounsbury (1956, 1964a, 1964b), Ward Goodenough (1965, 1967, 1970), and Anthony Wallace and John Atkins (1965; Wallace and Atkins 1960) explored the use of formal analysis of kinship terminologies as a tool to elucidate human cognition. Coming from the vantage point of symbolic anthropology, Clifford Geertz (with his wife, Hildred, as senior author) wrote his obligatory book on kinship in 1975. Then sometime during the mid-1970s, following an announcement by David Schneider that kinship did not exist in any culture known to humankind, kinship studies largely dropped from sight.[2]

While anthropologists were losing interest in kinship, however, scholars in other academic disciplines and ordinary people the world over continued to treat it as a vital concern. Sociologists, psychologists, political scientists, economists, and theologians still examine variations in household organization, making claims about a putative connection between poverty, crime, and allegedly pathological familial forms. Such kin-related issues as teen pregnancy, children born out of wedlock, and the absence of a "father figure" are held to cause violence, alcoholism, drug abuse, demoralization and despair, urban decay, and rural poverty. "Family values," meaning adulation of the nuclear family, has been a centerpiece of American political campaigns at least since the middle 1980s. Televangelists and op ed columnists continue touting a connection between an alleged moral breakdown, the elimination of school prayer, loss of personal responsibility, a decline of marriage and the family as the cornerstone of social life, and a plethora of social ills.[3] Meanwhile, in the natural sciences, sociobiology emerged claiming status as "the new synthesis." Treating kinship as a biogenetic fact rather than a cultural construct, E. O. Wilson and his followers introduced such notions as "kin selection" and "inclusive fitness" in their endeavor to account for social behavior in biological terms.

Other kin-related issues have captured popular imagination on an international scale. The women's and gay rights movements have challenged widely accepted definitions of marriage and parenthood, prompting heated conflicts among social policy makers and church leaders over whether homosexual partnerships deserve the religious sanctions and legal protections currently afforded heterosexual spouses. Whether adoptees are "real" or "fictive" kin is an increasingly compelling question as "right-to-lifers" advocate adoption in place of abortion and adopted children, with growing frequency, seek out their "birth parents." Perhaps most dramatically of all, new reproductive technologies—including sperm donation, surrogate motherhood, and, most recently, cloning—have brought to the forefront Schneider's (1968, 1972, 1984) questions: How are relatives to be defined? And "what is kinship all about?" Ironically, such questions are now being argued in the courts more often than in the halls of academe.

As a focus of concern in anthropology, cultural relativism is only slightly younger than the field of kinship studies, going back to the late nineteenth-century writings of Franz Boas in the United States (e.g., see several of the articles in his 1966 collection, *Race, Language and Culture*) and the early twentieth-century writings of Bronislaw Malinowski in England (e.g., 1929: chap. 13). Cultural relativism was introduced as an alternative to the mid- to late nineteenth-century's evolutionary perspectives, which held that cultures could be ranked according to their degree of "civilization" or moral and intellectual merit.[4] By contrast, most twentieth-century anthropologists have taken the position that each culture has its own merits, that each works in its own way, that our job as anthropologists is to try to understand others rather than make value judgments about them, and that most beliefs and practices, however strange they may appear at first, are eminently sensible when viewed in relation to their cultural context. Relativism in this sense has been the leitmotif of anthropology throughout the past century, and it continues to be taught as a central tenet in almost every introductory class in sociocultural anthropology. Yet relativism also has come under fire both within and from outside of the discipline.

Evolutionary schemas, although out of favor through most of the past century, never entirely disappeared from British and American anthropology, and their leading proponents—people like Leslie White and V. Gordon Childe—were never fully comfortable with relativism. Marvin Harris, at least as far back as 1968, complained that cultural relativism can serve as an excuse for anthropologists to avoid taking a stand against injustice and oppression; others with very different theoretical predilections (e.g., Hatch 1983; Turner 1997) have come to similar conclusions about relativism and its moral limitations.

In popular discourse, the attack on relativism has been still more strident and uncompromising. Political commentators from America's "religious right" have railed for years against "secular humanism" and its attack on the absolute moral standards propounded in the Bible. They hold secular humanism and relativism accountable for our alleged loss of compassion and moral responsibility, for the presumed breakdown of marriage and the family, and for the host of related social problems cited above. Thus, kinship and relativism are joined as much in public consciousness as they are in academic anthropology. That connection provides the backdrop for this volume.

Schneider, Kinship, and Symbolic Anthropology

David M. Schneider, who died in 1995, was an important figure in cultural and symbolic anthropology and in the study of kinship. He was among the strongest proponents of what might be called the "meanings and symbols" approach to culture, and he systematically advocated taking one's informants' statements as authoritative even when they were counterintuitive from the anthropologist's perspective. He has influenced the discipline through several articles and books, most notably *American Kinship: A Cultural Account* (1968) and *A Critique of the Study of Kinship* (1984), and through many students who have gone on to become prominent anthropologists in their own right.[5]

Schneider was born in Brooklyn, New York, in 1918. His parents were immigrants from Eastern Europe, who, for much of their adult lives, were active in the American Communist Party. Although they did not speak to their children about their party affiliation, they were open about their political sympathies, which David largely adopted as his own.

David's relationship with his family was, at best, ambivalent. He liked and respected his father, but he had a difficult time with his mother, and he resented his younger brother, who was born when David was six. In his autobiographical interviews, Schneider says that he expressed his displeasure by doing poorly in school, which eventually led his parents to send him to Cherry Lawn, a "progressive" boarding school in Darien, Connecticut. He viewed his parents' decision as an act of abandonment, and he appears never again to have felt close to members of his natal family.

Schneider remained at Cherry Lawn until his high school graduation, after which he entered the New York State College of Agriculture at Cornell University. He intended to major in agricultural bacteriology, but he disliked math and languages, and he reports that he could not pass the organic chemistry requirement. To get off academic probation he began to take social science courses, in which he did well; and during that period R. Lauriston Sharp introduced him to anthropology. It was also at college that he met his lifelong friend—and intellectual adversary—Ward Goodenough, and his wife, Addy. David and Addy were married on June 17, 1940, the day of their Cornell graduation. Their marriage appears not always to have been the happiest, but it endured until her death in 1982.

Schneider's undergraduate career was undistinguished, and he reports— undoubtedly with characteristic exaggeration—that he graduated with a D average. While Goodenough went on to Yale to study with George Peter Murdock, David remained at Cornell for an additional year, earning an M.A. under Sharp.

After receiving his master's degree, he briefly joined Goodenough at Yale. There he met Geoffrey Gorer, who introduced him to psychoanalytic anthropology. Through Gorer he also met Margaret Mead, who apparently saw in David a scholarly potential that others had missed. Shortly thereafter, he was drafted into the army. Treating the army as an opportunity for field research, he took notes on his experience and published his first two articles, "The Culture of the Army Clerk" (1946) and "The Social Dynamics of Physical Disability in Army Basic Training" (1947).

Because of a personal dislike for Murdock, Schneider did not return to Yale upon his discharge from the army but applied instead for a Social Science Research Council demobilization award. When this was unsuccessful, Mead prevailed upon Clyde Kluckhohn to have him admitted to Harvard's doctoral program in social relations. There, he worked with Kluckhohn and sociologists Talcott Parsons and George Homans. His initial interest was psychological anthropology and, in 1947, he co-edited with Kluckhohn and Henry Murray an important collection of essays in that field. A stint of fieldwork on the Micronesian island of Yap from 1947 to 1948 led Schneider to look seriously at kinship. At length, he concluded that his predecessors, Murdock, Rivers, Radcliffe-Brown, and others, "were absolutely all wrong about kinship terms" (1995:206). Nonetheless, much of David's early work on Yapese social structure (e.g., see 1953, 1962) can easily be fit into the traditional structural-functionalist mold.

Schneider's dissatisfaction with previous approaches to kinship led to a career-long preoccupation with the American kinship system. As he put the matter, "the simplest, most obvious way to demonstrate that they were all wrong was to use common American kinship terms as an example." In his first publication on this topic (Schneider and Homans 1955), he challenged the conventional distinction between vocative and referential kin terms and noted the variety of terms commonly applied to relatives, many of them outside the realm of what anthropologists typically recognize as kin terms proper. This work, in turn, led him to conclude that the definition of kinship was far more problematic than had generally been recognized—a theme to which he would return.

Schneider's collaboration with Homans also led to his first major public controversy. In *Marriage, Authority, and Final Causes* (1955), Homans and Schneider disputed Lévi-Strauss's explanation for the predominance of matrilateral over patrilateral cross-cousin marriage. Earlier, Radcliffe-Brown had noted a tendency for men in patrilineal societies to marry their matrilateral cross-cousins—their mother's brother's daughters. Radcliffe-Brown attributed this tendency to a warm, emotionally close relationship in many patrilineal societies between a man and his sister's son, and he suggested that a boy's sentimental attachment to his maternal uncle is then transferred to the uncle's daughter. Since patrilineal societies are far more common ethnographically than their matrilineal counterparts, it stands to reason that matrilateral cross-cousin marriage should be more common than the patrilateral variant.

In *The Elementary Structures of Kinship,* Lévi-Strauss argued (contra Radcliffe-Brown) that a cultural phenomenon such as unilateral cross-cousin marriage cannot be explained in terms of individual sentiments. Following the lead of Mauss and Durkheim, he proposed that a rule directing men to marry their matrilateral cross-cousins is, for structural reasons, more productive of social solidarity than the reverse. His alliance model was bolstered by the fact that it works equally well with either matrilineal or patrilineal descent and is, therefore, not tied to statistical vagaries.

Homans and Schneider objected that what Lévi-Strauss had presented was a *final* cause—that matrilateral cross-cousin marriage exists because it is "good for society." Marriage is contracted by people, they argued, not societies, and Lévi-Strauss had told us nothing about why a man would *want* to marry his matrilateral cross-cousin. The answer to that question requires the search for an *efficient* cause, and for that, one must return to individual sentiments, per Radcliffe-Brown.

Homans and Schneider's argument was widely accepted until the appearance of *Structure and Sentiment* by Rodney Needham, an equally irascible protagonist. After forswearing any hint of polemic or asperity (1962:viii), Needham proceeded to declare of *Marriage, Authority, and Final Causes* that "its conclusions are fallacious, its method unsound, and the argument literally preposterous" (1). Homans and Schneider failed to recognize, according to Needham, that Lévi-Strauss was really concerned with *prescriptive, not preferential* systems of cross-cousin marriage; and if a man has no choice as to whether or not he will marry his matrilateral cross-cousin, the issue of individual sentiments becomes irrelevant.

Schneider replied with his now-famous article, "Some Muddles in the Models: Or How the System Really Works" (1965), in which he disavowed the central argument of his book with Homans (he has since referred to it as "the Homans book") but contended that Needham was equally mistaken—that from a structural viewpoint it makes no difference how rigidly a rule is enforced; what matters is the rule's existence. Therefore, Lévi-Strauss's failure to make explicit that he was only concerned with prescriptive marriage systems was not an oversight; rather he had chosen not to distinguish between prescriptive and preferential marriage systems because the difference is irrelevant to his argument. In a perverse twist of fate, Lévi-Strauss (1969) proclaimed in the preface to the English edition of *The Elementary Structures of Kinship,* which Needham had edited and helped to translate, that Schneider was correct.

As all this was going on, Schneider worked to refine the culture concept that had been developed by Kroeber, Kluckhohn, and Parsons. Central to this view of culture was its separation from biology, individual psychology, and, perhaps most notably, the social system. Whereas the social system comprised regular patterns of behavior engaged in by concrete individuals, culture was a system of symbols and meanings. In important ways, this echoed the distinction between *langue* and *parole* (Saussure 1959). Culture, like *langue* or language, is an underlying code shared by all members of the community. Just as knowledge of a language does not tell us what anyone will say, to understand a particular culture does not necessarily tell us what someone will do. People immersed in different cultural systems may act similarly for very different reasons, and people sharing the same culture may behave quite differently if their situations differ in some salient way.

Schneider (1968:1) defined culture as "a system of symbols," and a symbol as "something which stands for something else, or some things else, where there is no necessary or intrinsic relationship between the symbol and that which it symbolizes." Since symbols are arbitrary social constructs, anything might be used as a symbol and attached to any meaning. The existence of a symbol in one community does not ensure that it will be recognized in any other, nor will the denotatum associated with a symbol in one community necessarily appear elsewhere. A cultural unit—that is, a category distinguished and defined by members of a particular community through the manipulation of symbols and meanings—is specific to a particular culture, and whether any construct exists cross-culturally is an empirical question. Thus, anyone attempting to apply Schneider's approach must listen to what his or her informants say and avoid making prior assumptions.

Perhaps Schneider's most widely cited book is *American Kinship: A Cul-*

tural Account. This book was in part the product of a survey of kin-term use among Chicago residents; more importantly, Schneider used it to illustrate how one might conduct and present an ethnography based on his culture concept. He attempted to look at American kinship in the same way that he would approach a foreign culture: by eliminating prior assumptions about the culture's units and their distinctive features; identifying the meanings and symbols through which members of the community define their own cultural units; and using his interpretive insight to discover the order underlying his informants' cultural system. The result was a view of American kinship that differs from the common sense perspective held by most American natives, but which was intended to make that common sense perspective intelligible to the critical observer.[6]

Above all, Schneider contended that kinship is a cultural system, not a set of biological facts. Americans use biological relatedness as a symbol in terms of which kinship is defined and differentiated from other cultural domains; but the application of that symbol is not dictated by any objective, biogenetic reality. Often people who have no biogenetic relationship to one another are considered kin, while others who are biologically related may be denied kinship status.

American culture, Schneider argued, encompasses two great orders which he termed the "Order of Nature" and the "Order of Law." Kinship for Americans, he said, is unique in that it partakes of both orders, being defined in terms of two distinctive features. These features are shared natural or biogenetic substance (Order of Nature) and a code for conduct involving diffuse and enduring solidarity (Order of Law). Americans commonly speak of the first in terms of "blood," as when they refer to "blood relatives" or say that "blood is thicker than water." In referring to the second, they use such expressions as "a relationship" and "love." The core symbol holding this system together is sexual intercourse or coitus. It is through the symbol of sexual intercourse that husband and wife express their love for one another, creating a "relationship in law," in the process joining their biological substance to create new relatives "by blood." Schneider called love between blood relatives such as parent and child "cognatic love"; it excludes sexual relations, which would be incest. Love between husband and wife is "conjugal love" and receives its highest expression in coitus or the act of "making love."

In cases where both substance and diffuse, enduring solidarity are present, the relationship is clearly one of kinship. People in such positions are "blood relatives" and would be typified by a woman who gives birth to a child, then nurtures and raises it. If only one component is present, Americans may or may not consider the person in question to be kin, either designation being correct according to the definitions and symbols that make up American culture. Thus, in the case of in-laws, shared substance is normally absent whereas adherence to the appropriate code for conduct is present, and Americans are divided as to whether or not in-laws are relatives. Similarly, adoptive relatives, characterized by diffuse, enduring solidarity but not shared substance, are sometimes differentiated from "real" relatives and sometimes considered to be "real relatives" of a special type. The inverse situation applies to a "natural" relative such as a woman who gives birth to a child and then gives it up for adoption; shared substance is present, but not diffuse, enduring solidarity. In this case, Americans may say that the woman is the child's mother because the natural relationship cannot be severed, or they may deny the mother-child relationship because the woman is not acting as a mother should.

American Kinship was followed by a pair of articles in which Schneider took his 1968 conclusions in unexpected directions. In 1969 he noted that kinship, nationality, and religion in American culture are all defined in terms of an articulation between shared substance and diffuse, enduring solidarity. If these three cultural domains share the same distinctive features, however, then those features do not distinguish any one from the other two. And if the three domains are indistinguishable from one another, the inevitable conclusion is that American culture has no one discrete domain deserving of the label "kinship." In 1972 he added that since kinship is an English word, and since anthropologists from Morgan onward have been involved in studying what they termed kinship, if it were to exist in any culture it should exist in ours. Since kinship does not exist in American culture, Schneider (1972:50) argued, "*In the way in which Morgan and his followers have used it, it does not exist in any culture known to man*" (emphasis in original). This declaration was perhaps Schneider's most enduring legacy. Upon reaching this startling conclusion, he noted with more than a touch of self-deprecating irony that he may have "devoted a good part of my intellectual life to the industrious study of a non-subject" (51). His last major work, *A Critique of the Study of Kinship,* explored the implications of kinship's nonexistence and how the illusion of its existence had distorted cultural analysis throughout the history of anthropology.

Symbolism, Kinship, and Cross-Cultural Comparison

Fundamental to Schneider's position is the characterization of culture as a system of symbols. Since the connection between a symbol and its referent, by definition, is arbitrary, the variation among cultural categories and systems is restricted only by the limits of human imagination. In contrast with the cognitive anthropologists of the 1950s, 1960s, and 1970s, who were interested in the different ways that culture could divide and organize reality, Schneider viewed culture as creating its own reality. Thus, a ghost is as real as a corpse in a culture that recognizes ghosts, and it should be taken just as seriously.

This is the point that he was making in his famous umpire allegory. The story, which Schneider repeated to almost every class he taught at the University of Chicago (see Leaf, this volume), has three umpires speaking at a meeting of their professional association. In order of experience and erudition, the three declared, "I calls 'em as I sees 'em," "I calls 'em as dey is," and "Dey ain't nuttin' 'til I calls 'em." The third umpire was right, not because he was better at calling balls and strikes than any of the others, but because he recognized that until a person, defined by the rules of baseball as an umpire, pronounces something to be a ball or a strike, all one has is a round object hurtling through space. The concept of "baseball," "pitcher," "batter," "umpire," "ball," "strike," and, indeed, the game itself, are all matters of cultural definition. In fact, such notions as "object," "movement," and "space" are also matters of cultural definition, making unthinkable the attempt even to discuss a presumably external reality in the absence of cultural presuppositions.

The most important lesson to be drawn from Schneider's deconstruction of kinship is an appreciation of just how difficult it is to put aside one's preconceptions and allow one's ethnographic analysis to proceed exclusively from indigenous cultural categories. After all, if kinship, which seems to be based on inescapable biological facts of life, does not exist as a cross-cultural universal, and arguably may not exist *anywhere*, then the existence of *any* cross-cultural universals must be called into serious question. This line of reasoning leads to a Boasian particularism—perhaps even solipsism—in which generalization, explanation, and any attempt at developing theory become all but impossible.

Schneider denied that he was opposed to cross-cultural comparison, and he claimed to support the formulation of general laws relating to human action. In several places he has identified himself as a materialist (e.g., 1995:6) and positivist (e.g., 79–83). As a graduate student at the University of Chicago in the early 1970s, I even heard him state on a number of occasions that he was, in the last analysis, a structural-functionalist—perhaps not entirely surprising for a devoted follower of Talcott Parsons. His objection to comparison, he averred, was not that it was being done, but that all too often anthropologists were trying to compare incomparable units. In order to do cross-cultural comparison, he proposed, one must first identify the symbols and meanings that exist in each community and then ask if the same (or similar) symbol systems also exist elsewhere. In one of his clearest statements on this point, Schneider (1976:160) said:

> The fundamental axiom of cultural analysis is that it is the native definition which is the basic data, it is the very stuff of which a cultural analysis consists. The imposition of *a priori* definitions . . . on a variety of different cultures is precisely what must be avoided. The solution is really quite simple and is one used all the time: starting with the Western European cultural definition and then looking in each culture for something that is vaguely like it, then proceeding to identify the similarities and the differences, and by continuing to compare, expanding the horizon to the point where there are a series of different cultural definitions, a series of different cultural meanings and an array of various symbols for those meanings. This provides not only a comparative study of the general area, but also should provide a series of intensive studies of particular cultures.

Similarly, in the same article where he denied the existence of kinship as a cultural category, Schneider (1972:48) explained how comparative work, in his view, should proceed. He declared that

> the key to the comparative problem is in locating the symbolic elements from a careful analysis of the units which the culture itself defines. We do not say, "Let's look at lineages," we ask instead what units this culture postulates, and the answer may have nothing whatever to do with lineages. We must then follow these symbolic elements throughout the particular culture, wherever they may lead and in whatever forms they may be found. In short, framing a question is the first step. It must then be answered for our own culture as an hypothesis. One then takes those cultural constructs and asks if any other culture has anything like it or not, how they differ, where and in what way, and where they appear to be the same. . . . it is fundamental to start with hypotheses about the analyst's own culture first because that is the first culture he can come to understand. . . . Ultimately, if he is really lucky, he may learn something about what Kroeber called "the nature of culture" or, if you prefer, the structure of the human mind.

Schneider's claims to be a positivist and materialist, and his denunciation of postmodernism (1995:8–10) seem more than a shade incongruous considering that his deconstruction of kinship as a cultural category (1969, 1972, 1984) is frequently cited as a forerunner of postmodern analysis in anthropology.[7] Yet some of the most productive work that Schneider inspired was comparative in nature. I particularly have in mind a series of monographs on such topics as adoption, incest, and siblingship, growing out of meetings of the Association for Social Anthropology in Oceania (e.g., Carroll 1970a; Brady 1976; Huntsman and McLean 1976; Marshall 1981). Moreover, Schneider thought highly enough of these enterprises to write an introduction to one volume (Schneider 1976) and a conclusion to another (Schneider 1981). Geertz (1966:5), whom Schneider often cited approvingly, has argued that symbols exist not in individual minds but at the level of interpersonal understanding, making them "as public as marriage and as observable as agriculture." And Schneider, himself, even at his most stridently solipsistic, contended that "systems of symbols and meanings can be compared as easily as systems of reproduction can be compared from one society to another" (1972:40).

While Schneider sometimes seemed to support comparative studies, however, his attitude was at best ambivalent, and some of his comments suggest that he was less than enthusiastic about the very conception of projects that he inspired and which were conducted by his students. For example, he devoted much of his introduction to the incest volume (1976) to the proposition that phenomena typically grouped together under the heading of "incest prohibitions" are so diverse that they belie the cross-cultural existence of such a category. And in his recent autobiographical interviews (1995; see also 1972:59), he suggested that anthropologists have ceased to study not just kinship but descent, alliance, the incest taboo, religion, economics, politics, and other supposed "institutions" for similar reasons. In short, despite Schneider's protestations to the contrary, cross-cultural comparison based upon shared symbols is, to say the least, a challenge to sustain.

A Critique of Schneider's Study of Kinship

> Well the first thing you know, Old Jed's a Millionaire.
> The *kinfolk* said, "Jed, move away from there."
> Said, "Californie is the place you oughtta be,"
> So they loaded up the truck, and they moved to Beverly.
> —"The Beverly Hillbillies"

I have argued elsewhere (see particularly Feinberg 1979) that Schneider's deconstruction of American kinship is mistaken on several grounds. This conclusion is inescapable, given his fundamental proposition that the natives are the ultimate authority on what exists in their culture. Every English-speaking American I know is familiar with such terms as "kin," "kinship," "kinsmen," "kinfolk," "relatives," and "family," and everyone has a fairly clear idea of what those terms mean. Therefore, by Schneider's criteria, kinship *must* be a cultural domain in America. If his distinctive features are incapable of differentiating kinship from nationality and religion, it shows not the absence of kinship but a defect in his analysis—he must be mistaken in his identification of distinctive features.

While Schneider, in my opinion, is correct that kinship has something to do with ideas about shared substance and diffuse, enduring solidarity, I would suggest that the distinctive features exist at a more specific level: relatives share a particular kind of substance and manifest solidarity in specific ways that are different from those in which one demonstrates solidarity with one's nation or one's church. Schneider's seemingly minor shift from talking about "shared biogenetic substance" to "shared natural substance" may be important in this respect since the substance one shares with one's compatriots is land or native soil, whereas the substance that one shares with kin is biogenetic.[8]

Although I believe Schneider to be mistaken in his contention that kinship does not exist in American culture, I am sympathetic to his admonition to begin one's analyses with native categories and avoid imposing assumptions deriving from one's own cultural background. And I agree with Schneider that if we are to take this admonition seriously, we cannot make prior assumptions as to what symbols, meanings, units, or categories we will find in any culture but our own. Thus, while kinship does exist in American culture, whether or not it exists anywhere else is an empirical question, the answer to which must be demonstrated, not assumed. In fact, it is unlikely that any other culture will have a domain identical with that which we in America call "kinship," and the question becomes whether the community under study has some cultural domain similar enough to the one we call kinship that it merits the same label.[9]

In this respect, I agree with Harold W. Scheffler (e.g., 1970, 1976) that kinship in the United States is fundamentally a genealogical phenomenon. Since "kinship" is an English word, denoting an American cultural category, and since that category (as I understand it) is genealogically defined, then other cultural systems must be defined at least partially in terms of genealogical relationships if they are to be termed "*kinship* systems."[10] I think it can be shown empirically that most communities do have systems of relationship that are defined at least partially in genealogical terms. Thus, kinship is, in fact, a viable unit for cross-cultural comparison. Along with Schneider, however, I am suspicious of claims to the universality of kinship. Indeed, by the criteria I have outlined here, it would appear that the Trobriand Islands as described by Susan P. Montague (this volume) are a community without a kinship system.

The suggestion that kinship is not a cross-cultural universal, and that it may not exist at all, has been troubling to many anthropologists, including those contributing to this collection. Many colleagues have responded by simply ceasing to study kinship in a systematic manner; hence, the paucity of books, articles, and conference presentations about kinship over the past two decades. Others have attempted to redefine it in such a way as to bring it back into anthropological focus. For example, Montague (this volume) treats Trobriand kinship as a "multiple slotting system" involving dietary rules, control of certain forms of magic, and reciprocal exchange. Dwight W. Read and Murray J. Leaf (both, this volume) see it as a system of logical relationships that can be usefully represented in terms of mathematical models. Robert McKinley identifies kinship as "a philosophy" and reverses Schneider by saying that others clearly have kinship systems; Americans are the ones for whom it may be absent. In our case, kinship's functions should be, but have not yet been, replaced by what C. Wright Mills called the "sociological imagination." Yet, despite these efforts, Schneider's problem is not fully overcome. McKinley may be right that kinship is (or at least that it involves) a philosophy, but surely not every philosophy is kinship. Likewise, not every set of logical relationships that can be represented mathematically is kinship. And if the Trobrianders do not calculate relationships on the basis of genealogy, in what sense can their system be described as one of kinship?

An alternative preferred by many anthropologists, including some contributors to this collection, is not to try to define explicitly what kinship is or to stipulate how it might be differentiated from other cultural domains, but to take the common sense view that "I know it when I see it." This seems to be the approach taken by Laura Zimmer-Tamakoshi (this volume). For many purposes, such a procedure may be adequate and even useful. But scholarly rigor ultimately requires that we define our terms; and if we are unable to do so, it makes our use of those terms suspect.

In light of discussions that have taken place over the years, it is worthwhile to clear up some points of confusion and specify what Schneider was *not* saying. First, he did not claim that kinship is nonexistent. Rather, he contended that it does not exist *as a cultural system*. As he (1972:39) makes quite plain:

> What "kinship" is all about is considered here only in its cultural aspects; it is "kinship" at a cultural level as defined here. I am explicitly *not* speaking of "kinship" at a psychological level. Nor am I speaking of it as a system for the organization of social groups, that is, not at the social system, social organizational or social structural level, for these are, by my definitions, *not* the same as the cultural system. The cultural level is focused on the fundamental system of symbols and meanings which inform and give shape to the normative level of action. . . .

The question I am asking, which follows directly from this theory is: What are the underlying symbols and their meanings in this particular segment of concrete action and how do they form a single, coherent, interrelated system of symbols and meanings?

However, while kinship "has no discernible cultural referent" (1972:50), kinship, religion, economics, and politics can be distinguished and defined "in the social or sociological system" (59). It is fine for anthropologists to observe domestic arrangements in different societies and to ask how people order relationships between men and women, or between women and their children (44). However, this is not to study culture; and if kinship is a cultural domain, then neither can it be to study kinship. If one studies institutions at the social level and fails to notice that they tend to merge as cultural domains, one risks "fragmentation of the cultural material into artificial segments which remain unlinked and unlinkable" (60). The result is to obscure the culture's fundamental integration.

A second common point of confusion is Schneider's attitude toward the natural sciences in general and biology in particular. He did not claim that biology fails to exist or that the study of biogenetic relationships should cease. In fact, he considered himself to be a materialist and a partisan of natural science. When he got sick he went to the hospital and was treated according to generally accepted biomedical practice. However, biology is not culture; culture and biology exist at different levels of analysis; one cannot be reduced to the other; and we should not deceive ourselves into thinking that we are learning about culture by studying biology. There is nothing wrong with studying genetics, but to study genetics is not to study kinship. Furthermore, we already have disciplines that study biological organisms (biology), the individual psyche (psychology), and social systems (sociology). If anthropology has a unique contribution to make to intellectual discourse, he contended, it is through the study of culture.

Schneider and Cultural Relativism

In an earlier, unpublished manuscript as well as his contribution to the present volume, Martin Ottenheimer has characterized Schneider as a "cultural relativist," a position he considers to be logically "self-destructive" and antithetical to cross-cultural comparison. Whether or not this is a fair critique can only be answered if we first define cultural relativism, a term that has been used by different commentators to denote a wide variety of procedures and assumptions.

One use of the expression refers to what might be called *contextual relativ-*

ism. This perspective simply holds that traits, beliefs, practices, and the like must be understood within their particular cultural contexts; thus, what appears superficially to be the same trait or practice may have different significance in different cultural settings. This point was articulated at least as far back as Boas in his essay on the limitations of the comparative method.[11] Contextual relativism serves as a warning that one must proceed with caution, but it has never been a barrier precluding *all* cross-cultural comparison.

A quite different matter is *ethical relativism.* This is the proposition that there are no good or bad cultures, values, ideas, or practices; that differences do not imply degrees of ethical merit or moral standing; that each extant culture works in its own way and should be understood in its own terms; and that we should not make value judgments. Ethical relativism, in turn, has several variants.

1. One version postulates that anthropology is a science, and that values are philosophical—not scientific—questions. Therefore, in our role as anthropologists we should not judge other peoples or their cultures. However, we are also human beings, each with his or her own cultural baggage. We have our own preferences, values, and predilections growing out of our respective cultural backgrounds, and we cannot be expected to discard our deeply held values when acting as private citizens. Thus, despite his commitment to cultural relativism as a professional anthropologist, Franz Boas spoke out strongly against eugenics, racism, and fascism; Ruth Benedict (1967 [1946]) studied Japan on behalf of the U.S. Office of War Information in an attempt to assist the allied military effort during World War II; and Margaret Mead (1963 [1935], 1949), made little effort to disguise her aversion to the hostile, competitive, aggressive, and internally fragmented Mundugumor of what is now Papua New Guinea.

2. A second version of ethical relativism holds that different cultures have different moral standards and different justifications for their standards. In case of fundamental differences, there is no objective basis for deciding among alternative moral values. One can point to inconsistencies in a moral code, or to someone's failure to act in accordance with his or her explicitly articulated ethical system. However, differing value systems come down to subjective preference, and there are no rational grounds for condemning another community whose moral sense differs from one's own. This perspective takes the previous point an additional step by denying us the prerogative of evaluating others by our own standards even in our capacity as private individuals.

3. A third variant of ethical relativism is what I would characterize as a version of self-determination. This view posits that each community has its

own values and ideas regarding how people should treat one another, and that regardless of our feelings about another community's values or its way of life, other people's standards are their business. Just as we would not like them to impose their values on us, we have no right to impose our views of right and wrong on them. Adherents to this position might well make the further point that we have enough ethical breaches in our own society that we are in no position to criticize anyone else; that our concern should be to set our own house in order.

Ethical relativism, in any of its guises, is an obstacle to moral judgments and actions based upon such judgments. However, it says nothing about the possibility of nonevaluative comparison.[12]

Another complex of ideas going under the heading of cultural relativism posits that no one can ever understand another culture in any truly meaningful way. We might call this position *epistemological relativism*. This notion is often associated with a form of linguistic relativism contained in the so-called Sapir-Whorf hypothesis and going back in some important ways at least to Nietzsche. Adherents to this view contend that the external world is not directly and immediately apprehended, but that sense data are always filtered in some manner. Each of us understands the world from his or her own perspective, and a major determinant of that perspective is one's language. People from different cultural backgrounds speak different languages and perceive the world in fundamentally different ways. The best that any anthropologist can hope to achieve, then, is a poor translation that inevitably distorts the Other's cultural reality by rendering it in the intended audience's language.

Schneider was a cultural relativist in some of the senses I have described but not all. He was not an ethical relativist by any recognizable definition. He took strong positions on political and ethical issues and never hesitated to speak his mind. Although his notion of culture was narrower than that of most contextual relativists, he accepted the idea that cultural units should be understood in terms of their relationships to one another. This idea, however, is not particularly controversial and it appeared as early as Tylor's identification of culture as a "complex whole" (1871:1). What is distinctive about Schneider is that, following Kroeber and Parsons (1958), he viewed culture as excluding people, patterns of behavior, and even norms, which are the rules that people utilize for translating meanings, symbols, basic categories, and understandings into action (Schneider 1995:79). In other words, one might say that he accepted a form of anthropological holism, but it was what one might call a partial holism!

The version of cultural relativism that is germane to Schneider's cultural analysis, then, is the third—or epistemological—relativism. This is the most clearly antithetical to cross-cultural comparison, and it anticipates postmodern skepticism and deconstructionism. Despite Schneider's vociferous protests to the contrary, his deconstruction of kinship as a cultural category is a direct forerunner of more general anthropological deconstruction, and his work pushes strongly toward the description pole of the description/comparison dichotomy (cf. Goodenough 1970). Thus, Schneider's approach does seem to militate in favor of a form of relativism that has a strong postmodernist and antiscientific bias.

This is what led to the comment by Ottenheimer that generated, and is forcefully articulated, in the present volume. Ottenheimer characterizes cultural relativism as "self-defeating" or "self-destructive" because what passes for relativism in the work of authors like Schneider simply substitutes one form of ethnocentrism for another. Anyone who insists that we study other cultures from the natives' point of view, while rejecting all other approaches as intrinsically invalid, is guilty of a form of absolutism; therefore, it is not relativistic.

In a sense, this argument is indisputable—and Schneider actually supported it. Human beings always view the world from the perspective of *some* culture; therefore, some form of ethnocentrism is inescapable. This is why Schneider rejected the emic/etic distinction: what passes for an etic account is, in fact, just the observer's emics. However, Schneider had another point. Western scholars since Herodotus have studied phenomena from a Western viewpoint and will, undoubtedly, continue to do so.[13] We have studied Western classics and continued to develop Western philosophical and scientific paradigms. But until recently, we have been inclined to draw conclusions about non-Western peoples without seriously and systematically considering how things look *to them*. Yet, one cannot adequately understand others, how they think, and what they do without knowing their perspective on the world. This reality does not negate the value of physics, chemistry, neurophysiology, or cultural ecology; instead, it provides otherwise unavailable data and analyses that are intrinsically valuable, and which might even prove useful to practitioners of Western science. Cultural anthropology, since Boas and Malinowski, has attempted to redress this lacuna; yet, however hard we try, our own cultural presuppositions tend to creep in and color our analyses. The value of a David Schneider is to remind us of this fact in stark, dramatic terms; to force us to return to the most basic questions; and to minimize our ethnocentric biases. These are issues that have only grown more urgent since Schneider began to write about them. They remain issues with which we must come to terms if we are to live comfortably upon our rich and diverse planet as we enter a new century.

What Was Schneider All About? Interpretations of His Work and Contributions to This Volume

Schneider was nothing if not controversial, as may be seen in the varied understandings of his work reflected in this collection. Indeed, his writings might be viewed as a kind of anthropological Rorschach test, revealing as much about the commentator's theoretical predilections as about Schneider himself.

In part, the disparate perspectives on Schneider's "cultural" approach, its soundness, value, insight, and profundity, are an inevitable consequence of the fact that he routinely took extreme positions on difficult and complex issues and resolutely defended them against all comers. Moreover, he was not entirely explicit, systematic, or consistent in portraying his position on such vital points as those at issue in this volume. Perhaps less transparent but equally compelling was his personal complexity and his often tense and contradictory relationships with colleagues and students.

Schneider's substantial charm and charisma, along with a dogged determination, made him arguably the dominant figure in the University of Chicago's anthropology department through much of the 1960s and 1970s. For many students he became almost a father figure as he shepherded them through the labyrinth of departmental politics, supported their graduate careers, and used his considerable influence to find them attractive professional positions in an increasingly tight academic job market. At the same time, he could be abrasive, and he often made life difficult for those around him. He was adept at the sarcastic put-down and was not always fair in his depiction of his adversaries' views. This feature of Schneider's persona was compounded by a certain unpredictability, so that more than a few of his associates alternately experienced warm encouragement and personal disparagement— as Raymond D. Fogelson (this volume) makes plain in his unsettling reminiscence (see also DeMallie, this volume). Consequently, one rarely knew what to expect of him on any particular occasion, and the insecurity generated by his mercurial demeanor caused many potential allies to keep him at arm's length. To some degree, then, people's views of Schneider's anthropology reflect the tenor of their personal experiences with him.

Most of the contributors to this collection had personal dealings with Schneider at some point in their academic careers. Raymond J. DeMallie,

Feinberg, Leaf, and Montague were students of his at the University of Chicago. This meant taking classes from him, conversing with him and, for some of us, working under his direction as a master's or doctoral committee member. Fogelson was, for many years, a colleague of Schneider's at the University of Chicago, and McKinley served as a reviewer of the manuscript that eventually was published as *A Critique of the Study of Kinship.* Goodenough, despite fundamental differences on important theoretical issues (see conclusion), was among Schneider's most enduring and consistent friends, dating to their undergraduate days together at Cornell University. Ottenheimer and Zimmer-Tamakoshi had no personal relationship with Schneider, although his writing influenced their thinking about this book's core issues.

My own association with Schneider was relatively short-lived and typically paradoxical; in many ways it parallels DeMallie's experiences (this volume). During my first year of graduate studies, Schneider served as my advisor. He supported my work and, in part because of that support, the department awarded me a much-coveted National Institutes of Mental Health (NIMH) Training Grant. He arranged for my initial fieldwork with the Navajo during the summer of 1970 and prevailed upon the kindness of Gary Witherspoon to ensure that I did not get into too much trouble during my brief foray into Native American ethnography. He and Fred Eggan were the readers on my master's paper, which I completed in early 1971. Over the ensuing year, as I prepared for doctoral fieldwork in the Solomon Islands, our relationship began to sour, and shortly before my departure, he proclaimed that he would no longer serve as my advisor. Although this forced me into the uncomfortable position of having to find a new committee chair while attending to other pressing logistical arrangements, I greeted Schneider's announcement more with relief than annoyance. From that time on, we never communicated directly beyond polite salutations when we met in public. Nonetheless, Schneider's view of kinship as a cultural system, along with his approach to culture as a system of arbitrary symbols that must be elicited from one's informants, has been a major influence on the way that I have conducted myself as a professional anthropologist over the past twenty-five years. While I regret not having been able to maintain a long-term collaborative relationship with Schneider, that has not altered my conviction that he correctly identified important problems and helped us begin to address them.

Other contributors' experiences have differed from mine, as do their assessments of Schneider's place in anthropological history. What they have in common is that Schneider forced each one to reconsider his or her own theoretical positions and the implications of those positions for conducting ethnographic fieldwork.

This volume begins with assessments by Fogelson and DeMallie of Schneider's place in the development of anthropological theory. In succeeding chapters, Leaf, Read, Ottenheimer, and McKinley provide more abstract, philosophical critiques of Schneider's theoretical position and explore potential alternatives. From there, it moves to two primarily ethnographic chapters in which Montague and Zimmer-Tamakoshi apply Schneider's lessons, respectively, to the Trobriand Islands and to the Gende of highland New Guinea. Lastly, Goodenough considers Schneider's work, examining their basic points of disagreement in light of issues raised by the other contributors.

Raymond Fogelson (chapter 1) discusses Schneider from the perspective of a departmental colleague and book review editor of the *American Anthropologist*. His chapter situates Schneider's work and influence in relation to major controversies in the history of anthropology and of kinship studies, with special reference to the debates surrounding componential analysis. He conveys the ambivalence shared by many of Schneider's colleagues and students: feelings of admiration for his keenly critical mind and willingness to flout convention that were offset by a distaste for his slash-and-burn style of cultivating interpersonal relations, his intellectual sleights-of-hand, and his occasional refusal to engage serious critics of his work. In making the latter point, Fogelson discusses at some length Anthony F. C. Wallace's review of *American Kinship* in the *American Anthropologist*. Finally, he credits Schneider for the presumed demise of kinship studies and notes Schneider's connection with postmodernist critiques of the anthropological enterprise.

Raymond DeMallie's essay (chapter 2) should be read in conjunction with and as a complement to Fogelson's. It is largely a historical ethnography, situating the issues, debates, and personalities in and around the University of Chicago's anthropology department during the 1960s and early 1970s, from a student's perspective. DeMallie lays out Schneider's reservations about componential analysis—and cognitive anthropology in general—and it reinforces Fogelson's discussion of Schneider's attempt to come to terms with formal semantic analysis. DeMallie clearly depicts Schneider's distinctive interpersonal style, the kind of personal loyalty that he demanded from many of his students and associates, and the political and interpersonal tone that he engendered in the department. He describes Schneider's position on history and historical explanation by contrasting it with that of Schneider's departmental colleague and theoretical adversary, Fred Eggan. Yet, despite DeMallie's many differences with Schneider, he acknowledges the contribution that Schneider's view of culture as a symbol system made to shaping his own understanding of Lakota kinship.

Murray Leaf (chapter 3) explores the philosophical underpinnings of

Schneider's theoretical stance, characterizing him, in the last analysis, as an idealist. He suggests that idealism and materialism are more closely aligned philosophically than most commentators recognize, both of them being monistic explanatory constructs. The opposite of idealism, he argues, is not materialism but empiricism. By rejecting empiricism, he contends, Schneider impeded his own ability to conduct, in practice, the kind of informant-based cultural analysis that he advocated in his programmatic statements.

Dwight Read (chapter 4) agrees with Schneider that kinship cannot be reduced to genealogy but disputes the conclusion that it, therefore, fails to exist. Rather, he suggests that it can be identified as a system of logical relationships among a discrete set of terms, and that those relationships can be represented in terms of formal mathematical modeling. In some cases the model may be mapped onto a genealogical grid, but that is not an essential feature of a kinship system. He illustrates his point by offering his own analysis of American kinship.

Martin Ottenheimer (chapter 5), like Leaf, offers a logical-philosophical critique of Schneider's analytic framework. Schneider, he argues, by insisting that his version of cultural relativism be adopted as the only acceptable approach to analyzing kinship, comes to embrace a form of absolutism, thereby rendering his position logically incoherent. Ottenheimer calls for us to move beyond both cultural relativism and biological reductionism and to adopt what he characterizes as a truly relativistic framework. By this he means more than a simple merger of the two opposing paradigms. Rather, he envisions a kind of pluralism which recognizes that no one has access to a culture-free, objective truth but that both frameworks provide useful insights: one is critical for understanding how the world appears to particular peoples; the other is essential for cross-cultural comparison and general illumination of the human condition.[14]

Robert McKinley (chapter 6) argues that kinship is best viewed not as a cultural system in Schneider's sense, but as "a philosophy" intended to answer the question, "How can one human being be morally obligated to another?" As he nicely states the case, "no matter how people count their relatives, relatives always count." Perhaps Schneider has a point when he contends that we distort important cultural realities by labeling as "kin" all those who "count." But if such persons are not kin, McKinley asks, "then why are the mythologies of peoples all over the world filled with such figures as pathetic orphans, incestuous mates, exotic spouses, heroic twins, fraternal strife, and supernatural in-laws?" Yet, while McKinley takes exception to Schneider's view that kinship is a figment, he accepts that it has come unraveled in America. In that light, he cites what C. Wright Mills termed "the sociological imagination" as having the as-yet-unrealized potential to accomplish in the West what kinship does in non-Western communities.

Susan Montague (chapter 7) offers the first of two ethnographically grounded discussions, illustrating the manner in which Schneider's approach may lead to fundamentally new and different ways of understanding kinship systems. She applies Schneider's admonitions about the meaning of kinship and the limitations of genealogical reckoning to the Trobriand Islands, a community that has occupied a central place in anthropological discourse and kinship analysis since Malinowski's pioneering work during the early twentieth century. Following Schneider's exhortation that we begin with indigenous categories and symbols, she examines Trobriand views of person-hood and bases for constructing interpersonal relationships. Those views draw upon weather patterns (particularly wind and rain), the magic that enables one to control those patterns, and the interconnections between weather magic and various food categories. Together, these produce an integrated system of symbols in terms of which persons are defined and linked to one another.

Laura Zimmer-Tamakoshi (chapter 8), like Montague, accepts Schneider's strictures concerning the limitations of genealogy for determining membership in putatively kin-based groups, which she glosses as "clans," among the Gende of Papua New Guinea. She suggests that Gende regularly "gerrymander" their genealogical networks in such a way as to maximize their short-term economic benefit. By following Schneider's directive to look for indigenous definitions, Zimmer-Tamakoshi comes to understand the flexible nature of Gende kinship, and she is able to resolve several apparent contradictions that emerged over her two decades of research with them.

Ward Goodenough concludes this volume by exploring the nature of his personal friendship and theoretical differences with Schneider, connecting the latter to issues raised in the earlier essays. Schneider, he contends, distorted what his predecessors and colleagues meant by "genealogy" in order to fabricate a straw man that he could then attack. He argues that kinship is grounded in the biological facts of sexual reproduction and childhood dependency, a point of genuine difference between Schneider and him. Genealogies, however, are cultural constructs, not biological facts. Since Schneider's critique of formal semantic analysis revolved around the use of genealogical components for purposes of cross-cultural comparison, and since he misconstrued what genealogy is all about, his rejection of componential analysis, in Goodenough's opinion, was fundamentally misguided. In challenging Schneider's cavalier dismissal of formal analysis, Goodenough revisits themes raised by Fogelson, DeMallie, Leaf, and Read. At the same time, he

joins Leaf, Read, Ottenheimer, and McKinley in protesting Schneider's ab-
dication of attempts at cross-cultural comparison in favor of an extreme form
of epistemological relativism.

Schneider's Contribution to Anthropological Discourse and Future Directions for the Discipline

Perhaps the most compelling contradiction to be found in Schneider's work
is that while his deconstruction of kinship as a cultural system sounded the
death knell for a certain kind of kinship study, it also provided the basis upon
which the subject would re-emerge as a centerpiece of anthropological theory and investigation. This has occurred on two fronts.

Schneider's first enduring contribution has been to Pacific Islands anthropology. He was a major force behind the proliferation of ethnographic research in Micronesia during the decades following World War II (see Marshall 1999:404–6). Not only did a number of his students (e.g., David Labby,
John Kirkpatrick, and Vern Carroll) conduct significant research on Yap and
its neighbors.[15] Schneider also was the dominant intellectual force behind
creation of the Association for Social Anthropology in Oceania (ASAO) in
the late 1960s and early 1970s. Vern Carroll, who ably represented Schneider's
vision of a sharply defined, symbolically circumscribed cultural anthropology, became the association's most important leader during the early years.
The first ASAO monograph, dealing with adoption in Eastern Oceania and
edited by Carroll, followed Schneider's lead and did much to free Pacific kinship analyses from their previous genealogical (in Schneider's sense) grounding.[16] This project was further advanced by a second ASAO volume on adoption (Brady 1976) as well as one on siblingship (Marshall 1981). If Schneiderian
symbolic anthropology should ever generate coherent, systematic cross-cultural comparison, these volumes will have paved the way.

The second area in which Schneider's work has had a lasting impact is
feminist anthropology and gender studies. Schneider's avowed commitment
to gender equality was sometimes hard to locate in his personal life.[17] Nonetheless, the implications of his theoretical framework were not lost on feminist scholars (see, e.g., Collier and Yanagisako 1987; Stone 1997). In much the
way that Lyell's geological chronology made room for Darwin and Wallace's
theory of organic evolution through natural selection, Schneider's freeing of
kinship from the limitations of biology provided a context within which feminist anthropologists were able to establish gender as a cultural construct (cf.
Peletz 1995:346). If gender definitions, roles, and power relations are symbolically constructed, they become culturally variable; they lose their aura of

biological inevitability, and true gender equality takes on an aspect of feasibility. In such an atmosphere, family roles and relations can be contested in a way that was previously impossible, and such notions as lesbian motherhood (Lewin 1993) are transformed from oxymorons into serious intellectual, social, and legal concerns.[18] Lastly, in addition to freeing kinship studies from their biogenetic underpinnings and thereby laying the groundwork for much subsequent work by feminist, gay, and lesbian scholars, Schneider's writings have helped to generate a renewed interest in adoption (e.g., Modell 1994), and they foreshadow many of the issues raised by new reproductive technologies (e.g., Ragoné 1994, 1997).

David Schneider was among the most complex and paradoxical contributors to modern anthropology. He was not always consistent in his own positions, nor was his personal life always consistent with the theory he espoused. His influence upon the discipline might have been greater had he mastered a style of interpersonal relations adapted to creating allies rather than alienating potential supporters. Yet, despite these limitations, he helped revolutionize the way in which we think of kinship, family, gender, and culture itself. This book reflects the paradox, ambivalence, and irony experienced by most of those who dealt with David Schneider and whose careers were shaped by his thought. It explores the many paths he charted, posts warning signs at several dead-end intersections, and suggests directions for productive research in the years to come.

Notes

1. That analysis was further extended in Morgan's famous and influential *Ancient Society* (1877).

2. Around the same time Schneider's arch antagonist, Rodney Needham, arrived at a similar conclusion.

3. Interestingly, those commentators who attribute our myriad social problems to moral degeneracy and a breakdown of family values are least likely to acknowledge the social consequences of an economic system based on private profit and individual competition, a system which requires many losers for each winner.

4. Even Sir E. B. Tylor, whose famous opening to *Primitive Culture* equates "culture" with "civilization," held that people differed in degree of civilization.

5. Among Schneider's distinguished former students are James Boon, Vern Carroll, Richard Handler, Bradd Shore, Roy Wagner, and Gary Witherspoon.

6. This turns out to be perhaps the critical difference between Schneider and Murray Leaf (this volume). Leaf not only insists that the anthropologist listen to his or her informants as sources of data, but he rejects any interpretation that is not readily recognizable to one's informants.

7. Schneider's influence, for example, is unmistakable in Linnekin's review of "con-

structionist" or "post-modernist" approaches to the study of tradition in Oceania (e.g., Linnekin 1992; also see Handler and Linnekin 1983).

8. My criticisms of Schneider are further spelled out in Feinberg 1979.

9. I have adopted this approach in my own ethnographic analyses (see Feinberg 1981a, 1981b, 1981c, 1990, 1996).

10. But cf. Read (this volume), who argues that, even in America, kinship is a system of logical relationships among terms and categories and is not reducible to genealogy.

11. E.g., see Boas's discussion of masks and clans in North America (Boas 1896:904–5).

12. I am not arguing here that it is possible for analysis and theory to escape evaluation; only that if it could be done as a practical matter, the endeavor would not be precluded by ethical relativism.

13. This is true despite the fact that just what constitutes a Western viewpoint has changed over time.

14. Ottenheimer's critique must be framed by Schneider's caveat that sociological, psychological, biogenetic, and other approaches to understanding human phenomena are legitimate and appropriate. Therefore, Schneider was not proposing that his was the only acceptable mode of scholarly inquiry. Rather, the difference between his and Ottenheimer's positions appears to revolve around Schneider's insistence on defining culture as a system of meanings and symbols. This narrow definition of culture, combined with the view that kinship is a cultural system, Ottenheimer notes, may preclude important insights that can only be obtained by opening kinship to investigation from such perspectives as cultural ecology or evolutionary biology. While a Schneiderian framework can be useful in addressing certain problems, Ottenheimer cautions anthropologists to apply it judiciously.

15. Labby and Kirkpatrick both conducted field research on Yap (see Labby 1976; Kirkpatrick and Broder 1976); Carroll (e.g., 1970b; 1975) worked on Nukuoro Atoll, a Polynesian outlier located in what is now the Federated States of Micronesia.

16. A theme that runs throughout the Carroll volume and its successors is the symbolic value of land, equating it with blood as a form of shared natural substance that underpins kinship in many Pacific Island communities. This insight was nicely captured in Martin Silverman's felicitous suggestion (1970, 1971) that Oceanic kinship is defined by "blood and mud."

17. E.g., for Schneider to have his wife spend months distilling and summarizing his data, only to discard those summaries with hardly an acknowledgment (see Schneider 1995:210–11; Fogelson, this volume) suggests a kind of exploitation belying his occasional feminist pretensions.

18. Thus, it is no accident that Schneider's last (posthumous) article (Schneider 1997) dealt with gay and lesbian kinship in contemporary America.

References Cited

Benedict, Ruth. 1967 [1940]. *The Chrysanthemum and the Sword.* New York: Meridian.

Boas, Franz. 1896. "The Limitations of the Comparative Method of Anthropology." *Science* 4:901–8.

————. 1966 [1940]. *Race, Language and Culture*. New York: Free Press.

Brady, Ivan A., ed. 1976. *Transactions in Kinship: Adoption and Fosterage in Oceania*. ASAO Monograph No. 4. Honolulu: University of Hawai'i Press.

Carroll, Vern, ed. 1970a. *Adoption in Eastern Oceania*. ASAO Monograph No. 1. Honolulu: University of Hawai'i Press.

————. 1970b. "Adoption on Nukuoro." In *Adoption in Eastern Oceania*. Ed. Vern Carroll. 121–57. ASAO Monograph No. 1. Honolulu: University of Hawai'i Press.

————. 1975. "The Population of Nukuoro in Historical Perspective." In *Pacific Atoll Populations*. Ed. Vern Carroll. 344–416. ASAO Monograph No. 3. Honolulu: University of Hawai'i Press.

Collier, Jane Fishburne, and Sylvia Junko Yanagisako, eds. 1987. *Gender and Kinship: Essays toward a Unified Analysis*. Palo Alto, Calif.: Stanford University Press.

Durkheim, Émile, and Marcel Mauss. 1967. *Primitive Classification*. Trans. Rodney Needham. Chicago: University of Chicago Press.

Eggan, Fred, ed. 1937. *The Social Anthropology of North American Tribes*. Chicago: University of Chicago Press.

————. 1950. *Social Organization of the Western Pueblos*. Chicago: University of Chicago Press.

————. 1972. "Lewis Henry Morgan's Systems: A Reevaluation." In *Kinship Studies in the Morgan Centennial Year*. Ed. Priscilla Reining. 1–16. Washington, D.C.: Anthropological Society of Washington.

Evans-Pritchard, E. E. 1940. *The Nuer: A Description of the Modes of Livelihood and Political Institutions of a Nilotic People*. Oxford: Clarendon.

————. 1951. *Kinship and Marriage among the Nuer*. Oxford: Clarendon.

Feinberg, Richard. 1979. "Schneider's Symbolic Culture Theory: An Appraisal." *Current Anthropology* 20 (3): 541–49.

————. 1981a. *Anuta: Social Structure of a Polynesian Island*. Lā'ie and Copenhagen: Institute for Polynesian Studies in cooperation with the National Museum of Denmark.

————. 1981b. "The Meaning of 'Sibling' on Anuta Island." In *Siblingship in Oceania: Studies in the Meaning of Kin Relations*. Ed. Mac Marshall. 105–48. ASAO Monograph No. 8. Ann Arbor: University of Michigan Press.

————. 1981c. "What Is Polynesian Kinship All About?" *Ethnology* 20:115–31.

————. 1990. "New Guinea Models on a Polynesian Outlier?" *Ethnology* 29:83–96.

————. 1996. "Sanctity and Power on Anuta: Polynesian Chieftainship Revisited." In *Leadership and Change in the Western Pacific: Essays in Honor of Sir Raymond Firth*. Eds. Richard Feinberg and Karen Ann Watson-Gegeo. 56–92. London School of Economics Monographs on Social Anthropology, No. 66. London: Athlone.

Firth, Raymond. 1936. *We, the Tikopia*. London: George Allen and Unwin.

————. 1957. "A Note on Descent Groups in Polynesia." *Man* 57:4–8.

————. 1964 [1954]. *Essays on Social Organization and Values*. London School of Economics Monographs in Anthropology, No. 28. London: Athlone.

Fortes, Meyer. 1945. *The Dynamics of Clanship among the Tallensi*. London: Oxford University Press.

————. 1949. *The Web of Kinship among the Tallensi*. London: Oxford University Press.

————. 1950. "Kinship and Marriage among the Ashanti." In *African Systems of Kinship and Marriage*. Eds. A. R. Radcliffe-Brown and C. D. Forde. 252–84. London: Oxford University Press.

————. 1969. *Kinship and the Social Order: The Legacy of Lewis Henry Morgan*. Chicago: Aldine.

Fox, Robin. 1967. *Kinship and Marriage*. Baltimore: Penguin.

Geertz, Clifford. 1966. "Religion as a Cultural System." In *Anthropological Approaches to the Study of Religion*. Ed. Michael Banton. 1–46. Association of Social Anthropologists (ASA) Monograph No. 3. London: Tavistock.

Geertz, Hildred, and Clifford Geertz. 1975. *Kinship in Bali*. Chicago: University of Chicago Press.

Goodenough, Ward H. 1965. "Yankee Kinship Terminology: A Problem in Componential Analysis." In *Formal Semantic Analysis*. Ed. Eugene A. Hammel. 269–87. Special issue of *American Anthropologist* 67 (5), pt. 2.

————. 1967. "Componential Analysis." *Science* 156:1203–9.

————. 1970. *Description and Comparison in Cultural Anthropology*. Chicago: Aldine.

Handler, Richard, and Jocelyn Linnekin. 1983. "Tradition: Genuine or Spurious?" *Journal of American Folklore* 97:273–90.

Hatch, Elvin. 1983. *Culture and Morality: The Relativity of Values in Anthropology*. New York: Columbia University Press.

Homans, George C., and David M. Schneider. 1955. *Marriage, Authority, and Final Causes: A Study of Unilateral Cross-Cousin Marriage*. New York: Free Press.

Huntsman, Judith, and Mervyn McLean, eds. 1976. *Incest Prohibitions in Polynesia and Micronesia*. Special issue of *Journal of the Polynesian Society* 84:149–298.

Kirkpatrick, John T., and Charles R. Broder. 1976. "Adoption and Parenthood on Yap." In *Transactions in Kinship: Adoption and Fosterage in Oceania*. Ed. Ivan A. Brady. 200–227. ASAO Monograph No. 4. Honolulu: University of Hawai'i Press.

Kluckhohn, Clyde, Henry A. Murray, and David Schneider, eds. 1953. *Personality in Nature, Society, and Culture*. 2d ed. New York: Knopf.

Kroeber, Alfred L. 1909. "Classificatory Systems of Relationship." *Journal of the Royal Anthropological Institute* 39:77–84.

————. 1917. *California Kinship Systems*. University of California Publications in American Archaeology and Ethnology, Volume 12. Berkeley.

————. 1936. "Kinship and History." *American Anthropologist* 38:338–41.

————. 1938. "Basic and Secondary Patterns of Social Structure." *Journal of the Royal Anthropological Institute* 67:299–310.

Kroeber, Alfred L., and Talcott Parsons. 1958. "The Concepts of Culture and of Social System." *American Sociological Review* 23:582–83.

Labby, David. 1976. *The Demystification of Yap*. Chicago: University of Chicago Press.

Leach, Edmund R. 1961. *Rethinking Anthropology*. London School of Economics Monographs on Social Anthropology, No. 22. London: Athlone.

————. 1970. *Claude Lévi-Strauss*. New York: Viking.

Lévi-Strauss, Claude. 1969 [1949]. *The Elementary Structures of Kinship*. Trans. James Harle Bell, John Richard von Sturmer, and Rodney Needham. Boston: Beacon Press.

Lewin, Ellen. 1993. *Lesbian Mothers*. Ithaca, N.Y.: Cornell University Press.

Linnekin, Jocelyn. 1992. "On the Theory and Politics of Cultural Construction in the Pacific." *Oceania* 62:249–63.

Lounsbury, Floyd G. 1956. "A Semantic Analysis of the Pawnee Kinship Usage." *Language* 32:158–94.

———. 1964a. "A Formal Account of the Crow- and Omaha-Type Kinship Terminologies." In *Explorations in Cultural Anthropology*. Ed. Ward H. Goodenough. 351–93. New York: McGraw Hill.

———. 1964b. "The Structural Analysis of Kinship Semantics." In *Proceedings of the Ninth International Congress of Linguists*. Ed. Horace G. Lunt. 1073–93. The Hague: Mouton.

Lowie, Robert H. 1920. *Primitive Society*. New York: Liveright.

———. 1929. "Relationship Terms." *Encyclopedia Britannica* (14th ed.). London.

———. 1930. "The Crow and Omaha Kinship Terminologies." *Verhandlungen des Internationalen Amerikanisten Kongersses* 24:102–8.

———. 1932. "Kinship." *Encyclopedia of the Social Sciences* 8:570.

———. 1948. *Social Organization*. New York: Holt, Rinehart and Winston.

Malinowski, Bronislaw. 1913. *The Family among the Australian Aborigines*. London: University of London Press.

———. 1929. *The Sexual Life of Savages in North-Western Melanesia*. New York and London: Harcourt, Brace, Jovanovich.

———. 1930. "Kinship." *Man* 30 (2): 19–29.

Marshall, Mac, ed. 1981. *Siblingship in Oceania: Studies in the Meaning of Kin Relations*. ASAO Monograph No. 8. Ann Arbor: University of Michigan Press.

———. 1999. "Ripples from a Micronesian Sea." In *American Anthropology in Micronesia: An Assessment*. Ed. Robert Kiste and Mac Marshall. 387–431. Honolulu: University of Hawai'i Press.

McLennan, J. F. 1970 [1865]. *Primitive Marriage*. Chicago: University of Chicago Press.

Mead, Margaret. 1949. *Male and Female: A Study of the Sexes in a Changing World*. New York: Dell.

———. 1963 [1935]. *Sex and Temperament in Three Primitive Societies*. New York: William Morrow.

Modell, Judith. 1994. *Kinship with Strangers: Adoption and Interpretations of Kinship in American Culture*. Berkeley: University of California Press.

Morgan, Lewis Henry. 1871. *Systems of Consanguinity and Affinity of the Human Family*. Smithsonian Contributions to Knowledge, No. 17. Washington, D.C.

———. 1877. *Ancient Society*. Chicago: Charles H. Kerr and Company.

———. 1969 [1851]. *League of the Iroquois*. New York: Corinth.

Murdock, George Peter. 1940. "Double Descent." *American Anthropologist* 42:555–61.

———. 1947. "Bifurcate Merging." *American Anthropologist* 49:56–69.

———. 1949. *Social Structure*. New York: Macmillan.

———. 1960. "Cognatic Forms of Social Organization." In *Social Structure in Southeast Asia*. Ed. G. P. Murdock. 1–14. Chicago: Quadrangle Books.

Needham, Rodney. 1962. *Structure and Sentiment: A Test Case in Social Anthropology*. Chicago: University of Chicago Press.

Peletz, Michael. 1995. "Kinship Studies in the Late Twentieth Century." *Annual Review of Anthropology* 24:343–72.

Radcliffe-Brown, A. R. 1950. "Introduction." In *African Systems of Kinship and Marriage.* Ed. A. R. Radcliffe-Brown and C. D. Forde. 1–85. London: Oxford University Press.

———. 1965 [1952]. *Structure and Function in Primitive Society.* New York: Free Press.

Ragoné, Helena. 1994. *Surrogate Motherhood: Conception in the Heart.* Boulder, Colo.: Westview Press.

———. 1997. "Chasing the Blood Tie: Surrogate Mothers, Adoptive Mothers, and Fathers." In *Situated Lives: Gender and Culture in Everyday Life.* Ed. Louise Lamphere, Helena Rangoné, and Patricia Zavella. 110–21. New York: Routledge.

Rivers, W. H. R. 1900. "A Genealogical Method of Collecting Social and Vital Statistics." *Journal of the Royal Anthropological Institute* 30:74–82.

———. 1906. *The Todas.* London: Macmillan.

———. 1907. "On the Origin of the Classificatory System of Relationships." In *Anthropological Essays Presented to E. B. Tylor.* Ed. N. W. Thomas. 309–23. Oxford: Clarendon.

———. 1910. "The Genealogical Method of Anthropological Inquiry." *Sociological Review* 3:1–12.

———. 1914. *Kinship and Social Organization.* London: Constable.

———. 1915. "Kin, Kinship." In *Encyclopedia of Religion and Ethics.* Ed. J. Hastings. 7:700–707.

———. 1924. *Social Organization.* New York: Knopf.

Saussure, Ferdinand de. 1959. *Course in General Linguistics.* New York: McGraw-Hill.

Scheffler, Harold W. 1970. "Kinship and Adoption in the Northern New Hebrides." In *Adoption in Eastern Oceania.* Ed. Vern Carroll. 369–89. ASAO Monograph No. 1. Honolulu: University of Hawai'i Press.

———. 1976. "The "Meaning" of Kinship in American Culture: Another View." In *Meaning in Anthropology.* Ed. Keith H. Basso and Henry A. Selby. 57–91. Albuquerque: University of New Mexico Press.

Schneider, David M. 1946. "The Culture of the Army Clerk." *Psychiatry* 9:123–29.

———. 1947. "The Social Dynamics of Physical Disability in Army Basic Training." *Psychiatry* 10:323–33.

———. 1953. "Yap Kinship Terminology and Kin Groups." *American Anthropologist* 55:215–36.

———. 1962. "Double Descent on Yap." *Journal of the Polynesian Society* 71:1–24.

———. 1965. "Some Muddles in the Models: Or How the System Really Works." In *The Relevance of Models for Social Anthropology.* Ed. Michael Banton. 25–85. ASA Monograph No. 1. London: Tavistock.

———. 1968. *American Kinship: A Cultural Account.* Englewood Cliffs, N.J.: Prentice-Hall.

———. 1969. "Kinship, Nationality, and Religion in American Culture: Toward a Definition of Kinship." In *Forms of Symbolic Action.* Ed. Robert F. Spencer. 116–25. Proceedings of the 1969 Annual Spring Meeting of the American Ethnological Society. Seattle: University of Washington Press.

———. 1972. "What Is Kinship All About?" In *Kinship Studies in the Morgan Centennial Year.* Ed. Priscilla Reining. 88–112. Washington, D.C.: Anthropological Society of Washington.

———. 1976. "The Meaning of Incest." In *Incest Prohibitions in Polynesia and Microne-*

sia. Ed. Judith Huntsman and Mervyn McLean. 149–70. Special issue of *Journal of the Polynesian Society* 84 (2).

————. 1981. "Conclusion." In *Siblingship in Oceania: Studies in the Meaning of Kin Relations.* Ed. Mac Marshall. 389–404. ASAO Monograph No. 8. Ann Arbor: University of Michigan Press.

————. 1984. *A Critique of the Study of Kinship.* Ann Arbor: University of Michigan Press.

————. 1995. *Schneider on Schneider: The Conversion of the Jews and Other Anthropological Stories by David Schneider, as Told to Richard Handler.* Ed. Richard Handler. Durham, N.C.: Duke University Press.

————. 1997. "The Power of Culture: Notes on Some Aspects of Gay and Lesbian Kinship in America Today." *Cultural Anthropology* 12 (2):270–74.

Schneider, David M., and George C. Homans. 1955. "Kinship Terminology and the American Kinship System." *American Anthropologist* 57:1194–208.

Silverman, Martin G. 1970. "Banaban Adoption." In *Adoption in Eastern Oceania.* Ed. Vern Carroll. 209–35. ASAO Monograph No. 1. Honolulu: University of Hawai'i Press.

————. 1971. *Disconcerting Issue: Meaning and Struggle in a Resettled Pacific Community.* Chicago: University of Chicago Press.

Stone, Linda. 1997. *Kinship and Gender.* Boulder, Colo.: Westview Press.

Turner, Terence. 1997. "Human Rights, Human Difference: Anthropology's Contribution to an Emancipatory Cultural Politics." In *Cultural Relativism and Universal Human Rights.* Ed. Terence Turner and Carole Nagengast. 273–91. Special issue of *Journal of Anthropological Research* 53:269–381.

Tylor, Sir Edward B. 1871. *Primitive Culture.* London: J. Murray.

————. 1889. "On a Method of Investigating Institutions: Applied to Laws Marriage and Descent." *Journal of the Royal Anthropological Institute* 18:245–72.

Wallace, Anthony F. C. 1965. "The Problem of Psychological Validity of Componential Analysis." In *Formal Semantic Analysis.* Ed. Eugene A. Hammel. 229–48. Special issue of *American Anthropologist* 67 (5), pt. 2.

Wallace, Anthony F. C., and John Atkins. 1960. "The Meaning of Kinship Terms." *American Anthropologist* 62:58–80.

1. Schneider Confronts Componential Analyses

RAYMOND D. FOGELSON

DAVID SCHNEIDER was Chair when I was hired at the University of Chicago in 1965. He made me nervous. On the one hand he could be generous and supportive and readily flash his not inconsiderable charm; when in his paranoid-oid mode, on the other hand, he could be vindictive, mean-spirited, destructive and self-destructive.[1] Over the years my sense of unease about him never abated. If he invited me to his house and presented me with a potted plant, a book, or some other seemingly gratuitous gift, I left wondering what he had done behind my back. The paranoia was contagious, and, as he frequently observed, "even paranoids have real enemies." Faculty meetings with David were never dull and could devolve into emotionally draining identity struggles. I confess that I felt more relief than sadness when he left Chicago for the warmer climes of Santa Cruz in 1982. In thinking about and writing this chapter, these feelings of nervous apprehension return.

I intend to focus on David Schneider's cultural approach to kinship, which culminated in his influential work on American kinship, a subject whose reality he later came to question. I will also stress the development of competing approaches to the study of American kinship, most notably componential analysis.

Schneider's Cultural Anthropology: Underlying Premises

As is generally acknowledged, Schneider possessed an acutely critical and analytic mind. We see this mind at work in his approach to kinship, an approach that has ramifying roots. One stem is traceable to neo-Boasian culturalism as mediated through Ruth Benedict, Margaret Mead, A. L. Kroeber, and his major professor, Clyde Kluckhohn.[2] He publicly espoused the broad theoretical position of Talcott Parsons (1957), however, in his heuristic separation of cultural, social-structural, and motivational or psychological levels of analysis.[3] For Parsons, as for Kluckhohn, culture consisted of norms and values; Schneider preferred to view culture as systems of symbols and meanings (although one would be hard pressed to conceive of meanings that were not expressed symbolically or of meaningless symbols).[4]

Schneider's viewpoints were also tempered by his interactions with British social anthropology. Indeed, what I regard as one of his best works, his relentless, talmudically argued analysis of the distinctive features of matrilineal descent groups (1961:1–29), comes out of theoretical concerns of British structural-functionalism. Moreover, the American kinship project was originally envisioned as a Chicago complement to the study of middle-class kinship undertaken by Raymond Firth and his collaborators in London (1968). However, while the London study examined kinship ideology, it was less concerned with symbolic meaning and more empirically grounded in behavioral data.[5]

Schneider clearly shares with his British colleagues the structural-functional disregard for culture history and for shorter or longer time perspectives. I recall that he often glibly dismissed history, in his noneventual shadowboxing with Fred Eggan, by asserting in proposal hearings and dissertation defenses that "history explains nothing"; the ghost of Radcliffe-Brown was heard appreciatively clanking in the congested steam pipes of the Anthropology Common Room. I secretly felt at the time that Schneider deserved the Henry Ford Chair of Historical Bunk. He was clearly uncomfortable with the emergence of historical anthropology as a central concern of Chicago anthropology, which in part displaced, if not completely defaced, symbolic anthropology as the collective representation of the Chicago department.[6]

Another feature of the Schneiderian cultural approach to kinship was its claim to remaining true to reported native conceptions and realities. Induction was favored over deduction; yet, as we know too well, an overdependence on induction can present insurmountable problems to production ("Don't bother me with data"). Schneider had to face this problem later in his major work on *American Kinship*. He displayed a chronic distrust of externally imposed categorical systems, such as economic, religious, political, and, most particularly, kinship systems. He also questioned the universality of such institutions as the family and the postulation of universally translatable elementary kin terms. Here the principal target of Schneider's scorn was George Peter Murdock and the kind of behaviorism and logical positivism spawned by Murdock's typological approach to the analysis of kinship systems and social structure (see Murdock 1949). Schneider effectively challenged the reality and meaning of Murdock's basic kin terms as minimal units, or building blocks, that would permit a scientific study of society. Ultimately Schneider (1984) would challenge whether kinship systems themselves possessed existential reality or were merely arbitrary artifacts of the Western analyst.

Behind this controversy over native realities lurked the influence of Kenneth Pike's linguistically derived etic/emic distinction. For Murdock's followers, who were to develop componential analysis, etics, by analogy with phonetics, became a methodological device to get at native cultural or psychological realities, by analogy their phonemics. Or to put the matter inversely, if not perversely, emics comprised an analytic method used to get at other people's etics. For Schneider, any categorical presupposition was suspect and thus biased the resulting account.[7]

While Schneider's position may possess abstract philosophic virtue, such an approach delays, if not denies, any possibility of comparison, controlled or otherwise, and leads to a kind of nihilistic ultimate relativism in which each case is unique (cf. Feinberg and Ottenheimer, both this volume). This extreme relativism flies in the face of the way "normal" sciences and most other scholarly disciplines proceed. They arbitrarily delimit an area of investigation and set up operational or heuristic definitions of the phenomena they wish to investigate, but the boundaries of these spaces may be redrawn and the operational definitions may be amended or even discarded as a result of subsequent examination. Hence, progress in science and the other disciplines depends on the ability to compare and, if necessary, reject results, something that Schneider's relativism would deny.

The American Kinship Project

Schneider's work on American kinship does, indeed, make assumptions and presumptions both in the formal collection of data (cf. Wolf 1964) and in the analysis of those data. Schneider's interest in studying American kinship goes back at least to his early collaborative work with George Homans at Harvard, "Kinship Terminology and the American Kinship System" (1955). In this paper, they hoped to show that, despite diversity, and historic and ethnic complexity, Americans do share at base level a system of symbols and meanings that define a distinctive kinship pattern. Their account is not an exercise in exoticizing the familiar, but rather is a fairly persuasive effort to show that cultural meanings and codes for conduct are fundamentally shared, while allowing for minor variations in particulars.[8] The data are culled from intensive interviews with 209 informants in and around Cambridge, Massachusetts. This reliance on interviews and survey research was essentially similar to Firth's methodology in the London study and is largely continuous with the modes of data collection followed in Schneider's later Chicago project.

Serious questions have arisen regarding the degree to which Schneider used the extensive empirical data collected for the Chicago project in arriving at the interpretation he advanced in *American Kinship: A Cultural Account* (1968), hereafter referred to as "the pamphlet."[9] In *Schneider on Schneider* (1995:209–11), he confesses that he wrote "the pamphlet" without reference to the thousands of pages of field data collected by his assistants and carefully distilled and summarized by his wife, Addy. She accused him of dishonesty and burned her compilations. He justifies his procedure by arguing that it would be equally fraudulent to bolster conclusions already formulated with selected supporting materials. Indeed, there is honesty in his dishonesty, but one is left wondering why he went to the trouble of mounting a massive research project if he intended to ignore the results of that research.

The partial summary of the data from the Chicago study, *The American Kin Universe: A Genealogical Study* by David Schneider and Calvert Cottrell, was published in 1975 in an ill-fated departmental monograph series of limited distribution. At best this work bears only a tenuous relationship to "the pamphlet." In fact, a close reading of *American Kin Universe* reveals many serious discrepancies with what "the pamphlet" reports. It is doubtless significant that *American Kin Universe* is cited but not discussed in the chapter "Twelve Years Later," appended to the second edition of "the pamphlet" (1980); moreover, *American Kin Universe* fades completely from Schneider's field of vision in his final major opus, *A Critique of the Study of Kinship* (1984).

In this final work, he fully articulates his argument that the reality of kinship is an illusion, a conclusion that is particularly ironic in that he devoted most of his intellectual career to pursuing this phantasma. I'm afraid that the final demolition of kinship more resembles Don Quixotish windmill tilting than Saint Georgian dragon slaying. But then again, as we might infer from Handler's interviews in *Schneider on Schneider,* Schneider's entire life embodied contrary contradiction, a kind of funny unfunniness, or unfunny funniness, if you will.

Critique of Componential Analysis

Schneider was sharply critical of interpretations of American kinship produced by componential analysts. Componential analysis, now consigned to the dustbin of anthropological history, had serious flaws that Schneider was quick to expose. The method emerged out of ethnosemantics and has a lineage that can be traced back at least to Charles Sanders Peirce as mediated through the neglected Charles Morris. The method was part and parcel of the ethnoscientific turn in American anthropology in the 1960s, a movement that shared Schneider's desire to get at native categories, metaphysics, and ontological realities. The method, however, involved formal operations rather than freely elicited informant testimony obtained through observation or interview. Ethnoscience explored many domains, but from the start it concentrated its efforts on the analysis of kinship.[10]

At a 1969 Wenner-Gren Symposium on Cognitive Studies and Artificial Intelligence, Schneider produced a paper entitled "Componential Analysis: A State-of-the-Art Review" (1969a). Four years earlier, Schneider had fired his first salvo against componential analysis in his critique of his friend Goodenough's analysis of Yankee kinship terminology (1965a). In that paper, he disagreed with Goodenough's rules for inclusion or exclusion of relatives by marriage. The Wenner-Gren paper is a further devastating critique that was never published but circulated in mimeograph form. To quote Schneider:

> Componential analysis made its appearance on the anthropological scene in 1956 in the first number of the 32nd volume of the journal *Language,* in the very same issue as Y. R. Chao's important paper on Chinese Terms of Address. That issue contained, side by side, Goodenough's Componential Analysis and the Study of Meaning and Lounsbury's A Semantic Analysis of the Pawnee Kinship Usage. Those two papers have since been regarded as a sort of Year One for Componential Analysis in Anthropology, and justly so. Chao's paper, on the other hand, has been ignored by anthropologists; at least I have seen no references to it in either the literature of componential analysis or of kinship terminology generally. (1969a:7)

Indeed, as Schneider slyly notes, who today reads Chao? For that matter, who today reads Spencer? Or better, Parsons? Schneider was as astutely aware of the shunning effect of silence as he was of the power of unbridled self-promotion. He goes on to note that

> it would be fair to say that componential analysis has not been overlooked, neglected, or ignored.
>   Rather than being neglected, a clear, clique-like group practice it with considerable vitality. The members of this group are with few exceptions, first-rate minds. It is certainly true that some of them are notably unproductive when measured by the ordinary standard of published or printed output, but if the proper libations are poured their verbal output is audible and within the

confines of the group or alleged clique they seem to exert a perceptible intellectual influence. If they don't speak to anyone else, they at least speak to each other. Some onlookers seem convinced that the clique-like character of the movement makes it impervious to criticism or to facts inconsistent with its theory or findings. In other words, say the onlookers, the practitioners of the art of componential analysis only read and quote each other, act as if they invented anthropology, and simply ignore facts they don't like. (1969a:8)

Schneider was nothing if not the master of innuendo, a dedicated (Groucho) Marxist who reveled in the paranoia of a one-man outgroup.

He goes on in this caustic essay to debunk componential analysis for resting on unwarranted assumptions, for failing to deal with both terms of address and terms of reference, for avoiding affinal terminology, for erecting premature boundaries and refusing to consider metaphoric kinship extensions or so-called fictive kinship, for neglecting issues of polysemy in kin terms, and perhaps most fundamentally, for failing to offer satisfactory definitions of kinship terms and to say what kinship itself is all about—a topic Schneider addresses in later essays (1970a, 1970b, 1972). He also sharply criticized the componential analyses of American or Yankee kinship produced by A. K. Romney and Roy D'Andrade (1964), by Goodenough (1965), by Anthony F. C. Wallace and John Atkins (1960), and by Philip K. Bock (1968). The criticisms are well directed, and the inconsistencies in the different analyses open up many disconcerting issues for dispute. Schneider takes his long-time friend, Ward Goodenough, to task more respectfully but no less critically than his other targets.

A. F. C. Wallace and American Kinship

Shortly after Schneider's *American Kinship* "pamphlet" appeared, and just prior to his unpublished Wenner-Gren critique of componential analysis, I found myself in a difficult position. As book review editor of the *American Anthropologist,* I had the unenviable responsibility to assign a reviewer to the "pamphlet." My general policy was not to go easy on colleagues: Robert McC. Adams was justifiably irate over being trashed by Karl Wittfogel (1967); and my close friend George Stocking thought Margaret Mead (1970) didn't do justice to his *Race, Culture and Evolution,* although he later relented and recognized that she said many things suitable for framing as book blurbs. If I learned anything during my tenure as book review editor, it was that there is nothing so delicate as the anthropological authorial ego. But what to do with David Schneider's book? I felt obliged to solicit a major-league peer reviewer, and someone who would give *American Kinship* a thorough reading. I thought Anthony Wallace, who had also written on the subject of American kinship, would be an ideal reviewer. Also I felt that I could persuade Wallace to accept the assignment. The review was received in timely fashion and published in the *American Anthropologist* (1969).

Wallace's review was fulsome, highly critical, yet not without praise for the significance of Schneider's stimulating and productive enterprise. Since the book is about American kinship, Wallace adopts the privileged role of a native informant and offers an alternative structural model to resolve the fundamental contradiction in American culture between nature and law that supposedly generates legal coitus, children, relatives, family, and the almost mystical quality of "enduring, diffuse solidarity."[11] Wallace's model emphasizes an opposition between freedom and constraint; he views love as an elemental force in nature involving intense attraction distinct from other more casual forms of love and lovemaking and not always integral to marriage. Wallace also offers an extended analysis of cousin-marriage and "kissing cousins" that Schneider neglects in his cultural account.[12] He finds other faults in Schneider's claims to authority (e.g., "Nothing which I say in this book is inconsistent with what I know"), in the adequacy of Schneider's sample, in the tenuous relation between data and theory, the empirical validation of ideal-typical ethnographic models, and the biases built into the initial selection of a particular type of model. Wallace hopes that the answers to many of his questions will be given in subsequent promised publications by Schneider.

Wallace would never get answers to his questions. His review was completely ignored by Schneider and by Schneider's students. I observed a cooling in our never-so-hot relations after the Wallace review appeared. When I finally asked him about his reaction to the review, the only response I could elicit suggested that Wallace didn't understand him and that the review was beside the point. Why the neglect? Why did Wallace become Schneider's Y. R. Chao? Schneider was rarely shy about public confrontation, as one can read in his published debates with the likes of Edmund Leach, Ward Goodenough, Rodney Needham, Ernest Gellner, and even Daniel Patrick Moynihan. Schneider, despite his sensitivities and insecurities, was an "in-your-face" kind of guy. Why did he fail to rebut Wallace? In his "Twelve Years Later" chapter in the second edition of *American Kinship,* when hopefully his temper had cooled and componential analysis was conveniently dead, if not buried, he still offers no response to a serious and highly critical review of his work in the major journal of American anthropology. Was this an instance of the unconscious psychic power of denial? Or was it a conscious tactical move on Schneider's part to silence serious criticism? How do we get into the mind of this anthropological native? Whatever the case, the silence worked. Until recently I have seen no published references to Wallace's review of *American Kinship* in the subsequent literature on the topic.[13] Not only was it ignored by Schneider and his followers, but Wallace's review is not even mentioned by Schneider's many critics, or by the cognitive anthropologists who are the direct heirs of componential analysis, which continues to exist under the euphemism "feature analysis" (D'Andrade 1995:21). As an informal test I asked several of the contributors to this volume about their recollections of Wallace's review; their memories of the review were vague at best.

Schneider's Legacy and the Future of Kinship Studies

Depending on your viewpoint, David Schneider's confrontation with componential analysis can be taken as high point or a low point in an evolving or devolving theoretical trajectory. A suitable starting point along this course could be his disagreement with Clyde Kluckhohn over the influence of biological determinants on personality; he soon extended this to a critique of biological influences on culture more generally. His critique was more than a replay of the eternal controversy over the relative importance of nature or nurture. Rather, it questioned the essential assumptions about the nature of the "natural" upon which so much of the promise of a comparative science of society, as envisioned by Murdock and others, insecurely rested. The venue in which Schneider chose to play out this struggle was the seemingly incontrovertible field of kinship.

Kinship had achieved an almost sacrosanct status in social anthropology as the "physics," if not the "physiology" of social structure. Primary kinship terms were considered elemental or minimal units that combined to form complex typological systems. Such systems could then be expressed abstractly and subjected to mathematical manipulation and formal analysis. Schneider was able to expose the limitations of such techniques by noting critical variations in assumed terms of reference and address, as well as violations of rules of usage.[14] While these limitations did not necessarily invalidate the efforts of the formalists to frame their analyses, they did help to legitimize a more intuitive approach, whereby native understandings of the meanings of kin terms were privileged. This leads almost directly to the epistemological problem of the locus of reality (also noted by Leaf, this volume): Does it reside in the mind of the native or the analyst? The formalists claim that their methods enable them to delineate rules or principles by which native realities can be accounted for, if not predicated. Schneider's cultural approach assimilates much data acquired through interviews and observations; yet the interpretations, as he grudgingly admits, are formulated in his own head without direct reference to the data. Thus, concepts like "diffuse enduring solidarity" are almost as alien to native informants as "bifurcate merging."[15]

Schneider's American kinship project was an effort to examine critically the domain of kinship. The move that he and Raymond Firth made to study kinship in modern urban settings was motivated less by a desire to prove the value of anthropological approaches to the modern world and its problems, and more by a wish to break out of the functionalist paradox that challenged the separate reality of kinship in so-called "primitive" or simpler societies. In such societies, kinship could not be clearly differentiated from other institutions in the political, economic, and religious realms.

However, Schneider argued that even in complex urban societies, kinship could not be neatly compartmentalized as a separate domain, recognized as such by the natives. He questioned the reality of the boundaries separating kinship from nationality and religion (1969b). While one can assume a certain amount of categorical leakage through metaphorized extension and logical anomalies, one can also legitimately question whether it was useful to throw the kinship baby out with the leaking bath water. By the time of his final magnum opus, *A Critique of the Study of Kinship* (1984), kinship no longer exists for Schneider as a valid, translatable, human cultural universal.

Indeed, the study of kinship, which played such a prominent role in the development of anthropological theory, now seems to be a dead topic. Its demise can be accounted for by a variety of overdetermined factors, including changes in the scale and scope of contemporary anthropology, the decline of fieldwork, critical views of scientific understanding, and the emergence of postmodern multiculturalism. Certainly David Schneider's developing critique was an influential, if not decisive, factor in the death of kinship studies. Only time will tell whether the subject will be revived, reincarnated, or reinvented.

Notes

1. After this was written, I discovered that Adam Kuper recently assessed Schneider in a similar fashion, calling him "an anti-establishment man, a maverick, a trickster, something of a troublemaker, out to shock the orthodox, never at peace with his colleagues or himself" (1999:122). I think at a deep level Schneider was very much an "establishment man," or wished to be.

2. Schneider's relationship with Kluckhohn was highly ambivalent, and he only faintly acknowledges Kluckhohn's influence on his thought. Schneider notes that they disagreed over the role of biological determinism in psychology (viz. Schneider 1995:70; Kuper 1999:125), claiming that Kluckhohn used it to rationalize his own closeted homo-

sexuality. Schneider seems to ignore the fact that, in his day, Kluckhohn was doubtless the most articulate and philosophically sophisticated champion of cultural relativism. However, Kluckhohn, along with many others, saw no contradiction in also recognizing the existence of human universals, some of which were biologically grounded, such as species characteristics, along with others grounded in distinctive cultural configurations. Indeed, for Schneider the nonbiological basis of kinship became a persistent theme in his work. It emerges clearly in his critique of Marion Levy's and other similar definitions of kinship as rooted in "blood" and reproduction (1965b:83–101), and it recurs in *American Kinship: A Cultural Account* (1968, 1980), and "What Is Kinship All About?" (1972). In the latter article and, finally, in *A Critique of the Study of Kinship* (1984), he questions the phenomenological reality of kinship itself as a valid comparative cultural category.

3. Parsons also came to recognize a "Behavioral Organism" underlying the "Personality System" in his subsystems of action (1966:28–29) and noted that his whole edifice rested on a biological substrate. In "Notes Toward a Theory of Culture" (1976), Schneider belatedly denies that culture is the sole determinant of social action, and he disclaims that levels of analysis can be judged as being higher or lower. Yet he introduces that astronomical term "galaxy" as a cultural concept to transcend more restricted notions of patterns, norms, or institutions. By your metaphors, so shall you be known.

4. Schneider's conception of culture breaks clearly from that of Kluckhohn, Kroeber, Parsons, and Geertz, all of whom emphasize norms, values, and patterns of and for behavior (Schneider 1976). His conception is more system oriented and less actor centered (cf., Schneider 1980:125–36). As McKinley (this volume) notes, Schneider also broke with Parsons in his refusal to consider how the cultural, social, psychological, and organic subsystems might be brought back together.

5. Despite the divergence of the two studies and the absence of cross-referencing, a retrospective comparison of the London and Chicago projects might prove valuable today in terms of methods and theory for the study of urban kinship.

6. Schneider's synchronic perspective severely limited his analysis of Yapese kinship, as his student, David Labby (1976), demonstrated. Schneider's first and second accounts of Yapese kinship, which take up part 1 and part 2 of *A Critique of the Study of Kinship*, are themselves thoroughly critiqued by Adam Kuper (1999:149–58).

7. Yet in his deconstructive quest to be free of presuppositions, it should be noted that Schneider never considers the concept of culture to be an ethnocentric construct far removed from the consciousness of most native peoples (cf., Kuper 1999:145).

8. Later, in response to criticism that *American Kinship: A Cultural Account* (1968) represented only middle-class patterns, Schneider and Raymond T. Smith (1973) examined lower class kinship and family structure. They report that "at the level of pure cultural conceptions in the domain of kinship, there is no variation of any detectable significance" (1973:103). However, the norms that provide rules for family structure and behavior show definite differences between the middle and lower classes (1973:105).

9. According to oral testimony, when *American Kinship: A Cultural Account* was finally published, Schneider went to Dean D. Gale Johnson's office and proudly slapped a copy of the slim volume on his desk. A few weeks later the Dean encountered David and thanked him for his pamphlet. Schneider non-self-deprecatingly refers to the incident in *Schneider on Schneider* (1995:220).

10. Somewhat paradoxically, perhaps, it was one of Schneider's heroes, A. L. Kroeber, whose categories of kinship relationship (1909) served as the cornerstone for much of the work in the componential analysis of kinship.

11. As Adam Kuper (1999:135–36) notes, Schneider fails to credit Talcott Parsons as the source of his quaint phraseology. In a similar manner, the catchy title of one of Schneider's most influential articles, "Some Muddles in the Models: Or How the System Really Works" (1965) may have been an unacknowledged appropriation from a statement by Robert Redfield in a general discussion of the use of the terms "structure" and "model" in theoretical anthropology. To quote the relevant passage, Redfield says, "As Dr. Kroeber has referred to his strictures on structure, I shall not meddle with this muddle of models" (Tax et al. 1953:120). What we may have here is a Max Müllerian (contagious) disease of language!

12. Even more germane to Schneider and Wallace's argument concerning the meaning of love in American kinship might be some discussion of the term "love child," which refers to a child born out of wedlock.

13. Adam Kuper (1999:136), my doppelgänger in this essay, makes a brief reference to a small part of Wallace's review.

14. Schneider's recognition of the problem of alternative terms and irregular usages can be traced back at least to the monograph he co-authored with John Roberts on *Zuni Kin Terms* (1956:15–18). A review of this carefully crafted study should dispel any misconception about Schneider's ability to conduct kinship studies in the traditional mode.

15. In his essay, "Kinship, Nationality, and Religion in American Culture: Toward a Definition of Kinship" (1969:120), Schneider does acknowledge Parsons's use of the adjective "diffuse" as well as recognizing that the phrase "diffuse, enduring solidarity" was his own invention and would be considered jargon by a native speaker.

References Cited

Bock, Philip K. 1968. "Some Generative Rules for American Kinship Terminology." *Anthropological Linguistics* 10:1–6.

D'Andrade, Roy. 1995. *The Development of Cognitive Anthropology.* Cambridge: Cambridge University Press.

Firth, Raymond, Jane Hubert, and Anthony Forge. 1968. *Families and Their Relatives: Kinship in a Middle-Class Sector of London—An Anthropological Study.* New York: Humanities Press.

Goodenough, Ward H. 1965. "Yankee Kinship Terminology: A Problem in Componential Analysis." In *Formal Semantic Analysis.* Ed. E. A. Hammel. 259–87. Special issue of *American Anthropologist* 67 (5), pt. 2.

Kroeber, A. L. 1909. "Classificatory Systems of Relationship." *Journal of the Royal Anthropological Institute* 39:77–84.

Kuper, Adam. 1999. *Culture: The Anthropologists' Account.* Cambridge, Mass.: Harvard University Press.

Labby, David. 1976. *The Demystification of Yap: Dialectics of Culture on a Micronesian Island.* Chicago: University of Chicago Press.

Mead, Margaret. 1970. "Review of *Race, Culture, and Evolution* by George W. Stocking." *American Anthropologist* 72 (2): 374–78.

Murdock, George P. 1949. *Social Structure.* New York: Macmillan.

Parsons, Talcott. 1957. *The Social System.* New York: Free Press.

———. 1966. *Societies: Evolutionary and Comparative Perspectives.* Englewood Cliffs, N.J.: Prentice-Hall.

Romney, A. K., and Roy G. D'Andrade. 1964. "Cognitive Aspects of English Kin Terms." *American Anthropologist* 66 (3): 146–70.

Schneider, David M. 1961. "Introduction: The Distinctive Features of Matrilineal Descent Groups." In *Matrilineal Kinship.* Ed. David M. Schneider and Kathleen Gough. 1–29. Berkeley: University of California Press.

———. 1965a. "American Kin Terms and Terms for Kinsmen: A Critique of Goodenough's Componential Analysis of Yankee Kinship Terminology." In *Formal Semantic Analysis.* Ed. E. A. Hammel. 288–308. Special issue of *American Anthropologist* 67 (5), pt. 2.

———. 1965b. "Kinship and Biology." In *Aspects of the Analysis of Family Structure.* Ed. Ashley J. Coale et al. 83–101. Princeton, N.J.: Princeton University Press.

———. 1965c. "Some Muddles in the Models: Or How the System Really Works." In *The Relevance of Models for Social Anthropology.* Ed. Michael Banton. 25–85. ASA Monograph No. 1. London: Tavistock.

———. 1968. *American Kinship: A Cultural Account.* Englewood Cliffs, N.J.: Prentice-Hall.

———. 1969a. "Componential Analysis: A State-of-the-Art Review." Paper presented at the Wenner-Gren Symposium on Cognitive Studies and Artificial Intelligence Research, March 2–8, Chicago.

———. 1969b. "Kinship, Nationality, and Religion in American Culture: Toward a Definition of Kinship." In *Forms of Symbolic Action.* Ed. Robert F. Spencer. 116–25. Proceedings of the American Ethnological Society. Washington, D.C.

———. 1970a. "American Kin Categories." In *Échanges et communications: Mélanges offerts à Claude Lévi-Strauss.* Ed. P. Maranda and J. Pouillon. 370–81. The Hague: Mouton.

———. 1970b. "What Should Be Included in a Vocabulary of Kinship Terms." In *Proceedings of the Eighth International Congress of Anthropological and Ethnological Sciences.* 2:88–90. Tokyo: Science Council of Japan.

———. 1972. "What Is Kinship All About?" In *Kinship Studies in the Morgan Centennial Year.* Ed. Priscilla Reining. 32–63. Washington, D.C.: Anthropological Society of Washington.

———. 1976. "Notes toward a Theory of Culture." In *Meaning in Anthropology.* Ed. Keith H. Basso and Henry A. Selby. 197–220. Albuquerque: University of New Mexico Press.

———. 1980. *American Kinship: A Cultural Account.* 2d ed. Chicago: University of Chicago Press.

———. 1984. *A Critique of the Study of Kinship.* Ann Arbor: University of Michigan Press.

Schneider, David M., and Calvert B. Cottrell. 1975. *The American Kin Universe: A Genealogical Study.* University of Chicago Studies in Anthropology Series in Social, Cultural, and Linguistic Anthropology No. 3. Chicago.

———. 1995. *Schneider on Schneider: The Conversion of the Jews and Other Anthropological Stories by David Schneider, as Told to Richard Handler.* Ed. Richard Handler. Durham, N.C.: Duke University Press.

Schneider, David M., and Kathleen Gough, eds. 1961. *Matrilineal Kinship.* Berkeley: University of California Press.

Schneider, David M., and George C. Homans. 1955. "Kinship Terminology and the American Kinship System." *American Anthropologist* 57 (6): 1194–208.

Schneider, David M., and John M. Roberts. 1955. "Zuni Kin Terms." Notebook No. 3, Monograph 1, Laboratory of Anthropology, University of Nebraska, Lincoln.

Schneider, David M., and Raymond T. Smith. 1973. *Class Differences and Sex Roles in American Kinship and Family Structure.* Englewood Cliffs, N.J.: Prentice-Hall. (Reprinted with a new introduction in 1978 by the University of Michigan Press, Ann Arbor.)

Tax, Sol, et al., eds. 1953. *An Appraisal of Anthropology Today.* Chicago: University of Chicago Press.

Wallace, Anthony F. C. 1969. "Review of *American Kinship: A Cultural Account* by David Schneider." *American Anthropologist* 71 (1): 100–106.

Wallace, Anthony F. C., and John Atkins. 1960. "The Meaning of Kinship Terms." *American Anthropologist* 62:58–80.

Wittfogel, Karl. 1967. "Review of *The Evolution of Urban Society* by Robert McC. Adams." *American Anthropologist* 69 (1): 90–92.

Wolf, Linda. 1964. *Anthropological Interviewing in Chicago: Analysis of a Kinship Research Experience.* American Kinship Project, Monograph 1. University of Chicago, Department of Anthropology.

2. Procrustes and the Sioux: David M. Schneider and the Study of Sioux Kinship

RAYMOND J. DeMALLIE

Fred Eggan, Raymond D. Fogelson, and Chicago Anthropology in the Mid-1960s

DAVID SCHNEIDER had a profound effect on my thinking about Sioux kinship. I have taken the invitation to contribute to this volume as an opportunity to reminisce about my experiences as a student at the University of Chicago from 1964 to 1971. I had not come to Chicago to study with Schneider, but I had come to study kinship. I am a native of Rochester, New York, and in spring 1964, during my senior year in high school, I had the opportunity to hear Fred Eggan deliver the first annual Lewis Henry Morgan Lectures at the University of Rochester.[1] Eggan's lectures presented biographical material on Morgan, an introduction to the study of kinship and social organization, and four substantial regional case studies—Southeast, Plains, Great Lakes, and Southwestern Pueblos—based on Morgan's work and subsequent anthropological investigations. The series concluded with a lecture entitled "Lewis Henry Morgan and the Future of the American Indian," which took a broader look at Morgan's studies in relation to the developing ideas of American Indian self-determination. Eggan's presentation of Rochester's most famous anthropologist drew me in, and his mesmerizing descriptions of kinship systems and what could be learned by comparing them hooked me. When he mentioned in one lecture the need for someone to do comparative work on the kinship systems of the various groups of Sioux, I knew I had found my calling. After that evening's lecture, mustering all my courage, I volunteered for duty and told Professor Eggan—it didn't occur to me to ask—that I was coming to Chicago in the fall to be his student and work on those Sioux kinship systems.

Once at the University of Chicago I realized that I would actually have to get a B.A. first, but Eggan never let that detail stand in the way. From my freshman year onward, I wrote papers for him every year on some aspect of Sioux kinship. The variations in kin terms fascinated me, as did the problem of the characteristic Dakota cousin terminology used by the Sioux. Fred Eggan derived the pattern historically from a hypothesized former practice of cross-cousin marriage (1966:98–100), while Alexander Lesser derived it structurally from the practice of the levirate and sororate (1958).

As a student of Eggan's, I felt throughout my undergraduate years that my main mission was to understand Radcliffe-Brown and the British social anthropologists, but Raymond D. Fogelson—who has always been my link to reality, especially the reality that lies outside the University of Chicago—had us read the Boasians; and studying with Sol Tax guaranteed a wide reading list with a solid Redfieldian base.[2] I read Clifford Geertz under the careful tutelage of Hildred Geertz, whose undergraduate seminar on functionalism was one of the high points of my college years. Another was Claude Lévi-Strauss's visit to Chicago in 1965, which inspired me to try to understand structuralism.

In the fall quarter of 1967, I wrote a paper for Fogelson titled "Lewis Henry Morgan and the Kinship System of the Dakota" in which I compared the schedules in Morgan's *Systems of Consanguinity and Affinity of the Human Family* (1871) with other published accounts, including Eggan's and Lesser's. I laid out the various kin term correspondences and tried to systematize my speculations about changes in the system. Fogelson's comments, written directly on the paper, were instructive, and supportive. Most insightfully, he suggested the possibility "of dual models existing in informants 'heads' and appropriately applied . . . in specific situations."

David M. Schneider and "Semantic Space"

At the start of the next quarter when I talked to Fogelson about my paper, he suggested I rethink it in terms of "semantic space." My blank look prompted him to draw a diagram—a large empty rectangle—which he proceeded to divide into boxes based on such criteria as consanguinity/affinity, generation, and gender. Then he offered a barrage of citations, including the classic article by Anthony F. C. Wallace and J. Atkins (1960).[3] My paper that quarter, "A Semantic Aspect of Dakota Kinship Terminology," offered a tentative componential analysis of the system based on Lesser's data and focused on cross-cousin and affinal terms. To make the analysis work, as I stated in my paper, I had to exclude terms for "child," "co-wife," and "co-parent-in-law." That left thirty-three terms, neatly differentiated each from the other by seven components, each component divided into as many as five subdivisions. Uncharacteristically, Fogelson wrote not a word on the paper but instead passed it on to David Schneider, who gave me three single-spaced pages of reaction.

Schneider laid out the ground rules in advance so clearly that they deserve quoting: "You must understand that I have a 'bias,' that is, I have a profound disagreement with the whole 'ethnoscience' or 'new ethnography' approach. . . . I simply alert you to the polemic bias, not to deny merit to my comment[s], but rather to warn you to use your judgment, not accept what might seem to be my 'expertise.'"[4] He pointed out that my exclusions were "traditional, but hardly for that reason justifiable." The thirty-three terms were thus the artifact of my analysis. "But 33 is a very nice number. How many kinship terms does American have? And what are they?"

Similarly, the components of my analysis were traditional in anthropology, having no other source than Alfred L. Kroeber's "Classificatory Systems of Relationship" (1909) and, therefore, having nothing at all to do with the Sioux. Schneider wrote: "Componential analysis . . . always insists it is trying to find out what the native culture is like. I submit that it always stuffs it into a Procrustean bed fabricated out of uncomfortable kintypes defined in terms of analytic notions like age, sex, generation, collaterality, lineality, sex of speaker[,] sex of person spoken [to,] and of course the condition of life of the intervening relative." Then, in reaction to my historical speculations about hypothesized changes in certain terms, Schneider continued: "Here is a truly illegitimate technique; anything that does not fit we explain as a carry-over from a former system. . . . To explain why [the son-in-law] term is an anomaly by saying it remains from what it was before only asks you to explain the rest of the terms. . . . Maybe nothing has changed in Dakota *except* [the son-in-law] term. Can you show that this is not true? History, if it is to 'explain' anything, must explain everything in the same way."

In the spring quarter of 1968 I pulled together everything I had on Sioux kin terminologies into a bachelor's honor's thesis. It offered a complete collection of known sets of terms, a more developed componential analysis, and further discussion of possible semantic meanings of particular terms. That summer, while working in the old Bureau of American Ethnology archives at the Smithsonian Institution, I received from Schneider another three-page letter, somewhat ominously dated "Bastille Day." He summarized the findings of my paper in a brief paragraph, noting that I had treated only "a small, narrow portion of the relevant data":

> Hence to "finish" this paper . . . you either must go to the rest of the domain of kinship or you yourself must concede that after almost 80 pages of manipulation of genealogical material all you have are vague hints of what the system is all about. . . . Part II must now be the material you said you left aside— the usages, the social organization, the behavioral patterns, the ideology of kinship, the religious material and so on. When these two parts are then collated, I predict that you will really have your hands on the kinship system. But not until then.

He began his critical commentary by discussing my separate treatment of terms of address and terms of reference. I had thought of them as distinct systems because of the constraints of Lakota grammar. Schneider, on the other hand, following his developing cultural theory, saw them as parts of a single symbol system (see Schneider 1995:207). It was an important point for his approach to kinship:

> First, the address[/]reference dichotomy. I think that the empirical material on this dichotomy in American [kinship] is perfectly clear. The assumption that these are two *distinct, distinguishable, unitary* systems is demonstrably false. Not only are these neither distinct, nor distinguishable nor unitary *systems,* but there is ample evidence that there are not two. Thus we have shown that how people actual[ly] use terms in reference depends on who is being addressed. (I call my father, when I talk to a stranger, "father," but the kinship term for father when I talk to my brother is "pop" . . . etc. etc. What "is" the reference term here? Further, how many different address terms are there? What contextual differences occur in address? etc. etc.).
>
> Hence to assume a distinct, coherent, unitary *address* system, distinct from but related to a distinct, coherent unitary *referential* system, seems to me to introduce further complexities, further assumptions, further "problems" in the task you have set for yourself that can only hamper the analysis. What you do, I think, is to *add data* when no data need be added, and further, never check to see if it is data inherent in the system or in the analytic procedures (by you I mean one who does such things, as has been done since [W. H. R.] Rivers).

Of greater immediate interest to me was his commentary on my discussion of cross-cousin marriage:

> It is an important and tricky question whether when FaBr = MoSiHu and FaSi = MoBrWi this must or must not co-occur with a bilateral cross-cousin marriage rule and whether, finally, these must also co-occur with any minimal actual rate of such marriages. That is, to draw one specific corollary from this

general statement, it may well be that for the given system there is no distinction between kin and affines, between relatives by blood and by marriage, even if cross-cousin marriage does not occur and there are rules against it. If the whole society is regarded as kin, then marriage must be (if it is endogamous) with a member of the society, i.e. with a kinsman—ok?

He had put his finger on a sore point. All the literature supported the cultural proposition that the Sioux were related in one vast web of kinship coterminous with the tribal boundary, and at the same time the literature asserted that marriages could not take place between relatives. How were these two ideas to be reconciled?

Graduate Student Life: Diffuse, Enduring Solidarity and the Study of Sioux Kinship

In the fall of 1968 I made the transition to graduate school, and with it came a sense of urgency to get along with the work. My financial support, however, came from a National Endowment for the Humanities grant to the Field Museum of Natural History, so I spent the majority of my days that year in the museum's archives, storerooms, and work spaces studying the manuscripts and artifacts from the Plains that George A. Dorsey so assiduously collected in the first decade of the century. On the University of Chicago campus I attended Schneider's "Systems" class, a two-semester introduction to social anthropology for entering students, which I had learned to think of as the crucible from which we either would, or would not, emerge as anthropologists. For Schneider's opening lecture—which he repeated on the second day of class, as he said, just in case we might have missed any of his major points the first time around—I collated my notes with those of two other students to try to arrive at a consensual version of the event. From moccasins and medicine bundles in the morning to Parsonian theory in the afternoon, I remember those first months as quite disjointed. How could this whole field, past and present, be tied together into a coherent whole?

At that time Schneider was writing his article "American Kin Categories" for the Claude Lévi-Strauss festschrift (1970), and in his "Systems" course he intended to acquaint us with the intellectual foundation for the argument elaborated in his monograph *American Kinship: A Cultural Account* (1968), which had just appeared. He had structured the course very carefully. The fall quarter dealt with the basics: Durkheim, Parsons, the fundamental problems of anthropology, and a "history" of the study of kinship from Morgan on. This was "not history the way George Stocking writes it," Schneider said, but "history as it ought to have happened." The fundamental problem of the course, he commented on October 17 during a discussion of social theory, was the "ordering of the many subunits of the whole."

On October 22 he began his lecture, according to my notes, by urging us to adopt one theory but to gain familiarity with others as well. He cautioned us against thinking of theory as "good" or "bad." He noted the cognitive bias in the then-current definition of culture, apparent in the work of the componential analysts. As an alternative, he offered these suggestions: "Culture is a special kind of action." "What the natives think is not culture." Occupied as I was with the thought of writing a symbolic account of Sioux kinship, I know I did not appreciate the significance of those remarks.

By November 26, the last day of the fall quarter, Schneider seemed to be ruminating on the relationship between symbol and norm. "What does a symbol tell you to do?" he asked, rhetorically. He concluded the lecture with his famous definition of kinship as "diffuse and enduring solidarity," arguing that kinship was a cultural universal "because you have to have a mechanism for raising children."

Winter quarter dealt with descent versus alliance and a series of ethnographic case studies focused on kinship. In the concluding lecture Schneider defined culture in terms of the most general concepts: "This is what life is, this is what is." Norms were defined as behavioral patterns: "Who has the right to do what and with which and to whom." Values were defined as an intermediate level linking norms with culture. The quarter ended with his famed vacuum-cleaner model: Without a problem for study the anthropologist goes to the field like a vacuum cleaner, sweeping up data randomly and hoping on his return that the gleanings will fit together in some coherent manner.

That spring semester Schneider invited a few of us to participate in a small seminar called "Virgin Birth," in which each of us investigated and reported on a matrilineal society with a particular emphasis on the definition of kin terms. Ellen Becker (later Basso), back from fieldwork in Brazil, joined us. Schneider offered to synthesize our papers and give us a general theoretical statement at the end of the quarter, but we overwhelmed him with data, and he ultimately begged off.

With Eggan off campus for the 1969–70 academic year in England, I asked Schneider to serve with Fogelson as my M.A. committee. My task was to continue with part 2 of the bachelor's honors thesis. I thought a reasonable and useful exercise for the thesis would be to attempt a cultural analysis in the manner of Schneider, defining and exploring the relationship among the cultural units that comprise Sioux kinship.[5] I wrote it while in residence at the Smithsonian, where I worked with William C. Sturtevant, proponent of the New Ethnography and author of an important survey of works using componential analysis (1964); his advice never failed to be valuable but also never failed to conflict with Chicago models. I dealt with the behavioral patterns, the values, and the symbols and found that, no matter how hard I struggled against it, "diffuse, enduring solidarity" summed up my understanding of the cultural meaning of Sioux kinship.

The reaction from Chicago to my thesis might have been considered amusing, but only for someone not so closely involved as I was. From his letter of March 18, 1970, I concluded that Schneider liked it, so far as it went, but he pushed me harder:

> You don't face it and perhaps you shouldn't in this work, but . . . you have showed that kinship = nationality = religion etc. In other words, the whole blooming thing is a single system which is NOT culturally differentiated into "institutions," separate institutions, of kinship, nationality and religion. O.k. . . . So all I ask, then, is this: Why keep calling them "kinship" terms? Why not "nationality" terms? Or is that just as restricted as "kinship." Could you consider them simply as "relationship" terms? Try it on for size.

In a revealing aside, Schneider made a useful comment on my misuse of terms relating to Indian warfare, long before anyone spoke of political correctness: "The word 'murdered' should be changed to 'killed' or 'kilt' as the case may be. There is a tradition, which I think should be changed at the earliest convenience, that when indians kill whites, the whites are 'murdered', but when white[s] murder indians, the indians are killed." I have always been grateful to him for this.

In contrast to Schneider's reaction, on April 6 I received Fogelson's marginal comments on the manuscript. Next to a section where I discussed the boundaries of the kinship system from a symbolic perspective, he wrote: "Highly speculative. I doubt whether Lakota would recognize this, even tho Schneider would be pleased." That day I wrote to Fogelson, trying to explain and justify the approach I had taken. I characterized my work as an ethnographic study that attempted to define the Lakota cultural domain of "relationship" (*wótakuye*) and to show its internal ordering. I suggested that this symbolic approach was complementary to the componential analysis I had used in my honor's essay. At about that time, without prompting from me, a Lakota I had met in Washington discussed "relationship" at a cosmic level that to him was essential to traditional culture. This fit with the argument in my master's thesis. In self-defense I wrote: "I hope you understand that I have not 'stretched' the Dakota data to fit any preconceived ideas of Schneider's; on the contrary, I have been shocked at how closely his general conceptualization of 'diffuse, enduring solidarity' fits the Dakota data."

Nevertheless, I made no headway with Fogelson. In reply, on April 17, he wrote: "I've never been convinced, even after reading and re-reading Schneider, that I understand what 'diffuse, enduring solidarity' means." Further, "there is the problem of symbols floating around unanchored in an indeterminate level of reality . . . the reality of symbols must be demonstrated, and in some context." He concluded, "I hate to see you follow a narrow path that may eventually lead to an ambush in some box canyon."

I had commented to Fogelson in my letter that the final "test" of my symbolic analysis "will simply be my own intuitive feelings after field work." His response to this was direct: "The problem of 'testing' ethnographic formulations—including such criteria as reliability, validity, and replicability—is a serious one; I remain unconvinced that one's own 'intuitive feelings after fieldwork' constitutes sufficient response to the problem."

After turning in my master's thesis, I spent May to November doing fieldwork on the Cheyenne River Sioux Reservation. Only when I arrived there did it dawn on me how little actual preparation I had for fieldwork. But within twenty-four hours of arriving there I was living with a Lakota-speaking family in a rural community, and during the ensuing months I came to understand something about Lakota kinship in a participatory sense. I spent much of my time studying the language, recording traditional narratives, and writing my impressions of family life. I returned to Chicago just in time to attend the American Anthropological Association meeting in San Diego, where, through Sturtevant, I met Vine Deloria Jr., then the most visible and vocal spokesman for Indian activists. He challenged me to think how the work I was doing as an anthropologist might be of some good to Indian people, as well as advancing my own career. I found the contrast between reservation and academic life to be more disconcerting than I had anticipated.

During the winter I drafted my dissertation proposal, again while in residence at the Smithsonian. By this time Eggan had decided that I should not continue fieldwork but, instead, apply for an NEH fellowship to spend 1971–72 at the Smithsonian. (I had spent very little money from the NIMH grant the department had awarded, he told me, and the department could fund another student with the remainder of it.) The catch was that my dissertation had to be completed by the end of summer. Knowing that I had only made a start at a field study of kinship, I decided to focus the dissertation on historical sources, including the field notes and writings of previous students of the Sioux, including Clark Wissler, James R. Walker, Ella C. Deloria, and H. Scudder Mekeel. In my proposal I outlined an elaborate reconstruction of the historical Lakota kinship system, with contemporary Cheyenne River to serve as a test case. (The latter portion of the planned study was never written.)

My doctoral committee was headed by Eggan and included Fogelson, Schneider, and George Stocking. I was indecisive about my theoretical approach, and the proposal showed it. I talked more about the ethnohistorical method than about theory. Perhaps fearing criticism from other faculty members, I wrote in the proposal: "The theoretical approach which I take borrows mainly from the work of Fred Eggan for the analysis of social systems. . . . [The] study has been inspired by the work of David Schneider, but differs from him in that I would not deny the essential genealogical basis of kinship." Commenting on the proposal draft, George Stocking began his letter of February 25, 1971, "Why are you so cautious?"

On February 16, I sent the proposal to Schneider. It is worth mentioning that he was recuperating at the time from a heart attack and had just completed the draft of his paper "What Is Kinship All About?" Since Schneider could not come to Washington, James Boon—a fellow Chicago graduate student marooned at the Smithsonian—read it to the Anthropological Society of Washington as part of the symposium celebrating the centennial year of the publication of Morgan's *Systems*. In my cover letter I told him a bit about my experiences in the field:

> Dear Dr. David,
>   . . . When I was amongst my friends and enemies (but, Vine D[eloria] warns me, never informants), Sioux all, I found out the real truth behind the meaning of "relationship." For the Dakota, at least, it means "diffuse, enduring solidarity." . . . In short, what I felt was at least partly hypothesis in my MA thesis was strongly born out by my experiences among the Sioux.
>   . . . I also discovered in South Dakota that contemporary Dakota kinship, while not best looked at in total isolation from its aboriginal tribal history, can really best be understood as a part of middle and lower [class] American kinship.

As an example, I discussed variability in kin terms. A consultant would use *lekší* "uncle" for father's brother; later, the same individual might give *até* "father." I first interpreted this as evidence of change creeping into the system, the Sioux taking over the kinship pattern of English:

> One day I thought to verify my hypothesis by asking [a consultant] what her FB's name was. She told me. What did you call him, when you met him? *Ate*, "father," she replied. But you said *lekší* the other day, said I, indignantly. Oh, that's right, she said, but that's the white way. *Lekší*, Indian way. *Ate*, white way. In short, it depends which language you're talking. And when you're translat-

ing from Indian to English, or the reverse, for the benefit of the whites you use the white system, because they laugh at you for the other system. So I asked other people, all ages, and they all said, yep: two systems, white and Indian. You can use white terms in the Indian system, or Indian terms in the white system, but to do either sounds funny. Change? As far as kin terms go, they're just bilingual!

In his reply on February 23, Schneider seemed less enthused about my findings than I had anticipated. He wrote: "Your point about there being a bilingual system rather than an acculturated system is nice, but then how do you go about that problem? Or don't you need to? For if it does assimilate closely to lower class forms, surely you will have to do some field work in that direction."

Method, Theory, Ethnohistory, and Culture

In my letter I had asked Schneider for comments on the dissertation proposal and tried to explain to him why I took the tack that I did. I mentioned the case of another student who had tried to bring together his and Eggan's theories and found himself in a politically untenable position. So, I added, "I have decided to emphasize the methodology: ethnohistory, and not worry about theory."

The latter was the portion of my letter to which Schneider replied at some length. His tone seemed melancholy, though not surprising to anyone who has passed a long Chicago winter. But I did not understand the subtext of his letter then. He wrote:

> I am sorry to say that I cannot offer any profound, grand-design changes or alterations in the thesis proposal. In fact, to put it simply, I think it is fine. I think that the main strategy decision you have already made and that is to steer a neutral middle of the road position between all significant shoals, to keep as you put it, to methodological and not theoretical issues. You may not notice until too late that methodology is dictated by theory, and so of course any methodological position you take is in reality a theory. But let's cross that bridge when it hatches. . . .
>
> Anyway, as you know I will support you all the way until you are out and on your own academic feet, so for both formal and informal purposes I strongly approve this proposal or any other that you bring in. Then, once you are out and on your own theoretical feet, we can begin to talk more directly about how one can steer (stear?) a course between the old r-b [Radcliffe-Brown] via eggan models and those I push so hard. And you must agree with Jim [Boon] that life is just a text—would that we could read it twice!—if not a drama, a rite, a ritual, a performance, a structure and a disaster.

> Otherwise all is well here. Or seems to be. The winter will never leave, the cold is set in for the duration of the eternity, the grey grime and chicago gloom pervades all, and we survive by means that are not entirely clear or rational.

When I returned to Chicago in April for my dissertation proposal hearing, I called Schneider the evening before to remind him of the time. To my surprise he said, "I don't think you want me there." With some urging he reluctantly came to my hearing. The exam was held in the old anthropology library on the second floor of the social sciences building, with the candidate at one end of an immensely long table and the faculty clustered at the other end. When Schneider arrived he sat apart from the rest of the faculty, at a separate table, and after I gave a brief synopsis of my proposed dissertation, the event soon turned into a verbal battle (in which I played no part) over the very possibility of cultural analysis. One faculty member asked me if I had any model in mind for a cultural analysis—a rhetorical question since he quickly added, "I've never seen an adequate cultural analysis of anything!" Nor did I receive any support from Schneider. When I talked about my intention to use past anthropologists' field notes as source material for my dissertation, Schneider flatly denied that one anthropologist could use another's field notes in any meaningful way (see Schneider 1995:213–14). Fred Eggan watched, somewhat bemusedly I thought, and said little. (Did I deserve this?) In the midst of the fray, Sol Tax saved the moment by asking me a solid ethnographic question.

I waited an eternity in the hallway before being called back in and informed that I had passed. Schneider came up to congratulate me and told me quietly that I would understand why he was removing himself from my dissertation committee. Otherwise, he said, he would have to delay me in Chicago as a student a good deal longer. "After you get your degree we can continue our debate," he commented with a gracious tone. This wasn't the type of support I had imagined on the basis of his letter. Naively, I hadn't realized the serious consequences of the intellectual disagreement between us. It seemed to me at that moment that he had made it into more an issue of personal loyalty than of anthropological theory. (But to quote David Schneider, writing me about the department's shoddy treatment of a classmate, "c'est la guerre academique or sumthing.")

Sioux Kinship as a System of Symbols

In my field studies of kinship I have never forgotten the issues Schneider raised with me. I have come to see kinship as the core symbol for Sioux culture, but a symbol that embraces all the meanings of nationalism and religion, just as Schneider suggested. I have convinced myself of the reality of diffuse and enduring solidarity as the central meaning of kinship for the Sioux, even though contemporary Sioux speak in terms of blood. I have at times been tempted to see this as clear evidence of cultural change. (No, I can't prove that it isn't everything else that has changed.) By lucky chance I met a Yanktonai Sioux woman who liked to talk about kinship in the abstract more than any other Sioux I have ever met; and I remember thinking of David as I sat at her kitchen table, trying to figure out how this particular native thought. She insisted that blood was the defining feature of kinship, with a founding male at the root of the family. But she sensed my disappointment— or desperation—as I sought to define the subunits of this cultural concept. She sat back and seemed to appraise what I wanted and said, "Like, if someone were to come here and they had no place to stay and I took them in and fed them, they would be relatives to me; if you feed someone, if they depend on you, they are related to you." I smiled, and she seemed gratified by my reaction. Perhaps we were now related.

In the spring of 1979 I found myself back in the anthropology library at the University of Chicago where I had defended my proposal and later my dissertation. Fogelson had invited me to give a Monday afternoon seminar since I was in Chicago that year as a fellow at the Center for the History of the American Indian at the Newberry Library. I decided to talk about Sioux kinship and to present the cultural model that emerged from my studies. By this time I had taught seminars in kinship at the University of Wyoming and Indiana University, and had spent additional time in the field as well. I was ready to attempt a summary of my understanding of Sioux kinship, and this was the perfect place to do it. In the process I abandoned my quest to find indications of change in the system and critiqued the way I had presented the system in my dissertation. My talk (finally published as DeMallie 1994, in greatly revised form) concluded as follows:

> It now seems to me that in a cultural, i.e., symbolic, sense, biological relationships are at the basis of the Lakota kinship system. Yet sexual relations and the genealogical network they produced are continually overlooked and overridden by the kinship system. . . .
>
> In coming to this conclusion, I have essentially followed the method laid out by Schneider in his paper "What Is Kinship All About?", that is, I looked at the Lakota definition of the domain of kinship, studied the available behavioral and normative data, and abstracted from them the cultural system. My earlier analysis was incomplete because I focused too narrowly on the kinship system and so was unable to discover fundamental cultural symbols revealed through the

examination of Lakota sexual beliefs and religious concepts. This, of course, is thoroughly in line with Schneider's assertion that kinship itself is not a cultural system, but rather a part of the system that is culture.

I had not expected Schneider to be in the audience, but he was. Had I known he would be there I probably would not have made such direct reference to him. But he smiled and fairly beamed throughout my talk and afterward was flattering and supportive. I had seen the light! In a way I had. But by then the issues that seemed so critical a few years earlier had been eclipsed by others, and I had the uncomfortable feeling that the students in the audience perceived my talk as a historical relic.

During his years at the University of Chicago, Schneider's theories and his personality were inseparable. He demanded, it seemed to me, a level of personal loyalty that I found impossible to give. Nonetheless, he was an inspiring teacher who unabashedly used his own work as a model for students. His influence on my thinking has become clearer to me as time passes, and writing this commemoration of my interactions with him as a student, brief though they were, has brought that influence into focus.

Notes

1. These lectures were later published as *The American Indian: Perspectives for the Study of Social Change* (Eggan 1966).

2. For Fogelson's view of Chicago anthropology in the 1960s and 1970s, and Schneider's role in the University of Chicago Department of Anthropology, see Fogelson (chapter 1, this volume).

3. For systematic discussion of the formal analysis of semantic space in relation to kinship and its implications for Schneider's view of culture, see Leaf (chapter 3) and (especially) Read (chapter 4, both this volume).

4. All correspondence and lecture notes cited in this chapter are in the author's files at Indiana University. I have quoted material from David Schneider as he wrote it, only correcting obvious spelling errors, to reflect the quick pace of his thought as expressed in his hurried typing.

5. Susan Montague, another veteran of Schneider's "Systems" course and of the "Virgin Birth" seminar, was likewise inspired to attempt a cultural analysis of kinship, in her case in the Trobriand Islands. Montague's conclusions are presented in chapter 7 of this volume.

References Cited

DeMallie, Raymond J. 1994. "Kinship and Biology in Sioux Culture." In *North American Indian Anthropology: Essays on Society and Culture.* Ed. Raymond J. DeMallie and Alfonso Ortiz. 125–46. Norman: University of Oklahoma Press.

Eggan, Fred. 1966. *The American Indian: Perspectives for the Study of Social Change.* Chicago: Aldine.

Kroeber, A. L. 1909. "Classificatory Systems of Relationship." *Journal of the Royal Anthropological Institute* 39:77–84.

Lesser, Alexander. 1958. "Siouan Kinship Systems." Ph.D. dissertation, Columbia University, New York.

Morgan, Lewis Henry. 1871. *Systems of Consanguinity and Affinity of the Human Family.* Smithsonian Contributions to Knowledge 17. Washington, D.C.: Smithsonian Institution.

Schneider, David M. 1968. *American Kinship: A Cultural Account.* Englewood Cliffs, N.J.: Prentice-Hall.

———. 1970. "American Kin Categories." In *Échanges et communications: Mélanges offerts à Claude Lévi-Strauss.* Ed. Pierre Maranda and Jean Pouillon. 370–81. The Hague: Mouton.

———. 1972. "What Is Kinship All About?" In *Kinship Studies in the Morgan Centennial Year.* Ed. Priscilla Reining. 32–63. Washington, D.C.: Anthropological Society of Washington.

———. 1995. *Schneider on Schneider: The Conversion of the Jews and Other Anthropological Stories, as Told to Richard Handler.* Ed. Richard Handler. Durham, N.C.: Duke University Press.

Sturtevant, William C. 1964. "Studies in Ethnoscience." In *Transcultural Studies in Cognition.* Ed. A. Kimball Romney and Roy Goodwin D'Andrade. 99–131. Special issue of *American Anthropologist* 66 (3), pt. 2.

Wallace, Anthony F. C, and John Atkins. 1960. "The Meaning of Kinship Terms." *American Anthropologist* 62:58–80.

3. Schneider's Idealism, Relativism, and the Confusion of Kinship

MURRAY J. LEAF

Philosophy, Ethnography, and Umpires

DAVID SCHNEIDER did not demand ideological conformity in his students, and they varied greatly in the critical distance they chose to maintain. What attracted me to him in 1961 was not his positive theory so much as his ability to lay out and interrelate a wide range of critical issues in ethnographic theory while also dealing with the problem of saying what constituted internal consistency in an ethnographic description. But to state problems is not necessarily to solve them. In the end Schneider's analyses did not escape his own critiques, particularly insofar as those critiques were based on whether and how a given statement was actually provable. The difficulty with Schneider's analyses centered on idealism.

In the philosophical sense, idealism consists in a well-established bundle of simple but far-reaching ideas, images, implied purposes, and modes of argument that posits a real world of ideas or forms that lies beyond and shapes a somehow less real or less intelligible world of appearances. It is a characteristic of this well-formed and historically ingrained bundle that if you pick up elements of it and use them, however offhandedly or opportunistically, you are likely, in the end, to find yourself committed to their implications.

The historical and logical complement of idealism is materialism. Although idealists and materialists commonly pretend that their positions are fundamentally opposed and comprise all possible philosophical positions, they are, in fact, fundamentally interdependent and make up one specific cotradition. As Aristotle said of his disagreements with Plato, they are an argument among friends. They depend on one another and, within a framework of common assumptions, mirror one another. Both are dualistic. They share a philosophical vocabulary and a set of epistemological assumptions that radically distinguish the world of our experience from a real world that lies beyond it, and both hold that we cannot explain experience except by reference to that latter world or system. They differ only in how they construe this other world beyond experience.

The true opposite of idealism is not materialism. Rather, the opposite of idealism and materialism, together, is the line of epistemological development from sophism to skepticism, its various descendants through Kant, down to modern pragmatism. All positions in this line reject the idea of reality beyond experience in all forms. For skeptics, there is no world apart from the world of appearances—anything said to lie beyond it is an arbitrary imputation, a dogma, and any such dogma can always be countered by an opposite dogma. In a strict historical sense, "empiricism" is but another name for this same skeptical tradition. The name evokes both the Greek term for knowledge based on experiment and the name of Sextus Empiricus (c. 200 a.d.), the skeptical philosopher whose encyclopedic *Against the Dogmatists,* recirculated from 1465 onward, fostered empiricism's resurgence during the enlightenment. A very important aspect of the difference between the dualists and the skeptics consists in the way each tradition approaches the recognized fact of relativism in perception, both individual and cultural. The way we perceive things is bound up with, and cannot be detached from, our individual perspectives and our cultural presumptions. Dualists since Plato have consistently argued that because relativism characterizes ordinary experience, real knowledge must lie beyond it. Skeptics, by contrast, have seen this same quality as showing that what is taken as common knowledge depends not only on individual perception and judgment but also on the way individuals must interact in pursuit of practical ends. In the skeptical view, perception is not a reflection of experience but a tool for managing it.

I never asked Schneider directly to identify his philosophical preferences. He did not appear to welcome such questions. But his unwillingness to discuss formal philosophy does not mean that he was free of its assumptions, and sometimes he expressed those assumptions fairly clearly. One of those times was in a conversation shortly after I returned from my first fieldwork in the Punjab village I have described as Shahidpur, in the spring of 1966. My original research proposal had called for twenty-four months in the field, within which time I would complete the first draft of my dissertation and review it with the villagers.

After about eighteen months, I received a strongly worded letter from Schneider urging me to return at once. Since there had just been a war be-

tween Pakistan and India, it seemed possible that he had reasons for the demand that he felt he should not put in the letter. I therefore rushed to com-
ply, although I still completed the analysis, discussed the parts I thought
might be questionable with groups in the village, and incorporated their
reactions in a completed draft thesis. When I returned, I delivered several
copies to David immediately, to his evident surprise. He read it, and we met
to discuss it.

By that time it was clear that we had significant differences of opinion on
two major, interrelated questions. The first was whether culture consisted of
one system or several. The second concerned the depth and level of coherence we could expect in informants' accounts of their own systems and
whether, as a consequence, we should impose or avoid imposing our own
ideas of what such a system was in place of the ideas we might elicit. In my
thinking, the field experience had confirmed beyond any reasonable doubt
that communities did not contain one cultural system, but multiple, distinct,
and mutually incompatible cultural systems. Moreover, these systems generally corresponded to what anthropologists had consistently recognized as
separate institutions and put in separate chapters in ethnographies, without
being able to explain why they did so in general terms and while often still
asserting that all these patently different sets of ideas, values, and relations
were part of one single totality.

Schneider clearly rejected "total system models," but he was not clear about
what they were or what the alternative was. I was convinced that we could
rely entirely on indigenous ideas to provide the substantive content of social accounts, confining "theory" to descriptions of the way such ideas were
used and to our understanding of where and how to find them. If we were
careful to follow where our informants led by not disrupting the account with
our own preconceptions, we could not only elicit the cultural systems in some
surface sense—ideas about kin, gods, government, and so on—but also the
indigenous ideas of "system" and, indeed, of "culture" itself (or rather their
local counterparts) that lay behind them.[1] Kinship systems include their own
definition of what a kinship system is, religious systems their own ideas of a
religious system, and so on. Theory, in the sense of substantive sociocultural description, could thus be replaced by fact. My draft thesis had not bela-
bored these differences, but they were clear. In the discussion, however,
Schneider confined himself closely to ethnographic details. I supposed that
I should have expected this and that it reflected his sense of propriety—that
he saw his job as making sure that I was responsive to the facts, not to him
personally. Yet I was interested in his reactions on what seemed to be the larger
questions, and in the end he did indicate what these reactions were. After our

meeting had formally ended and he had risen to see me out, he stopped in front of the secretary's desk outside his office door to tell the anecdote about umpires that Richard Feinberg (this volume) also recounts: "There were three major league umpires: a young one just starting out, a middle-aged one who had been around, and an old veteran. They were discussing how to do their jobs, how they called balls and strikes. The young umpire said: 'I calls them the way I sees them.' The middle-aged umpire said: 'I calls them the way they *are.*' A pause, and the veteran said: 'They ain't *nothing,* 'til I calls them.'" A little questioning left no doubt that Schneider thought the veteran had it right and the beginner was wrong. It was not necessary to ask who the greenhorn might actually correspond to and who the veteran.

Although the story does not say explicitly where the concepts of balls and strikes ultimately come from, it is clear that Schneider would place them in the minds of the umpires because that is the only place they exist in any "real" or important sense.[2] Order must be imposed, and does not exist until it is imposed. But note that the imposer is a single individual in isolation, and what order is imposed on is not objects as we see them culturally (a pitch), but as Schneider construes them on the basis of his personal epistemological scheme (a culturally unclassified object in flight). Note also that the latter is not an empirical category, and neither are its implied conceptual complements. The notion of a culturally unclassified object, a purely material object in some sense, and of an idea in someone's mind that might be applied to it are not categories that arise within the data but that lie, he supposes, beyond it. The way Schneider thus sets aside experience and refers for an explanation of it to a "reality" outside it constitutes a form of dualism. His notion that the categories are the dominant part of this reality is idealism.

This is not an extreme philosophical idealism like that of Berkeley, Leibniz, or Whitehead, who argued that we cannot know that a material world exists apart from mind at all, but it is very much the more common variety that began with Plato and Aristotle and runs through Hegel, Comte, the German and French positivists, and J. S. Mill. It assumed the existence, beyond the shifting world of appearances, of both pure mind and pure matter and construed the problem of knowledge as equivalent to the problem of characterizing their interaction: mind over matter or matter over mind. More specifically, it most often construed the problem of knowledge as the problem of locating "essences," the distinguishing features by which we recognize general classes. The idealist position is that they must be inherent in mind rather than matter. Idealists usually recognize that locating these essences in the mind can make interpersonal agreement logically problematic, which is precisely why they usually drive toward one of two types of general conclusion: subjective idealism (solipsism) or objective idealism. Either mind is my mind alone, which is solipsism. Or mind is not the same as individual minds at all but some general or super mind that individual minds reflect, participate in, or are shaped by: God, society, the state, the collective consciousness, universal reason, and so on. The main alternative to this view has been the Hobbes-Locke type of materialism, the notion that essences lie in matter, and agreement exists because the categories arise in individual minds by the uniform action of impressions of this matter from without. From a skeptical point of view, however, both positions have the same catastrophic failing: they are fantasies. There is no warrant for either view in experience because there is no warrant for the basic distinction between mind and matter and the ancillary ideas of essences, categories, and the like. Real experience is shot through with relativism and that is all there is to it. Mind and matter in the idealist's and materialist's senses are absolutes, and we simply never encounter such things.

We do not perceive by taking some pure category and applying it to some material object. We can impute such a process to ourselves, but we do not experience such a process. In fact, perception is not the sort of interior process this suggests at all. It is, as Kant stressed, an exterior process: what we experience is the world around us, not some construction within us, and in this world we do not encounter either pure ideas or pure matter, whether in the form of universes, or a "buzzing blooming confusion," or moving objects that have no identity at all until an umpire assigns them one. What is it that the veteran calls a ball or strike? Is it experienced as some kind of raw or pure object in motion or is it experienced as a pitched ball? If the latter, it is not "nothing" until he calls it. To see it as a pitch is to see it with certain instructions attached regarding how we must react to it. A pitch must be called just one of two ways and everyone in the game is privy to the difference. Can he call any moving object whatever a ball or strike—say a gray feathery moving object with popcorn crumbs on its beak? Can he stand at the plate and call balls or strikes if the teams are not yet on the field? Can he call them if everyone in the stands says they are not there—or even not what he says? If it was truly "nothing" before he called it, logically he could. If it is a pitch, a culturally structured and also physical event, then he cannot. In the recognized running context of a baseball game, the umpire has the final say under the rules; but everyone else can judge how he uses that final say, and in fact if he calls too many the wrong way he will not remain an umpire very long. The veteran's position makes his calls seem logically unassailable and conveys an admirable air of authority, but the greenhorn has a much better grip on the social construction of reality.

Kinship Analysis

Schneider's approach to kinship and culture was broadly consistent throughout his writings, from his 1955 collaboration with George Homans, through his review of the alliance-descent debate (Schneider 1965a), to *American Kinship: A Cultural Account* (1968), and finally to its defense in *A Critique of the Study of Kinship* (1984). I will concentrate on the middle two.

Like most participants in the alliance-descent debate, Schneider recognized that key figures on the side of alliance theory aligned themselves with idealism and on the side of descent, they aligned with positivism. What he apparently did not recognize is how closely these two positions were philosophically interrelated and how similar they were in what they refused to consider. The problem is nicely encapsulated in a quote from Claude Lévi-Strauss that Schneider cites approvingly at the beginning of "Some Muddles in the Models." Lévi-Strauss is attacking Maybury-Lewis (wrongly) as a positivist, and then expands his remarks:

> Mr. M. L. remains, to some extent, the prisoner of the naturalistic misconceptions which have so long pervaded the British school . . . he is still a structuralist in Radcliffe-Brown's terms, namely, he believes the structure to lie at the level of empirical reality, and to be a part of it. Therefore, when he is presented a structural model which departs from empirical reality, he feels cheated in some devious way. To him, social structure is like a kind of jigsaw puzzle, and everything is achieved when one has discovered how the pieces fit together. But if the pieces have been arbitrarily cut, there is no structure at all. On the other hand, if, as is sometimes done, the pieces were automatically cut in different shapes by a mechanical saw, the movements of which are regularly modified by a camshaft, then the structure of the puzzle exists, not at the empirical level (since there are many different ways of recognizing the pieces which fit together); its key lies in the mathematical formula expressing the shape of the cams and their speed of rotation; something very remote from the puzzle as it appears to the player, although it "explains" the puzzle in the one and only intelligible way. (qtd. in Schneider 1965a:26)

There is serious confusion here, deriving from the dualists' radical dichotomization of the ideal and the material. It lies in the way Lévi-Strauss unites "naturalistic" with "empirical" and contrasts them with what is mathematical in order to imply that the patterns that are truly important, and truly controlling, cannot be revealed by empirical methods. Lévi-Strauss suggests, and Schneider accepts, that "the level of empirical reality" is very much like a physical picture or scene—objects we see, noises we hear. Lévi-Strauss clearly means to suggest that because the mathematical formulas are not "empirical" in this sense (since they are ideas), they cannot be discovered by empirical methods of any sort whatever. And if this reason is not sufficient, he offers a second: they are not known to the "players," presumably because the players too are confined to this merely empirical level. So asking the players about *their* ideas will not reveal *these* (important, controlling) ideas. These suggestions are, empirically, rubbish. Ideas are at least as observable as physical objects, although of course in a different way, as one would think a scholar who writes for others to read would recognize. There is no reason to think that the ruling ideas in a society are not as observable as any other ideas.

Lévi-Strauss and Schneider are right in suggesting that A. R. Radcliffe-Brown, E. E. Evans-Pritchard, Meyer Fortes, and a few other principals on the descent side of the debate were positivists, but wrong to equate positivism with materialism and much more wrong to equate materialism with empiricism. Positivism is less the opposite of idealism than it is an application of it. Émile Durkheim, Marcel Mauss, and others cited by Schneider as progenitors of idealism identified themselves as both idealists and positivists, and Radcliffe-Brown was as much a descendant of Comte and Durkheim as Lévi-Strauss was. In fact, the entire alliance-descent debate descended directly from the neo-Hegelian jurisprudent Joseph Köhler, who first advanced the idea of a prescriptive marriage system in *On the Prehistory of Marriage* (1897). Durkheim praised this work extensively in one important review published in *L'Année Sociologique* in 1897 and a second in 1905, and repeated Köhler's argument virtually point for point in the *Elementary Forms of the Religious Life* in 1912 (Durkheim 1915), although this time without citation. Lévi-Strauss's *Elementary Structures of Kinship* was nothing if not an attempt to revive it. The idea, most simply put, was that society began with radical social determinism: the first and most basic form of society was a single absolutely monolithic system of clans that gave each individual one and only one all-encompassing social identity and controlled literally all the individual's thought. Both the idealists and the positivists in the debate, but not the occasional actual empiricist like Maybury-Lewis, were happy to accept this basic imagery, and both accepted the further idea that such a social structure was ultimately to be imposed by the analyst and not discovered in nature. It was my theoretical model, and yet it controlled their behavior. The disagreement was only about what that imposed system should look like or to what it should be imputed. Should it lie in a theoretical model of "concrete" descent groups that somehow control the relations of those within them without being in any important sense psychological or cognitive, or should it lie in a theoretical model of social relations as a conceptual pattern that manifests itself through symbolic behavior?

Without a distinction in principle to make between the two positions, it is not surprising that Schneider's criticisms were localized and piecemeal and that his conclusions were more intuitive matters of taste or balance than decisive proofs or disproofs. He held only that we needed to confine ourselves to "partial system models" (otherwise undefined) in place of total system models and commended alliance theory as "capable of dealing with the symbol system as a system apart from, yet related to, the network of social relations" (1965a:79).

Schneider's (1965b, 1965c, 1969) critique of componential analysis was similarly partial and incomplete. He recognized that the componential analysts were treating a terminology as if it was only a taxonomy rather than a system for labeling reciprocal relations, as if a name applied in the domain of relatives was no different from a name applied in the domain of fruit. But this problem was not the focus of his attention, even though the difference between terminologies that are reciprocal and those that are not has far-reaching implications for the different ways they form conceptual structures. He focused only on defining the domain itself, the notion that there was a set of universal "kin types" based on genealogy by which its elements could be consistently and exhaustively defined. These "kin types" were basically a reification of the supposed relational primitives that one found in Murdock and could trace back to Morgan: father of, brother of, wife of and so on. Schneider's criticism—the veteran umpire notwithstanding—was that the componential analysts' assumptions and conclusions were circularly related. The possible genealogical relations were defined by their own a priori notions, and the components they used to gloss the kin terms were constructed with the same relations, so of course kin types could translate the names assigned to relatives. As Schneider said in his introduction, his main point was that "you are what you eat." Now we phrase the same idea as "garbage in, garbage out." Unfortunately, however, his argument did not stop there, and he appears to have carried away from it several unwarranted conclusions about kinship itself, rather than just the componential approach to it. Specifically, Schneider seems to have concluded that genealogy was irrelevant to kinship, and kinship terminologies did not exist.

American Kinship (1968) incorporates conclusions from both earlier critiques. It involves two major claims. First, culture is autonomous in a Durkheimian sense and consists in a system of symbols. Second, these cultural systems are shaped by what Schneider calls "central symbols." In the case of American kinship, the central symbol was "sexual intercourse" (59), further described as what is taken as "natural" sexual relations between a husband and wife (108). It was out of this central symbol that the rest of the system was "refracted." Schneider's use of the term "symbol" does not consistently carry the usual sense of a conventional sign or conventionally designated sign. He makes no effort to say, as a pragmatist might, why and how such symbols would be used; they are simply "constructs in American culture" (116). The main reason for calling them symbols is to distinguish them from facts of nature, specifically facts of biology. They are rather "constructs which depict these biological facts" but also "represent something other than what they are, over and above and in addition to their existence as biological facts and as cultural constructs about biological facts. They serve in this respect as symbols precisely because there is no necessary or intrinsic relationship between them and what they symbolize" (116). What they symbolize is "diffuse, enduring solidarity. They symbolize those kinds of interpersonal relations which human beings as biological beings *must* have if they are to be born and grow up. They symbolize . . . a special kind of trust which is not contingent and which does not depend on reciprocity. They stand for the fact that birth survives death, and that solidarity *is* enduring" (116, emphasis in original).

Schneider is not saying here that solidarity is a cultural construct which is imputed to interpersonal relations by symbolic means (as Victor Turner, Fred Bailey, or Harold Garfinkel, for example, might). He is saying that this solidarity "must" exist, does in fact exist, and that the symbol represents it. That is, diffuse solidarity in his analysis occupies precisely the place that the idea of the unity of the collective consciousness occupied in Durkheim's, and the focus on the sexual nexus between husband and wife is the precise counterpart of Durkheim's totemism. The argument is Durkheim's Hegelian social determinism merged with Freud's idea that the key to family relations lies in the patterns of sexual relations.

Solipsism

Schneider's ultimate repudiation of the possibility of an objective study of kinship systems has appeared to many to have extremely worrisome implications for anthropology as an objective science in general. The worry evaporates, however, when you recognize that the difficulties he pointed out spring only from the assumptions he shared with those who were the main targets of his criticism and that these assumptions are both unwarranted and unnecessary.

Relativism, again, is a fact. What is at issue is only what step one takes after that fact is recognized. For most idealists, the next step has been to argue for *absolute* idealism by postulating universal and unchanging ideas, forms, or categories, that actual perception manifests only dimly and imperfectly. Thus, while relativism affects the manifestation of the true bases of knowledge, it does not affect those bases themselves. With Durkheim and the French school, this absolute external mind became localized society, not an absolute for all but only for the particular group in question. The same position is implicit in Schneider's idea that American culture is an autonomous singularity as well as in the idea that one should look for such things as relatives and then ask what they are called (that is, first find the material things and then the categories applied to them). And this, it seems to me, is precisely where his analysis comes to grief.

In the 1960s, Lévi-Strauss's view that his theoretical models controlled the natives' actual behavior gave Schneider pause. After a short trip up the Amazon, Lévi-Strauss was not embarrassed to devote an entire book to arguing that "savage thought" was a type of *bricolage,* a puttering about (1962), but Schneider was culturally egalitarian. In his work, there was never a whisper of trying to show that "our" thinking is more evolved, complex, or autonomous than "theirs." We are they; it is simply a matter of where one stands. Even in Schneider's last discussions with Handler, when he seemed to have disavowed all else, this egalitarian stance remained. But it posed a problem. Rodney Needham's ethnocentrism had been clear to him when Needham, analyzing Purum, imposed his ideas of neatly bounded clans on Purum marriage patterns.[3] The componential analysts' ethnocentrism had been equally clear to him when they insisted that all terminologies be analyzed in terms of a genealogical grid. So why was it not also ethnocentric to impose the idea that American kinship was what you arrived at by questioning Americans about their relatives, or by imposing the idea of a symbol system or of (proper) coitus as a central symbol?[4] In the end, he evidently decided that it was.

If you accept idealism and reject the idea that you can claim to speak for some sort of absolute mind or consciousness "out there," the only other logical possibility is the view that the ordering mind is "in here," your own, and this is solipsism. Accordingly, after rejecting the universality of genealogical grids, the idea of kin terminologies, and apparently the idea of kinship itself, Schneider went on to reject what he called the "quartet" of traditional types of institutions (kinship, economics, politics, and religion) (1984:181n) and finally the ability of fieldwork to play a decisive role in any theoretical determination whatever. For Schneider it came down to the conclusion that "you could mostly make any goddam informant say anything you wanted him to" (1995:210). This leaves nothing. Anthropology is either an illusion, a phony science, or simply has got it wrong and has to start over.

The real problem was that Schneider saw no epistemological alternative to the componential analysts' view that the meanings of terms must lie in their "denotata," things not in ethnographic reality but beyond it. Nor, more importantly, did he see an alternative to the underlying dualistic distinction between ideas as radically subjective and things as radically objective.[5] Since he could not find kinship, economics, politics, and religion as "things" in this sense, his only remaining option was his complementary conception of ideas, that is, taking them as his own inner and individual imaginings. It is precisely as though the veteran umpire took the next two logical steps. If the balls and strikes ain't *nothing* till he calls them, then why not the whole game? And then where is he?

The Empirical Alternative

I will conclude with a brief demonstration of the empirical alternative Schneider chose to ignore. In a nutshell, what he says about the ideas attached to sexual intercourse in the American kinship system can be explained by looking at precisely what he said did not exist—the American kinship terminology.

The confusions about this system begin with the notion that "terminology" is the best way to speak of it. This notion implies that we should view our topic as a set of verbal tags (words) to be connected to a set of things (kin), rather than something else. In fact, it is something else: a conceptual architecture established in consensus. Kinship is a system of interrelated definitions of a set of interrelated social positions. Kinship terms are not, in the first instance, names for things (actual people who are kin) but for these conceptual positions. Such positions have standard or formal names as well as informal names. The formal names commonly, perhaps always, fall into well-ordered and highly redundant linguistic patterns that support the definitional relations. The informal names may convey emotional coloration or may be artifacts of language evolution such as surviving archaisms. But it is not necessary to use any of them to invoke the ideas of the positions, and it is, again, in the definitions of the positions, not the terms, that we find where the system hangs together.[6]

As kinship analysts since Lewis Henry Morgan and Ely Parker have suggested, and as I think all of us have actually experienced, there are in fact systems of kinship positions and they are in fact based on relational primitives. What has not been clear is what these primitives are and whether they are endogenous to the systems themselves or exogenous. Morgan's view, framed by a developmental view of society derived from historical jurisprudence and Roman law, was that they were endogenous. But his perspective did not require him to say what they were. He was more interested in the way any one terminology seemed to merge or split the categories of another terminology, which would allow them to be arranged in an evolutionary sequence of increasing specificity. Of course he also felt that there was a common natural basis that these distinctions captured, which he represented with English kin terms, but there was no more need for him to specify some set of ultimate distinctions than there would be for a historian of physics to specify once and for all the ultimate realities that physical theory has been progressively approximating. But since Schneider and the componential analysts rejected Morgan's developmental perspective, they found themselves having to discuss the bases of these classificatory distinctions as timeless and cross-cultural absolutes. Since they also shared the widely accepted but largely unexamined presumption that all the ideas salient in a culture must somehow be peculiar to it and therefore restricted to it, it followed that such cross-cultural absolutes could only be "etic" or analytic categories applied from without. They disagreed only over what these absolutes were—genealogical for the componential analysts, vaguely psychodynamic for Schneider.

Neither imputation is necessary. Empirically, the primitives are uniformly endogenous and readily elicited. They are the definitions of kin *directly* related to ego; that is, no other relations intervene between the primitive relation and ego. The definitions of the other positions flow from them the way the definitions of the various figures of geometry flow from the basic elements of a right triangle. They are the first positions learned in life, and it is through them that people growing up in a relational system learn the others.

The core positions with the recognized standard English names are given in figure 3.1. The ideas they entail, the indigenous equivalent of the componential analysts' "components," are given in the definitions of the elements that make up the drawing: lines for descent or "blood" relations, levels for generations, parallel lines for marriage, and triangles and circles for male and female. In English, an ego can have just one type of male sibling and one type of female sibling, and the definitions assume that one's male and female parents are also married to one another. Other societies can have quite different starting definitions. Tamil, for example, has distinct elder and younger siblings, and Purum counts only elder male siblings as brothers. Sometimes common property defines those who are related, or common clanship, and so on.

With such a core pattern, whatever it is, one can proceed outward to elicit the rest of the system just as users actually teach and learn it, as a system of relative products. Start by eliciting the relations defined as father of father, mother of father, brother of father, sister of father, son of father, daughter of

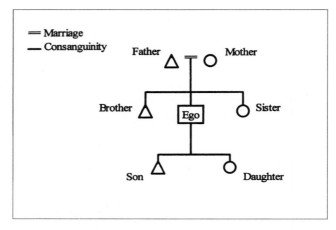

Figure 3.1. Core kinship positions with standard English names.

father, then do the same for each of the other core terms, then query each new position this yields in the same way, and so on outward until nothing more can be elicited. At first, this gives numerous seemingly diverging strings, but these strings can be gathered and redrawn, with the agreement of one's informants, into patterns that leave just one position for each term, which is to say one graphically symbolized idea for each term. When this method is applied to English, the results are as in figure 3.2.

Even if they did not participate in the elicitation, English speakers should readily understand this diagram and intuitively recognize its dominant features. Chief among these features is the pattern of extension indicated on the chart as rule 1, which holds that the line of terms with the stems -*father* and -*mother* or -*son* and -*daughter* can be extended upward or downward indefinitely by prefixing an additional "great" for each generation, and that all people so designated are relatives. Rule 2 holds that the -*uncle*/-*aunt* and -*nephew*/-*niece* terms can be extended in the same way as the terms in rule 1, and that all people so designated are relatives. Rule 3 states that the children of *uncles, aunts,* or *cousins* are *cousins*.[7] The arrows indicate direction of reckoning, which in English must be specified. A *grandfather* is any *father* of *father* or *mother,* but not all sons of *grandfathers* are *fathers.* This graphic structure represents all the positions of English as reciprocal pairs. To find what, say, a mother's mother's brother is to ego, start at ego and follow the three links up and over: great uncle. To find the reciprocal, sister's daughter's son or daughter, start again at ego, reverse the chain, and follow the links over and down: grandnephew or grandniece.

This is neither a total nor a partial model in Schneider's sense. It is not my interpretation of the whole or a part of something different and distant, with

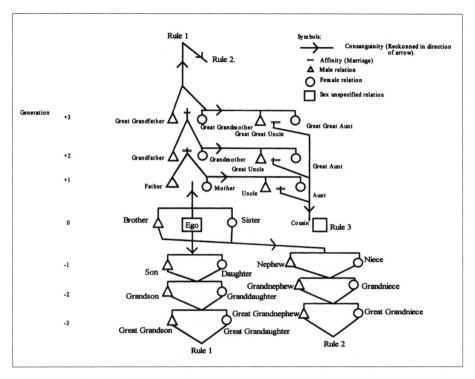

Figure 3.2. American kinship positions.

no definite operational connection between that distant thing and this representation. It is, rather, the ethnographic equivalent of an experimental record in the physical sciences, a procedure that does not merely represent or mirror some part of nature in some way but actually isolates and captures it. It is an experimentally created cultural artifact precisely parallel to an experimentally created physical or chemical artifact. Moreover, it is a cultural artifact that I can bring to you from the situation in which it was created by an unbroken chain of evidentiary steps. And finally, it is an artifact of a procedure designed to test a specific question, namely, to find out, first, if the definitions are systematic as a whole and, if so, to say what that systematic character consists in. Such a question is not important in normal usage, and therefore normal usage does not proceed in exactly this way or leave exactly this kind of trace. But this particular trace is crucial to understanding what makes your normal usage and my normal usage and everyone else's normal usage hang together, and to see whether or not the unity of cultural systems— the *systemness* of them—must be imposed or can be elicited. The answer, evident from the chart, is that the definitions form a system that is coherent

in itself and that its unity is defined by internal consistency based on use of
the core relations to define all subsequent relations; its internal reciprocal
coherence is defined by the fact that if x is the reciprocal of y, then y is the
reciprocal of x; and its external closure is defined by the ideas that relatives
end with cousins laterally but go on vertically from the indefinitely distant
first ancestor to the last descendant. This system allows the terminology to
provide clear criteria for what would count as a kinship relation or idea (that
is, something considered the same as or defined in terms of its constituent
elements) and what would be outside it.

Of course it is possible that this pictorial unity and cohesiveness might be
an illusion, but Dwight Read's mathematical analyses (1984; this volume).
demonstrates that it is not. He shows that the core definitions and generative procedure can be accurately restated as mathematical set relations, which
can then be turned into repeatable operations that a computer can use to
generate the same logical structure. Read's work with computers is important because while people might make unconscious or willful leaps of inference, computers cannot. In short, the American kinship terminology is a
cultural system, with "system" meant in a very strong sense. It is not the whole
of the American kinship system, but it is an important part of it.

With respect to Schneider's insistence that all kinship solidarity is diffract-
ed out of the core "symbol" of sexual intercourse between husband and wife,
and only between husband and wife, the key feature of the chart is precisely
the clear central line of terms indicated by the -*father* and -*mother* stems as
distinct from the collaterals whose descendants disappear into the blur of
"cousins." The line was recognized by Romney and D'Andrade (1964) when
they attempted to establish the "psychological reality" of their componential analysis, even though the analysis itself had not exposed it.[8] It is in fact a
dominant feature of English and most other Indo-European terminologies
of Western Europe, as contrasted, for example, with the Indo-European terminologies of Central and South Asia, which have distinct bilateral, two-
winged shapes that are limited vertically but extend indefinitely to the sides
(cf. Murray J. Leaf 1971 for Punjabi; Sylvia Vatuk 1972 for Hindi). In Punjabi
and Hindi, the father of your father's father's father is not a relative, but everyone in your father's generation is some kind of father's brother or mother's brother.

The connection between this structure and Schneider's psychoanalytic
convictions emerges if we ask to which relations the American incest rule
applies preeminently. Let people give examples; on what relations do they
focus? Read stories; what relations are they most often about? Not relations
within the village, as in most of South Asia. Not within the clan or lineage.

Not among all kin, and not between collaterals. Sexual relations are most clearly forbidden within the kinship core, with a particular emphasis just where Freud noted: relations between son and mother and father and daughter. To an American it may seem that there could hardly be an alternative, but of course other systems often have quite different rules. The question, then, is why Americans (and Europeans) have this one, and the answer is not the importance of some extrinsic "substance." It lies in asking what would happen to the terminology without it.

One need only inspect the chart for a few moments to realize that this is the same as asking what would happen if there were not an absolutely clear and unequivocal understanding that the generations are separate and that descendants of collaterals can never be lineals. The answer is that the entire structure would collapse. Its main contrastive dimensions would cease to exist. The *father/mother–son/daughter* line, going, as people readily say, "back to Adam," is precisely where we find the logical weight-bearing column of this particular conceptual structure, and the terminology, as a system of conceptualized positions and not just labels or noises, is the framework on which a host of other kinship ideas are hung.

In short, incest is indeed symbolic, but not as a mysterious embodiment of an even more mysterious "solidarity" that lies beyond the reach of any merely empirical method. It is symbolic because the rule that defines it is a vital conceptual dimension of a semantic structure we learn with our language, and use as a part of language, to define a crucial set of contexts within which we create important mutual relationships and expectations.

Notes

1. The observation that culture, itself, is an anthropological construct which may or may not resonate with indigenous categories is also made by Fogelson (this volume).

2. Feinberg suggests a slightly different reading, namely, that Schneider meant that they were nothing until the umpire called them within the rules of the game. That is, Schneider had the umpire speaking for the rules of the game as cultural system rather than for a general epistemology. Feinberg's reading is probably right as a statement of the way Schneider would respond to my characterization, but it does not in the end require me to revise my reading. It merely provides an additional argument about baseball itself that has to be peeled away. The notion that the pitched ball is "nothing" until the umpire calls it actually violates the rules of baseball, which provide procedures for dealing with wrong calls and even bad umpires. Yet even if this were not so, the real focus of the story is obviously not baseball but anthropology, and the implication is still that a fact is nothing until the anthropologist calls it, so in the end the position under two readings is the same.

3. Schneider had been suspicious of Needham's analysis, and I took the occasion of my master's paper to review the original ethnographies. In fact, Purum marriage ceremonies

marked the brides' father's status in terms of his social "age," which was symbolically indicated by the number of men in an attendant group composed of his daughter's spouses and the spouses of the daughters of his younger male siblings. They were not clan relations as such at all and a fortiori not relations prescribed by clan (Leaf 1963). Schneider was referring to this problem when he noted that Purum "fit only loosely into Needham's type" (1965a:69), and then more flatly that the types were in effect nothing but reified impositions (69–71).

4. Ottenheimer (this volume) makes a similar point in arguing that Schneider's avowed relativism ultimately devolves into a form of absolutism.

5. At the time the American kinship project was beginning, Schneider very graciously offered me a choice of working on it or on a different project concerning the analysis of Hopi and Navaho dreams. I chose the latter, in part because it would allow me to work alone but mainly because it seemed to me that the way the kinship research was being organized would not produce the results sought, precisely because of the assumptions I am describing. Schneider's purpose was to investigate kinship as a system in its own right. His method was to identify families and then interview their members about their relationships with each other and/or kinship in general. This procedure assumed at the outset that kin terms took their meaning from what they referred to, and in practice was bound to mix together all the different relations such people might have had with each other on all their various bases: economic, religious, political, or what have you. Once such ideas were so intermixed in the interview reports, there would be no objective way to separate them back out. I tried to suggest as much, but the alternative idea of starting out by trying to elicit the kinship ideas by direct inquiry, as one might elicit religious or mythological ideas and before seeing how they might be used, did not strike a responsive chord.

6. Read (this volume) makes this same point when he contends that the meaning of kinship terms is found in the logical relations among the terms, since what Read means by "logical" is the relationships of interdependency among the positional definitions.

7. It can be demonstrated that there is no systematic way to combine the recognized marks of degree of relatedness, that is, the ideas of "removal" and "first," "second," "third," and so on, while maintaining self-reciprocity. Hence it appears evident that while these ideas may be important with respect to other matters, such as the reckoning of inheritance, they are not part of the logic of the terminology as a system of reciprocally defined positions.

8. For example, they received the following responses when they asked high school students to say which of several types of relatives were "closer":

father-uncle-cousin: "a father is the most different; uncles and cousins are both off-shoots"

father-son-brother: "brother is most different because a father has a son and a son has a father, but a brother has a brother or sister"

brother-son-grandson: "a grandson is most different, because he is moved down further"

nephew-son-grandson: "a nephew is most different because he is offside. (I: What is offside?) Not in the same line." (Romney and D'Andrade 1964:164)

References Cited

Durkheim, Émile. 1897. "Köhler—*Zur Urgeschichte der Ehe*. Totemismus, Gruppenehe, Mutterrecht (Contribution a l'histoire primitive du mariage)." *L' Annee Sociologique* 1:306

———. 1905. "Köhler—*Zur Urgeschichte der Ehe*." *L'Annee Sociologique* 9:378.

———. 1915 [1912]. *The Elementary Forms of the Religious Life*. Trans. Joseph Ward Swain. London: George Allen and Unwin.

Köhler, Joseph. 1975 [1897]. *On the Prehistory of Marriage*. Trans. R. H. Barnes and Ruth Barnes. Ed. R. H. Barnes. Chicago: University of Chicago Press.

Leaf, Murray J. 1963. "'Age' in Purum Social Structure." Master's thesis, University of Chicago.

———. 1971. "The Punjabi Kinship Terminology as a Semantic System." *American Anthropologist* 73 (3): 545–54.

Lévi-Strauss, Claude. 1962. *La Pensée Sauvage*. Paris: Plon.

———. 1969 [1949]. *The Elementary Structures of Kinship*. Trans. James Harle Bell and John Richard von Sturmer. Ed. Rodney Needham. Oxford: Alden and Mowbray.

Read, Dwight W. 1984. "An Algebraic Account of the American Kinship Terminology." *Current Anthropology* 25 (4): 417–49.

Romney, A. K., and Roy G. D'Andrade. 1964. "Cognitive Aspects of English Kin Terms." *American Anthropologist* 66 (3): 146–70.

Schneider, David M. 1965a. "Some Muddles in the Models: Or How the System Really Works." In *The Relevance of Models for Social Anthropology*. Ed. Michael Banton. 25–85. ASA Monograph No. 1. London: Tavistock.

———. 1965b. "A Critique of Goodenough's Componential Analysis." In *Formal Semantic Analysis*. Ed. E. A. Hammel. 288–316. Special issue of *American Anthropologist* 67 (5), pt. 2.

———. 1965c. "Kinship and Biology." In *Aspects of the Analysis of Family Organization*. Ed. Ansley J. Coale et al. 83–101. Princeton, N.J.: Princeton University Press.

———. 1968. *American Kinship: A Cultural Account*. Englewood Cliffs, N.J.: Prentice-Hall.

———. 1969. "Componential Analysis: A State-of-the-Art Review." Paper presented at the Wenner-Gren Symposium on Cognitive Studies and Artificial Intelligence Research, March 2–8, Chicago.

———. 1984. *A Critique of the Study of Kinship*. Ann Arbor: University of Michigan Press.

———. 1995. *Schneider on Schneider: The Conversion of the Jews and Other Anthropological Stories, as Told to Richard Handler*. Ed. Richard Handler. Durham, N.C.: Duke University Press.

Schneider, David M., and George C. Homans. 1955. "Kinship Terminology and the American Kinship System." *American Anthropologist* 57:1194–208.

Vatuk, Sylvia. 1972. *Kinship and Urbanization: White Collar Migrants in North India*. Berkeley: University of California Press.

Yengoyan, Aram A. 1997. "Yengoyan on Handler's Schneider on Schneider." *American Ethnologist* 24 (1): 208–10.

4. What Is Kinship?

DWIGHT W. READ

DAVID SCHNEIDER rejects the assertion that "kinship . . . has to do with reproduction" (1984:198) and its corollary, the "Doctrine of the Genealogical Unity of Mankind" (119), because of his deep-seated conviction regarding the need to understand cultural phenomena using their own terms, meanings, and references. Schneider comments that "*the first task of anthropology,* **prerequisite to all others,** *is to understand and formulate the symbols and meanings and their configuration that a particular culture consists of* " (196, emphasis in the original). Kinship, Schneider argues, has not been approached from this perspective, and so "kinship . . . is essentially undefined and vacuous: it is an analytic construct which seems to have little justification even as an analytic construct" (185) and hence "'kinship' . . . is a nonsubject" (Schneider 1972:51; see also Needham 1971).

More than a half century earlier, when W. H. R. Rivers considered four modes by which kinship might be defined, he began in a similar vein by asserting that blood relationship (consanguinity) is inadequate for a definition of kinship because it does not account for adoption and other practices which show that "fatherhood and motherhood depend, not on procreation and parturition, but on social convention" (Rivers 1968 [1924]: 52). The second mode for defining kinship—the one he decided upon—was through genealogy, which could determine kinship through consanguinity as well as some other social procedure. Next he considered the possibility that kinship is defined through the terms of relationship, but found this mode lacking when he considered that pedigree and genealogy determine the terms of relationship and not the reverse. His fourth mode was by social function, whereby "persons are regarded as kin of one another if their duties and privileges in relation to one another are those otherwise determined by consanguinity" (53). But, as Schneider has pointed out, Rivers' notion of genealogy reintroduced the consanguinity he initially had rejected because in his genealogical method he limited the genealogical terms father, mother, child, husband and wife to "their English sense" (Rivers 1900:75). Schneider comments that "all Rivers really does, then, is to say that kinship is in the first instance defined in terms of consanguinity . . . and that sometimes social convention alone may confirm a kinship relationship even in the absence of a relationship of consanguinity but that, when it does, it is created in the image of a consanguineal tie" (1972:54).

This insistence on a consanguineal tie led Schneider to reject kinship as a domain of study. He asserts that "the way in which kinship has been studied does not make good sense" (1984:201) since "it exists in the minds of anthropologists but not in the cultures they study" (1972:51). What Schneider rejects is not the possibility of there being culturally identified relationships of one person to another, but the presumption that these relationships, if they are to be called "kinship relationships," are biological/reproductive, with biology's attendant genealogical grid, allegedly relevant to all cultures.[1] The presumed biological/reproductive basis has been introduced, he suggests, because "kinship has been defined by European social scientists, and European social scientists *use their own folk culture as the source of many, if not all, of their ways of formulating and understanding the world about them*" (1984:193, emphasis added). Schneider does not question the *existence* of a *citamangen-fak* relationship among the Yapese, with whom he did his fieldwork, but only whether it is meaningful to call it a father-son relationship as would be done under the "received view" of what is meant by kinship. Hence he questions whether it is a kinship relationship "*within* the framework of the conventional kinship theory" (67, emphasis added) because, as he argues, "the Yapese definition of the relationship between *citamangen* and *fak* remains radically different from the European cultural conception of kinship" (73), which presumes that reproduction is the critical defining property. That the relationship is neither genealogically construed nor arrived at through reproduction is evidenced, according to Schneider, by the fact that the "rights of the *fak* in the *citamangen*'s land . . . [is not] based on their kinship or genealogical connection," but "is based largely on the interaction, the doirg, of the exchange and less on the state of being, of having some substance, quality, or attribute" (75). To put it simply, what constitutes being a *fak* is cultural specification (what I will call "rules of instantiation"), not satisfaction of a universal genealogical relationship.

What would make concepts such as *citamangen* or *fak* kinship terms in view of my analysis is neither any purported genealogical property they may be said to satisfy nor how they relate to a genealogical grid. Rather, their status as kin terms would stem from their inclusion as symbols within a system of symbols that has abstract structure of a particular kind, namely, a structure that is generative and based on an abstractly definable property that links one symbol to another as its reciprocal.[2] This analytic framework frees kinship as a system of relationships from the assumption that the relationships are first of all genealogical and reproductive and, instead, considers them as they are culturally specified, both in terms of the structural form of the system of symbols through which the relationships are expressed and the "meaning" of those symbols. In other words, we must rethink at the most basic level what kinship is.

Schneider's arguments contrast strongly with Ward Goodenough's observation made about the same time:

> We anthropologists have assumed that kinship is universal, that all societies have kinship systems. If we are correct in this assumption, if every society does have some set of relationships whose definition involves *genealogical considerations of some kind,* then genealogical space must be constructed of things that are common to all mankind. These, we have seen, are parenthood and socially recognized sexual unions in which women are eligible to bear and from which women and especially men derive rights in children and thus establish parent-child relationships. (1970:97, emphasis added)

Goodenough, following in the footsteps of Rivers, takes as self-evident that kinship relations are to be defined using genealogical criteria.

Subsequently, with the formal approach to the study of kinship terminologies introduced by Floyd G. Lounsbury, the assumption of genealogy as the basis of kinship took on the aura of definition. Thus, Harold W. Scheffler and Lounsbury equate kinship and genealogy in comments such as "Relations of genealogical connection, or kinship proper" and "Where the distributional criteria are genealogical and egocentric, we speak of relations of kinship" (1971:38). But Schneider had noted that "the genealogically defined grid is the only analytic device that has been applied to most of the systems which anthropologists have studied. There has been almost no systematic attempt to study the question without employing this device. To put it simply, it is about time that we tested some other hypotheses" (1972:49).

Although Schneider never made it clear what would constitute these other hypotheses, another hypothesis about the source of the structuring of kinship terminologies—the subject of this essay—has, in fact, been tested and verified through its application to the analysis of three very different terminologies, namely, the American-English, the Shipibo of Peru, and the Trobriand Islander terminologies. The hypothesis upon which these analyses are based asserts that the set of kin terms for a particular terminology constitutes a structured system of symbols, and that such a system can be defined without reference to a genealogical grid. Further, mathematical analysis will demonstrate that the kin-term structure may be generated from a few symbols and from certain structural equations. In brief, these analyses provide strong evidence for a claim that terminological structures are cultural constructs whose features are explicable through the logic governing their generation as abstract structures without reference to a genealogical grid. In addition, linkage between the terminological space and a genealogical grid is elucidated by analytically mapping the terminological space onto the genealogical grid. That mapping, then, determines for each of the abstract symbols in the terminological structure its definition as a class of associated kin types. Contrary to Rivers's argument that kin terms are defined through genealogical relationships, the mapping going from the structure of kin terms to the genealogical grid establishes the independence of the definition of the kin-term structure from the grid. Rather than viewing either the terminological space or the genealogical grid as primary and the other as secondary, the results of the analysis argue for viewing the genealogical and the terminological spaces as co-existing conceptual structures with overlap arising through application of the symbols from these two conceptual structures to the same domain of persons. Distinguishing these cultural constructs is the degree of abstraction involved in their definition as conceptual structures.

The analysis also makes evident the way rules of instantiation of abstract symbols in concrete terms may provide a means whereby static structure takes on dynamic and malleable properties. The structure must allow for transition from the abstract domain of culture at the ideational level to the more concrete level of individuals and their social relationships. In that transition, the instantiation of abstract symbols can be changed and redefined without altering the underlying conceptual structure, namely, the terminological space. I hypothesize that the terminological space, contrary to Rivers's argument, provides a framework for defining the world of kin for egos and their alters through mapping of kin terms onto concrete alters and egos. This mapping provides a way to define a kinship world without presupposing the basis for that kinship world to be genealogical as defined by the genealogical grid, in accord with Schneider's argument. Recognizing that there are rules of instantiation giving abstract symbols concrete reference and that the content of these rules is culturally defined circumvents the problem of presuming that biology/reproduction or some cultural interpretation of it

(Keesing and Keesing 1971:157)—provides a universal basis for kinship. The terminological space is constrained by general, structural properties that make it a "kinship space" and structural equations that give it its particular form. The instantiation of the symbols can, but need not, be framed in terms of parenthood modeled on reproduction. But even if the instantiation is not culturally based on reproduction, it is still possible to construct a mapping from the terminological space to the genealogical grid under a straightforward mapping of the generating symbols of the terminological structure onto the primary kin types.[3] This implies that it will be possible to provide a genealogical "meaning" of the kin terms regardless of whatever may be the culturally formulated meaning of the generating symbols. Whether the genealogical "meaning" so constructed has cultural salience is, of course, at the heart of Schneider's critique of kinship based on a presumed universal genealogical grid.

Definition of Kin

The argument that reproduction—a universal—is the basis upon which kinship relations are defined via the parent-child relationship is appealing in its simplicity. Biologically for each person there must be a genetic father and a genetic mother.[4] If it is the case that all persons everywhere recognize at least a physical father and a physical mother (genitor and genetrix) modeled upon biological reproduction, then the genetic connections (via genetic father and genetic mother) can be replaced by genitor and genetrix, and kinship can then be viewed as modeled upon biological reproduction but freed from the requirement that one know the identity of the genetic father and the genetic mother. Presumably, the genitor and the genetrix are those persons posited by the local theory of reproduction through whom reproduction takes place. If so, then the repeated use of the reciprocal relationships *parent of* and *child of* permits genealogical tracing. From this vantage point, Rivers's genealogical method is but a small, additional step and seems to imply that kin terms can be considered as cover terms for sets of genealogical positions as Rivers and others have argued. But, as Schneider has shown, all of this presumes the universality of the relation *parent of* as the cultural "interpretation" of the biological fact that there must be a male and a female involved in procreation.

Schneider used his ethnographic work among the Yapese to illustrate that, at least for them, coitus is not culturally recognized as relevant to reproduction; hence, in their conceptual framework it would appear to be erroneous to assert that they have a concept of kinship modeled on biological reproduction. However, it might be asserted that even if reproduction were removed from the argument, as long as the Yapese have a concept that can be reasonably translated as *parent of* and *child of* in a genealogical sense, then the key aspect of the genealogical grid would still be present. It simply would not be founded upon a local theory of biological reproduction. Of course, Schneider's point is precisely that: Do the Yapese have a term that can be reasonably translated as "father," in a genealogical sense? His answer is that they do not have such a term: "The relationship between *citamangen* and *fak* may not properly be translated as 'father' and 'child,' and is indeed not even a kinship relationship according to certain [genealogical] definitions of that term" (Schneider 1984:78).

The problem with trying to maintain the genealogical grid as a primary referent for kinship in the absence of a local theory of biological reproduction based on coitus, hence the problem with trying to define kinship in terms of a genealogical grid, is also highlighted in other ethnographic accounts. For example, Jane Goodale in her comments about the Tiwi concept of "mother" notes that the Tiwi, like other Australian groups, attribute pregnancy to a dreaming on the part of her husband. The dreaming is crucial, as it is the means by which the social identity of a *pitapitui*, the unborn child, becomes established. The dreaming act identifies for a *pitapitui* its maternal social identity and through the dreaming act the dreamer's wife becomes pregnant. While the Tiwi, like the Yapese, deny that reproduction is simply a matter of coitus, they are perfectly well aware of the biological basis of reproduction. As Goodale puts it, for the Tiwi coitus is the basis upon which *humans* are made, but while this is a necessary, it is not a sufficient, condition for the reproduction of a *Tiwi child*: "Although the Tiwi recognize that either a husband or a lover can make a baby by having sexual intercourse with its mother, they also assert that such activity cannot alone create a *Tiwi* child. A Tiwi must be *dreamed* by its father, the man to whom its mother is married, before it can be conceived by its mother" (Goodale 1994 [1971]: 138, emphasis in the original). An unborn Tiwi must be dreamed as otherwise it would not know the maternal social identity that it must have to be fully part of the Tiwi social world: "*Pitapitui* do not know which woman in their sib is their particular mother and can only obtain this information from their father, whose identity they do know" (139). Interestingly, there is a parallel here between the Yapese notion that it is by doing work that a Yapese is formed and the Tiwi idea that it is by dreaming that a Tiwi is formed. For both groups, what it means to be a "child" does not derive so much from a local theory of biological reproduction as from a cultural concept of what is required to make a Tiwi or Yapese child as opposed to making another instance of *Homo sapiens*.

Goodale makes it clear that the Tiwi term, *innari*, which we might translate as "mother," does not easily lend itself to a genealogical grid because the term refers not to a single person but to a category occupied by any one of several women without distinguishing which woman from the category is the topic of a conversation. She comments: "I am fairly certain that it is completely unnecessary for Tiwi to make such [a genealogical] discrimination, which is one that *they not only do not, but also cannot, ordinarily conceptualize*" (Goodale 1994 [1971]: 73, emphasis added). If the Tiwi do not make a distinction among these women in terms of their different genealogical relationships to ego, then it is difficult to see how it can be argued that their kinship concepts are first of all grounded in genealogical relationships.

It does not require a group that excludes coitus in their concept of reproduction to find problems with the assumption that the persons identified by the same kin term have a prior genealogical identification. In her discussion of !Kung San kin terms, Lorna Marshall observes that the way they conceptualize their kin terms does not fit into a genealogical framework. She comments: "The !Kung were apparently not always assiduous in teaching their children the exact biological position of their kinsmen (whether a given man was FaBr or MoBr, for instance), and a person would not always know *why* he applied a certain term to someone, but he would know that the term he used was proper, and he would know the proper joking status to observe; that would have been well taught him by his parents" (1976:204, emphasis in the original). She goes on to say:

> !Kung informants showed no interest in generation as such. What a !Kung says, when he associates his relatives with each other in the pattern I have called generational, is that they are "like" each other. . . . That they are alike because they occupy the same "step or stage in the succession of natural descent" (as Webster defines "generation") apparently *does not concern the !Kung.* Instead it was the joking relationship they spoke of, and they pointed out the parallel position of their kin in its terms. (208, emphasis added)

While Marshall found it convenient to describe their kinship system in generational terms, it is evident from her comments that the !Kung do not conceptualize them in such terms. And according to their naming system, the whole system of terms of reference and address depends not on genealogical relationship but on one's name: "Names may be changed, and, when they are, the person is reclassified and the kin terms applied to him or her are changed accordingly" (Marshall 1976:236). When !Kung San who do not know each other meet, they establish their kinship relationship not by tracing their respective genealogies until they find a relative in common, but by determining a third person to whom each has a kinship relationship by virtue of a term of reference: "Gao [a Nyae Nyae !Kung] had never been to Khadum [to the north of the Nyae Nyae region] before. The !Kung who lived there at once called him *ju dole* [*dole:* 'bad,' 'worthless,' 'potentially harmful']. He was in haste to say that he had heard that the father of one of the people at Khadum had the same name as his father and that another had a brother named Gao. 'Oh,' said the Khadum people in effect, 'so you are Gao's *!gun!a*'" (242). In effect, they determined a kinship relationship, *!gun!a,* (a person in the name giver–name receiver relationship with ego) through a kin-term calculus that does not depend upon a genealogical grid for its computation.

Ethnographers working in New Guinea have also noted problems with assuming that kinship is first of all genealogical. L. L. Langness comments: "a man might hold rights in the group into which he was born, equivalent rights in a group in which he was raised, the same rights in a group in which his father was raised, his mother's group (either her natal group or one she happened to be raised in), and so on . . . *the sheer fact of residence in a . . . group can and does determine kinship*" (1964:170, 172, emphasis in the original). Similarly, Cherry Lowman-Vayda notes that for the Maring "first-generation non-agnates in residence are usually considered members of other clans. Their children, however, appear to be considered members of the clan with which their father resides. The rationalization of this is that *these children have been nourished by and grown on the products of local land and therefore may be claimed as members of the clan*" (1971:322, emphasis added). Laura Zimmer-Tamakoshi, in her contribution to this volume, notes that for the Gende

> the production and maintenance of ancestors through funeral payments (*kwiagi*) and pig feasts . . . is an old Gende custom. Contributors to a *kwiagi* are often biological descendants of the deceased. Affines and unrelated persons, however, may also contribute with the idea of obtaining the deceased's land rights as well as ancestral protection and other benefits the deceased may bestow. . . . Though the rhetoric surrounding these rites uses reciprocal kin terms . . . the meanings of the terms are not focused solely on biological relationships. Rather, the meanings stress the [actual or alleged] caring and exchange that exists between the two reciprocals, without which—biology notwithstanding—there can be no viable or positive relationship.

Interestingly, Rivers also noted that the users of a classificatory kinship terminology might not be able to justify applying a term to particular persons on the basis of blood or marriage, but he apparently failed to see the contradiction between this and his conviction that genealogy is the basis of kinship. He observed that while the use of a classificatory term was often

justified by its users in terms of "blood or marriage ties," this was not always
the case and "in other cases in which the terms were used they denoted merely
membership of the same social group and [the correct usage] *could not be
justified by distinct ties of blood or marriage relationship*" (Rivers 1924 [1968]:
191, emphasis added).

   Although a genealogical basis does not appear to be crucial to the meaning and definition of terms in these examples, some theorists such as Scheffler
and Lounsbury have, nonetheless, argued otherwise. For example they consider neither the !Kung terminology nor other terminologies that use a name
giver–name receiver relationship to determine kin-term usage to be coun-
terexamples to their thesis that genealogy is the basis of kinship. Instead, they
argue that "the system of name sharing and all it implies about social relations and the extended use of kinship terms is founded quite simply on the
(presumed) 'biological' (genealogical) facts" (1971:59). As evidence for their
claim, they note the presence of core terms in the !Kung San terminology that,
they argue, can be reasonably glossed as parent, child, and sibling. But if a
collection of persons can take on kinship status vis-à-vis ego without knowing any genealogical relationship, as occurred in Marshall's example of Gao,
then it is difficult to see in what sense a !Kung San term "is the 'name' of a
genealogically established category" (13, emphasis added), as they assert must
be the case for a kin term. Merely to assert that the terminology has a "core"
term that allegedly meets this criterion hardly suffices to justify the claim that
all "kin terms" are names for "genealogically established categories."

   Yet another means used to maintain the purported primacy of genealogy
as the basis of kinship in the face of the terminologies that seem to deny a
special position for genitor and genetrix has been to maintain that even if
the term glossed as "mother" is also properly applicable to females who are
not in a reproductive relationship with ego, nonetheless the female who gave
birth to ego is distinguished through reference to "true mother, genetrix"
(Scheffler and Lounsbury 1971:44). Such an argument, however, makes the
unwarranted assumption that a linguistic form that might be translated as
"true mother" necessarily refers to genetrix. While the Sirionó may use the
expression *ezi te* to mean "proper mother" in the sense of genetrix, as claimed
by Scheffler and Lounsbury, other groups do not make the same association
between "true" and genitor and genetrix. For the South Fore of New Guinea, Glasse comments that "when the genealogies were assembled it became
apparent that classificatory and *kagisa* ('fictive') kin were often listed as true
MBD [mother's brother's daughter]. . . . Even the daughters of MB's [moth-
er's brother's] age-mates were sometimes counted this way . . . their distinction [between 'true' and 'tenuous' relationships] refers to the *importance and*

solidarity of the bond and not necessarily to its genealogical closeness" (1969:33, emphasis added). Similarly, Zimmer-Tamakoshi (this volume) comments for the Gende of New Guinea that "regardless of who an individual's biological parents are . . . whoever is (or are) significantly more nurturing assumes the role of 'true parent(s)' in an individual's life. The reverse is also true, with a 'true child' being one who does what is expected for his or her 'parents' (biological or otherwise)."

However, to remove genealogy as the necessary basis for "kinship" immediately poses the problem addressed by Rivers: Upon what basis is kinship defined or definable? Schneider avoids this question by rejecting kinship, but he is rejecting a particular construal of kinship based upon what he calls the "Doctrine of the Genealogical Unity of Mankind." Whether or not we call it kinship, it is evident that all cultural systems have a culturally constructed means by which relationships between pairs of individuals are defined in a manner that not only defines a relationship between the pairs, but allows for calculation of a system of relationships through recursive use of a few relationships. The genealogical method "works" as a means of eliciting a corpus of terms that are used for reference and for address because the set of persons who can be considered with regard to genealogy and the set of persons who are identified with regard to terms of reference and address are overlapping sets. But the fact that the terms of reference and address can be elicited through the genealogical method does not establish the priority of genealogy as the basis for kinship. It is certainly possible to have more than one conceptual structure, each with its own definition as a structure that can be applied to the same domain. The problem is: If our idea of kinship is not based on genealogy, then what is its conceptual basis?

To address this question, we first need to show that genealogical reckoning involves more than simple replacement of genetic father and genetic mother by genitor and genetrix, since genealogical tracing occurs even when genitor and/or genetrix are not recognized culturally. Underlying the difference between the genetic and the genealogical is a shift from the phenomenological domain of empirical structures to the ideational domain of structures built out of abstract relations. Genetic father and genetic mother refer to empirical individuals (whether we can actually identify them or not) who must have existed as the source of the spermatozoon and ovum that create a biological person. Genealogical tracing only requires that to each person there be linked a single male person, whom we can call, following F. K. Lehman (n.d.) the *genealogical father* of ego, and a single female person, whom we can call the *genealogical mother*.[5]

This shift from the phenomenological to the ideational domain also provides the starting point for considering the terminological structure as a cultural construct distinct from the genealogical grid. To see this distinction, we need first to show the structure entailed by genealogical father and genealogical mother, and to show how the shift from genetic father and genetic mother to genealogical father and genealogical mother provides a basis for the widely occurring, if not universal, practice of genealogical tracing. Secondly, we will see that the genealogical grid involves yet another shift to a cultural construct formulated in accordance with an underlying logic. This shift involves more than a simple extension of the idea of genealogical tracing. The genealogical grid involves a different kind of structure than is produced through genealogical tracing, namely, a structure defined through equations that provide the structure with its particular form. Universality of the genealogical grid depends, then, upon the universality of the structural equations, and not just the presumed universality of genealogical father and genealogical mother as the basis for genealogical tracing. Thirdly, further abstraction leads us to the terminological space as a system of abstract symbols constrained only by structural properties that are to be satisfied, rather than properties exhibited by the generating symbols. In the analysis that follows, it will become evident that the terminological space no longer need be considered as modeled directly on genealogical or biological relationships.

Biological Model

We can model the relationships determined by genetic father and genetic mother by specifying that genetic father and genetic mother define a local structure that can be extended recursively. This model is defined locally by the fact that biological reproduction links one person (a node in the structure) with two persons (two other nodes in the structure), with the stipulation that two of the persons have opposite sex and each contributes directly to the genetic makeup of the focal person (see figure 4.1).

We can formally represent these two biological properties of sex difference and contributor of genetic material as follows. Let S be a set of persons. Let $\{m, f\}$ be a set with two symbols that we interpret as "male" and "female" respectively. We stipulate that there is a mapping σ from S to the set $\{m, f\}$ (that is, a rule that specifies for a person, s, in S whether the person should be linked to m [male] or to f [female]) which we write symbolically as: $\sigma{:}S \rightarrow \{m, f\}$ (read: "σ maps each element in the set S to the set $\{m, f\}$") for the set S, taken as a whole, and as $\sigma(s) = m$ (or $\sigma(s) = f$) (read: "σ maps s to m" or "σ maps s to f") for an element s in S. Let S_m be the subset of S such that if $s \in S$ (read: "s is a member of the set S") then $\sigma(s) = m$. The set S_m consists

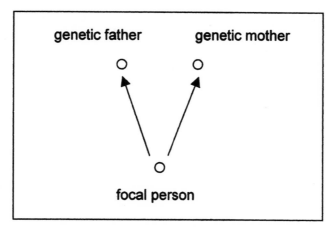

Figure 4.1. Triadic structure linking the focal person with biologically determined genetic father and genetic mother.

of those members of S linked to the "male" symbol, m. Similarly, let S_f be the subset of S such that if $s \in S$ then $\sigma(s) = f$. Now suppose there are two mappings, G (for genetic father) and g (genetic mother) with $G: S \to S_m$ and $g: S \to S_f$. Then for each $s \in S$, $G(s)$ is a male person and for each $s \in S$, $g(s)$ is a female person. We will call G the genetic father mapping and g the genetic mother mapping in the case where S is a set of actual persons and G and g are defined empirically for any person s in S by the fact of who in S (if anyone) is the genetic father of s and who in S (if anyone) is the genetic mother of s.

While the mappings G and g can be applied recursively—e.g., we can compute $G(g(s))$, or the genetic father of the genetic mother of person s—there is no structural restriction on such computations beyond the definitions of G and g—only the restriction imposed by the empirical facts regarding who copulated with whom and thereby created a pregnancy and a birth. Other than the local structure shown in figure 4.1, the structure determined by repeated application of genetic father and genetic mother (a family pedigree) has form dependent upon the empirical facts of who impregnated whom and cannot be specified in advance of knowing those facts.

The structure provided in figure 4.1 is what I call (Read 1992) a Model$_D$ (data model), that is, it is a model of empirical reality encompassing the biological fact of sex difference at the chromosomal level and the respective roles of each sex in providing a gamete with the haploid number of chromosomes such that when a pair of gametes unite, usually via coitus, the resulting zygote now has the diploid number of chromosomes. Other facts about biological reproduction (e.g., that the woman who conceives the child need not be the woman who produced the ovum) are not included; hence it simplifies reality. The validity of a Model$_D$ rests in its congruence with empirical facts and not with regard to its relationship to some theory about those empirical facts. For example, the assumption that all persons can be neatly divided into either biological males or biological females is a valid assumption only to the extent that it accords with biological facts. In actuality, such an assumption is not consistent with the biological fact that there are persons with extra X or Y chromosomes, which affects their phenotypic, sexual characteristics, nor with the fact that there are individuals lacking alleles responsible for full sexual development as males, or individuals who may even have an apparent shift in the sexual phenotype of the "male" person. We accept the simplification that all persons are either biologically male or biologically female in the model on the grounds that the biological exceptions are relatively unusual cases and so can be ignored for a model representing the majority of cases. In contrast, the genealogical grid posits symbols that are marked male or female regardless of the degree to which what they signify accords with the biological reality. In the genealogical grid, kin types are labeled male or female not to simplify the complexity of biological sex, but to fit them into the conceptual framework that the genealogical grid expresses. In our Model$_D$ we change our definition of what is a biological male or a biological female in accordance with the biological facts. Assertions such as "Reproduction requires a biological male and a biological female" are valid only to the extent to which it actually does require a gamete from a male and a gamete from a female to produce a viable zygote. But once we shift to culturally based definitions, we no longer use congruence with empirical evidence as the arbiter of a definition's validity.

The assertion that the model shown in figure 4.1 can be applied to any person implies that we can construct, from an initial person, a "tree," possibly with intersecting "branches" as we move upward in it, by applying the model recursively to each person identified in a prior application of the model. Thus, if we begin with person A, we know that there are persons B and C who are the genetic father and genetic mother of A, respectively, so that $G(A) = B$ and $g(A) = C$. But B and C are persons to whom we can apply the model, and so there must be persons D and E who are the genetic father and genetic mother of B, respectively, and persons F and G who must be the genetic father and genetic mother of C, respectively. Although we know that $B \neq C$, $D \neq E$, and $F \neq G$, it is possible that $D = F$. This result implies that while we can link each of A, B, C, D, E, F, and G via recursive application of the model in figure 4.1, we can know only some aspects of the resulting structure in advance (e.g., a genetic father cannot equal a genetic mother) and we can determine other aspects (such as possibly the fact that $D = F$) only from the empirical facts of who begot whom.

A second aspect of figure 4.1 is that recursiveness is not indefinite because the recursive argument is also historical, arguing what happened evolutionarily as we trace back through our ancestry. If we insist that the genetic father and genetic mother be members of the species *Homo sapiens,* we know that should we apply the recursive property enough times, we would arrive at biological "ancestors" who would not be classified as members of the species *Homo sapiens.* Further, even if we had the factual information on ancestral entities evolutionarily prior to *Homo sapiens,* we would also be unable to determine when to make the shift from ancestors who are *Homo sapiens* to ancestors who are not. While a species such as *Homo sapiens* has a well-defined biological boundary at a given point in time through capability of biological reproduction, the evolutionary boundary for *Homo sapiens* is arbitrary because it does not refer to a single event, but to change taking place over a period of time.

While the problem of establishing biological boundaries may seem remote from the question, Who is a kin?, it has the following important implication. The biological model given in figure 4.1, even with recursion, does not model the facts of ancestry once we categorize the persons identified by the model. Once we specify the set S of persons of interest, then the set S will not be closed under the genetic father and genetic mother mappings for the reasons already specified. There must be a person s in S for whom $g(s)$ or $G(s)$ is not in the set S. This fact is evident if we think of S as the set of persons that might be obtained, say, through collecting the genealogies of persons in a village. However exhaustive our attempts, there will be persons in our genealogy for whom the genealogical father and genealogical mother are not known, hence there surely must be persons for whom the genetic father and genetic mother biologically existed but are not in our set S of persons identified through the genealogies. Nor can we correct this limitation by defining S to be the set of all *Homo sapiens.* Even if we define S to be the set of all *Homo sapiens,* recursive sequences of the form, say, $g(g \ldots (g(s) \ldots))$, must eventually arrive at ancestors who are not members of the species *Homo sapiens* and so are not in the set S.

The genealogical grid has no such limitation. Built as it is upon the ideas of genealogical father and genealogical mother, it can be extended back indefinitely without running into boundary problems because it is not a Model$_D$, but a Model$_T$; that is, it is a model for a theory, not empirical data (see D'Andrade 1970:90 for an elaboration of this theory in terms of "a set of imaginary persons plus a number of genealogical relations"). Further, the genealogical grid will have properties, such as indefinite extension of kin-type products, that do not correspond to biological reality. That is, the rationale for the genealogical grid lies not in its ability to serve as a Model$_D$ for the empirical reality of the biological relationships between genetic father and genetic mother, but as a Model$_T$ for a theory of genealogical relationships.

We can identify that theory in two ways. One is via the concepts that are part of a cultural system and the relations among those concepts. The second is to identify the elements needed to make the transition from the biological tree as a Model$_D$ to a theory that would yield the genealogical grid as a Model$_T$. We will follow the second method here.

Genealogical Structure

The distinction between genetic father and mother and genealogical father and mother refers to a shift in the definition of the mappings G and g. Suppose we now drop the genetically defined mappings G and g and substitute in their place culturally defined mappings m and f, where we define $m(s) = t$ if, and only if, t satisfies an appropriate cultural criterion for t to be recognized as the genealogical mother of s, and $f(s) = u$ if, and only if, u satisfies an appropriate cultural criterion for u to be recognized as the genealogical father of s, but we leave unspecified the specific cultural criteria. Just as we can, in principle, construct a genetic tree by beginning from a focal person and tracing out along paths of genetic fathers and genetic mothers, so we can create the familiar genealogical tree by beginning from the focal individual and tracing along paths of genealogical fathers and genealogical mothers. As with the genetic tree, the particular form taken on by the genealogical tree depends upon who is identified as genealogical father and who is identified as genealogical mother to whom. That identification instantiates a conceptual system expressed in terms of symbols and relationships among symbols.

While at first glance it may appear that the shift from the mappings G and g to the mappings m and f merely substitutes a cultural definition for a biological one, the shift has more profound implications than that. Consider a focal individual, s, and two other individuals, t and u, from the set S of persons. Even if it should be the case that $g(s) = g(t) = g(u)$ and $G(s) = G(t) = G(u)$, that is, s, t, and u each have the same genetic mother and the same genetic father, t and u are still genetically distinct and cannot be equated genetically with one another in terms of their relationship to s. Each of t and u will be genetically distinct from each other and from s, regardless of sharing the same genetic mother and the same genetic father. In contrast, if $m(s)$

$= m(t) = m(u)$ and $f(s) = f(t) = f(u)$, that is, t and u have the same genealogical mother and the same genealogical father as does s, then from a genealogical perspective t and u are genealogical siblings with respect to s and are not distinguished in terms of genealogical specification. From a genealogical viewpoint, t and u each have the same kind of genealogical relationship to s, in that each is a sibling of s. The shift to the genealogical domain allows the biological distinctiveness of the persons t and u to be erased. This erasure is conceptual rather than empirical and follows from creating yet another structure—the genealogical grid—that represents only the kind of relationship one person may have with another. In this structure logic asserts that when the relationship of person s to person t is the same as the relationship of person s to person u, then s and t are instances of that relationship regardless of their empirical distinctiveness. Or, to put it another way, the genealogical grid is a conceptual construct abstracted from the genealogical tree with structure determined by its underlying logic and not by the empirical facts of how particular individuals are linked. As Lehman and Klaus Witz (1974:127) have commented: "There is abundant motivation . . . to hold not only that people do their kinship reckoning by a process that can be described as composition of relations, but also that they are able to generate an abstract, free floating positional schema which can be imposed on any given kinship situation and on which kinship reckoning is carried out." The "positional schema" can be taken to be the usual genealogical diagram, or grid.

Now let f, m, s, and d be kin-type symbols that are to be interpreted as representing genealogical father, genealogical mother, genealogical son and genealogical daughter, respectively. We may express the relationship of person t to person s when both are persons in the same genealogical tree in the usual manner by taking appropriate kin-type products of these four symbols; for example, t might be s's genealogical father's genealogical son. Let u be the genealogical father of s. Whereas "genealogical father" presumably refers to a single person, u, with respect to s, "genealogical son of u" refers to any male for whom u is the genealogical father. More formally, if we think of each of f, m, s, and d as a mapping of the set S of persons into the set S of persons, then f and m are one-to-one mappings whereas s and d may be one-to-many mappings. That is, if s is a male person, then s is a son of u and so the expression "s's genealogical father's genealogical son" could be used for s or for t. The ambiguity is resolved in the genealogical grid through the sibling kin types genealogical brother (b) and genealogical sister (z) since t can be called the genealogical brother of s but s cannot refer to himself as a "genealogical brother." Of course, genealogical brother (genealogical sister) may still be a one-to-many mapping and so the kin type genealogical brother will still group more than one person under the same term should u have more than one son.

In terms of persons, distinctiveness as persons is not at issue. Rather, the ambiguity arises from applying a conceptual structure (the genealogical grid) to a group of persons even though the grid does not model the group's actual genealogical pattern as it might be expressed in a genealogical tree. Applying the structure imposes theory (Model$_T$) rather than modeling empirical data (Model$_D$).

We may formally construct the consanguineal genealogical grid as a Model$_T$. We begin with a special symbol *ego* and the set of symbols { *f, m, s, d, b, z*}, which refer to the kin types genealogical father, genealogical mother, genealogical son, genealogical daughter, genealogical brother, and genealogical sister, and use the concatenation operation to construct strings of symbols from them that will represent kin-type products; that is, we would read the symbol string *fmf* as genealogical father's genealogical mother's genealogical father.[6] We stipulate that *ego* is a right identity with respect to concatenation, which yields the equation

$$(x)(ego) = x, \text{ for all } x \in \{ego, f, m, s, d, b, z\}. \quad \text{(eq. 1)}$$

For example, $(m)(ego) = m$ indicates that genealogical mother's ego is genealogical mother. Equation (1) ensures that the symbol, *ego,* will neither be embedded within a symbol string nor be the terminal symbol in a symbol string. Now let *G* be the set of all symbol strings that begin with the symbol, *ego.* The set *G* is closed under concatenation; that is, if *ego(xy . . . z)* ∈ *G* (read: "*ego(xy . . . z)* is a symbol string in *G*") and *ego(st . . . u)* ∈ *G,* then the concatenation of these two symbol strings, namely, *ego(xy . . . z) ego(st . . . u)*, reduces to the symbol string *ego(xy . . . zst . . . u)* (since *ego* is a right identity and so *z ego = z*), and the latter symbol string is an element of *G* because it begins with the symbol *ego.* More precisely, since the concatenation operation is a closed, associative[7] operation over the set *S,* the set *S* of all symbol strings that begin with *ego* forms what is known algebraically as a semigroup.

We now introduce the equations:

$$fs = ms = b \quad \text{(eq. 2)}$$

$$fd = md = z^8 \quad \text{(eq. 3)}$$

$$sf = df \quad \text{(eq. 4)}$$

$$sm = dm \quad \text{(eq. 5)}$$

$$bz = z \qquad \text{(eq. 6)}$$

$$zb = b \qquad \text{(eq. 7)}$$

$$sb = s = db \text{ and reciprocally, } bf = f = zf \qquad \text{(eq. 8)}$$

$$sz = d = dz \text{ and reciprocally, } bm = m = zm.^{9} \qquad \text{(eq. 9)}$$

Using these equations, we reduce symbol strings in G that contain the symbol strings on the left side of these equations by replacing any such embedded symbol string with the symbol appearing on the right side. For example, we would reduce the symbol string, *ego fsmd,* to *ego z* via *ego fsmd = ego bz = ego z.* The interpretation of each of these equations in the form of kin-type products should be evident.

Equations 1–9 are needed to ensure that the structure imposed on the set G, of symbol strings is isomorphic to the genealogical grid expressed in the form of the standard genealogical chart. That chart makes implicit assumptions about genealogical calculations such that the positions it displays are the same as the positions obtained through the kin-type products that make up the genealogical grid. For example, in the genealogical chart, ego's genealogical father's genealogical son has the same position as ego's genealogical mother's genealogical son and, in both cases, is ego's genealogical brother, which presumes that equation 2 is valid.[10] However, when a genealogical tree is constructed for a set of individuals from empirical data, the resulting tree structure need not be consistent with the genealogical grid. As individuals divorce, remarry, have offspring outside of marriage, and so on, they contribute to the features of the empirically based tree structure. These features are not part of the grid. Thus the genealogical tree may contain relationships that, while describable in genealogical terms, are not consistent with those displayed in the genealogical grid. The "discrepancy" arises from the fact that the former has structural properties that arise from empirical events (Model$_D$) whereas the latter has structural properties as a consequence of the logic upon which it is constructed (Model$_T$).

The genealogical domain has, then, two levels between which we, as culture bearers, easily shift. One level involves the substitution of genealogical father and genealogical mother for genetic father and genetic mother (see figure 4.2) and the structure determined empirically by repeatedly applying genealogical father and genealogical mother (and their reciprocal relations) to the empirical facts of reproduction in their culturally interpreted form. Let us call this *genealogical kinship.* This level is characterized by genealogical tracing using the concepts of genealogical father and genealogical moth-

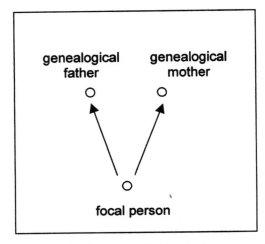

Figure 4.2. Triadic structure linking the focal person
with culturally determined genealogical father and
genealogical mother.

er and leads to the usual diagrams showing how the individuals in a set of
persons, such as an extended family, are linked genealogically. The second
level involves the conceptual structure created by kin-type symbols; such a
structure arises not from empirical context but from an underlying theory
that specifies which kin-type products define new genealogical positions and
which can be reduced to already defined genealogical positions as expressed
in certain equations (e.g., equations 2–9). At the second level, we shift from
the phenomenological (genealogical tree) to the ideational (genealogical
grid) domain.

It is possible to interpret the constituent elements of the structure so generated as other than kin types presumed to be the cultural interpretation of
the underlying biological system of reproduction. The linkage between a
symbol and a kin type is, as Schneider so forcefully argued, specified culturally, not by necessity, and it serves as a means to map the structure's symbolic elements onto actual persons in a manner consistent with that shown
in figure 4.2. Thus, if the genealogical symbol *ego* maps to the focal person,
then so long as the genealogical symbol *f* is mapped to that person's genea-
logical father, and genealogical *m* maps to that person's genealogical mother, then the genealogical grid is consistent with figure 4.2 no matter how ge-
nealogical father and genealogical mother might be defined. Whether or not
the kin types genealogical father and genealogical mother constitute "*biolo-*

gy interpreted through culture" (Vivelo 1978:150, emphasis in the original), as one introductory text on kinship phrases it, is not crucial for this process of mapping to individual persons. All that is needed is a way to link the symbols via cultural constructs that interpret them to be actual individuals in a manner consistent with the structure given in figure 4.2. In other words, from a formal perspective the "genealogical grid" does not require that genealogy be taken to represent actual or putative biological parent-child links. Rather, it represents genealogy in this sense only to the extent that genealogical father and genealogical mother are culturally modeled on biological parent-child links.

It should be noted that genealogical tracing exists without formulating the genealogical grid. Genealogical tracing through repeated use of genealogical father and genealogical mother does not require that the logic of a genealogical grid also be part of the cultural repertoire. Further, unless there is a group that truly is unaware of the biological basis of procreation, genealogical tracing may very well be universal, as Lehman (Lehman 1992:98) has argued. If so, then genealogical kinship defined as the set of relationships determined through genealogical tracing would also be universal. But unless the further step of constructing a genealogical grid as a conceptual structure is also recognized culturally, then there is no reason to assume that a genealogical grid, as opposed to genealogical tracing, is universal. Schneider's objection to the "genealogical grid" as universal appears to be an objection to assuming that the culturally defined genealogical grid is universal. Not considered by Schneider is the possibility that genealogical tracing may be universal when it is separated from genitor and genetrix as its basis.

We can summarize the consanguineal genealogical grid as a cultural construct that can be modeled through: (1) a set of symbols $\{ f, m, s, d, b, z \}$ along with a special symbol, *ego,* (2) a concatenation operation for forming symbol strings, (3) definition of ego as a right identity with respect to the concatenation operation, (4) identification of a set, G, of symbol strings that commence with the symbol *ego,* and (5) stipulation of certain equations (e.g., equations 2–9) that specify which symbol strings can be reduced to other symbols. The genealogical grid is the structure that arises from the application of those equations to the symbol strings in G. The resulting structure is a $Model_1$; hence its validity for a particular culture is ascertained not by reference to empirical data in the form of genealogical tracings, but by identifying cultural constructs that can be abstracted as the symbols required for constructing the genealogical grid along with cultural recognition of the equations that structure the space.

The structure so determined uses two abstractions from the empirical structures produced through genetic father and genetic mother. These are (1) the replacement of genetic father and genetic mother by genealogical father and genealogical mother along with abstraction of genealogical father and genealogical mother to the symbols f and m, respectively, and (2) abstraction of the recursive application of the structure shown in figure 4.2 to the concatenation operation on symbol strings to produce new symbol strings from the set of symbols used in the construction. The first abstraction also requires that there be a rule stipulating how the symbols shall be given instantiation when the structure is to be mapped onto a set of persons. While it might appear evident that f maps to father, m maps to mother, and so on (with father, mother, etc. referring to genealogical relations), given the intent that the structure defined conceptually should serve to determine the genealogical grid, this is not a formal necessity. We could, in the case of the Yapese for example, map f to *citamangen* and build a structure that would be based on "products" of the term *citamangen;* alter, for example, could be referred to as ego's *citamangen's citamangen.* The question whether the structure so produced is a *genealogical* structure lies at the heart of Schneider's critique of the notion that genealogy universally determines what constitutes kinship relationships.

Terminological Structure

The assertion that a structure based on constructs such as ego's *citamangen's citamangen* would be a genealogical structure rests on the claim that what we call kin terms are labels for sets of kin types. This claim implies that what we consider to be kin terms should be defined by their constituent kin types. The most developed, formal account taking genealogy as the means for defining kinship has been the rewrite/extension methodology introduced by Lounsbury (1964). Briefly, in a rewrite analysis the first step is to identify the kin types associated with each kin term. The next step is to reduce the set of kin types for a kin term to the focal kin type(s) for that set. Next, the focal kin type(s) in the reduced sets are given componential definitions (see Kronenfeld 1996). Lastly, rewrite rules are formulated that reconstruct the full range of kin types for the kin terms from the focal kin types for a kin term.

Insofar as the rewrite rules are not theoretically constrained, the last step can always be completed, regardless of the validity of the methodology's underlying assumptions, by adding whatever rewrite rule is needed to achieve closure. In this sense, the methodology is too powerful because it can be carried out on any collection of sets of kin types, regardless of how they were constructed. More problematic, though, is that the procedure must begin with a structure—the kin terms reduced to focal kin types—that has no a priori definition. The analysis has circularity because it assumes that terms are defined via kin types, but the structure from which it begins relies upon the kin terms for its specification. The circularity can be seen in the rewrite-rule analysis of the Sirionó kinship terminology. The Sirionó are a group from northeastern Bolivia, originally studied by Allan Holmberg (1948, 1950), whose terminology was extensively analyzed by Scheffler and Lounsbury using rewrite rules (1971). In their analysis, the structure to which the rewrite rules apply consists of the eleven terms in the terminology with their focal kin types as shown in table 4.1.

To derive the list of sets of focal kin types (the second column in table 4.1) requires first knowing the specification of the kin terms as sets of kin-type products; hence recovering the full range of kin types for each kin term from this list via rewrite rules does not fully establish the basis upon which the kin terms are defined as sets of kin-type products. The basis for the list of focal kin types is not specified. Unless we can specify why, for example, a female's *fzs* should be a focal kin type other than by appeal to the term *yande* and the range of kin types to which this term can be applied, the analysis has not succeeded in showing the basis upon which kin terms are associated with sets of kin types.

Ellen Woolford (Woolford 1984) asserts that to generate all kin classification systems, all we need are a grammar based on the five kin types parent, nuncle (sibling of parent), grandparent, sibling, and cousin, a fixed set of rewrite rules, reciprocity of kin types, and a partition operation (e.g., rewriting parent as mother and father), but her process works only by using rules that merely restate kin-term properties. For example, in her analysis of a Turkish terminology, she introduces rules such as "Divide by relative age of

Table 4.1. Siriono Kin Terms and Focal Kin Types

Siriono Kin Terms	Focal Kin Types
Ami	{ *ff, mf* }
Yande	{ *female's fzs* }
Ari	{ *fm, mm* }
Eru	{ *f* }
ezi	{ *m* }
anongge	{ *b, z* }
edidi	{ *s, d* }
ake	{ *ss, sd, ds, dd* }
akwani	{ *female's bd, male's zd* }
yande	{ *male's mbd* }
akwanindu	{ *female's bs, male's zs* }

ego versus alter: Sibling" and "Divide by sex of relative: Parent, Nuncle, Grandparent, Elder Sibling, Child" (779). She does not give any rationale for these rules other than the fact that they are necessary because the terminology has terms that distinguish between older and younger sibling and the kin types listed in the second rule correspond to terms that are sex marked. These ad hoc rules merely identify the ways in which the terminology differs from the purportedly universal analytic framework for all terminologies and use the properties of the kin terms to establish the rules.

If Scheffler and Lounsbury's assertion that a kin term "is the 'name' of a genealogically established category" (1971:13) is valid, then it must be possible to begin with the genealogical grid and next determine those categories of kin types for which the kin term is the "name" without appealing to properties derived from the names. Otherwise, we are implicitly recognizing that the kin terms are not simply the names for already determined categories but the means by which those categories are defined. Either we should consider the possibility that the kinship terminology has embedded in it the basis upon which the kin-type categories are constructed (the cultural rules, or what Meyer Fortes has called "a distinctive set of customary axioms" [1969:53]), or we must identify the cultural "rules" that have led to the categorization of kin types. In either case, the rewrite-rule analysis has to use the kin terms as the means to identify the consequences of those cultural rules when they are applied to the genealogical grid in order to form the categories of kin types allegedly "named" by the kin terms.

If it is the kin terms, along with their structural relations as kin terms, that carry the cultural information about how to categorize kin types, then we no longer need to assume that kinship is genealogy. Rivers rejected the possibility that kinship might be defined through kin terms on the grounds that kin terms are defined through genealogy. But if that assumption is incorrect and it is the kin terms that determine the genealogical categories—as I (Read 1998) have demonstrated to be the case for the American-English kinship terminology (AKT) and the Shipibo terminology—then it also follows that kinship may be defined by mapping the kin terms onto a collection of persons without necessarily making reference to genealogical claims. As the examples from Marshall and Goodale given earlier illustrate, calculations are in fact made to establish kinship without reference to genealogical claims through a kind of kin-term product.

Scheffler and Lounsbury call this process "pragmatic kin-class reckoning," but they go on to note that such reckoning is based on genealogy: "The relations between kin categories (narrow and broad) are such that partial genealogical knowledge suffices for their proper use" (1971:142n.3). Yet they also recognize that "the users of the system may not be accustomed to speaking or 'thinking' in the abstract of lengthy genealogical chains, e.g., of father's father's brother's son's sons" (142n.3). But if the user of the term is not thinking in terms of lengthy genealogical chains, then it is not clear how the user would know the genealogical relationship of one term to another unless this relationship was learned for every pair of terms—a daunting prospect to say the least. By their argument, a user of the AKT presumably would know that if alter is a person related to ego and referred to by ego's cousin as Grandfather, then ego would also know to use the kin term Grandfather to refer to alter by virtue of the calculation that a cousin's father's father or a cousin's mother's father is a grandfather when both ego and ego's cousin recognize alter as a kinsperson and even if ego does not know the genealogical kin-type product strings that "define" who is a Cousin.[11] But the calculation that a cousin's father's father or cousin's mother's father is a grandfather is not self-evident from the consanguineal kin-type definition for Grandfather, namely, $\{ff, mf\}$, in the absence of knowledge about the kin-type definition for Cousin, hence the genealogical calculation that links the kin term Cousin to the kin term Grandfather would have to be learned for this pair of terms. It seems more plausible that by experience ego is likely to know that a person that one's cousin calls Grandfather is a person that ego also calls Grandfather when both ego and ego's cousin recognize that person as a kin person, hence a Grandfather of a Cousin is a Grandfather as a kin-term product. In his critique of the assumption that kin terms first of all refer to genealogically related individuals, Lawrence A. Hirschfeld (1986:271) makes a similar observation: "It simply seems to be empirically the case that establishing the appropriate use of kinship terms involves reference to how the individuals use other kinship terms . . . not how those individuals are genealogically related." In this kind of learning through experience, ego knows the correct term to use to refer to alter without having to know the genealogical relationship of (to continue the example) ego to ego's cousin or of ego's cousin to ego's grandfather, or even of ego's genealogical relationship to grandfather. Let us refer to this kind of calculation that only uses kin terms and does not refer to genealogical relationships as a *kin-term product.*

More precisely, I have defined the kin-term product as follows: "Let K and L be kin terms in a given kinship terminology, T. Let ego, alter$_1$, and alter$_2$ refer to three arbitrary persons each of whose cultural repertoire includes the kinship terminology, T. The kin-term product of K and L, denoted $K \circ L$, is a kin term, M, if any, that ego may (properly) use to refer to alter$_2$ when ego (properly) uses the kin term L to refer to alter$_1$ and alter$_1$ (properly) uses the kin term K to refer to alter$_2$" (Read 1984:422, 1998:10).[12] For example, in the

AKT, if K is the kin term Father and L is the kin term Mother, then M = Father ∘ Mother is the kin term Grandmother.

The computation of the kin-term product does not depend upon genealogical relations; instead, unlike kin-type products that are assumed to be universal, it depends upon informant knowledge. Kin-term products are thus culturally specific and convey cultural concepts about how the kinship relations identified by the terminology may form a system of relationships.

If the cultural information load is embedded in the kin-term products, then it follows that we need a means to display that informational load directly rather than indirectly through mapping kin terms onto the genealogical grid. The means for so doing was originated by Murray Leaf, who illustrated his method using the American/English kinship terminology and the Punjabi kinship terminology (Leaf 1971, this volume). I have modified the kin-term map (Read 1984) in order to make it consistent with graphs showing the consequence of taking symbolic products by using arrows labeled to represent the symbol. Construction of kin-term maps has been implemented in the software program, Kinship Algebraic Expert System (KAES) (Read and Behrens 1990; Read 1998).

The kin-term map displays kin terms as nodes in a graph (mathematical sense) and traces their computation from a small set of kin terms using arrows (one term for each kind of arrow). For the AKT, the terms Self, Parent, Child, and Spouse suffice to generate all other kin terms (Read 1984). The kin-term map for the AKT constructed with the software program, KAES, is shown in figure 4.3. The upward arrows show the consequence of taking kin-term products with the kin term Parent. The downward arrows show the consequence of taking kin-term products with the reciprocal kin term Child. The kin-term products with the kin term Spouse, are shown with an equals sign. The kin-term map is a Model$_D$ as it represents informant information about kin-term products. Leaf's Punjabi example is of particular interest in this regard because it was elicited directly through informants and displays a structure that they found satisfactory as a map of their kinship world.

That it is possible to display the relationships among kin terms by means of products with the use of but a few kin terms suggests that the terminology structure may have an internal logic giving it its form and that the structure can be generated through repeated application of the kin-term product in a logically consistent and exhaustive manner. More precisely, it may be possible to model the kin-term map abstractly as a structure generated from a set of symbols (the generating elements) by taking a binary product defined over the set of symbols and using equations to determine the structure's form. Unlike the situation with rewrite rules, this claim about the kin-term map is

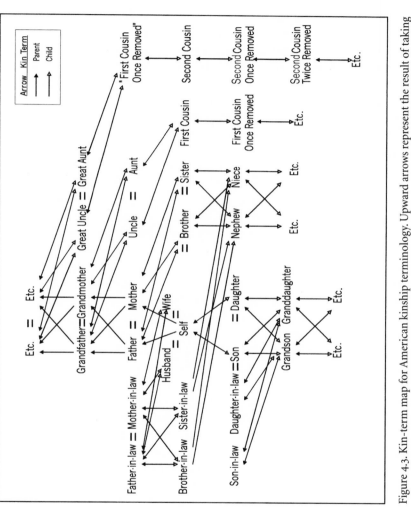

Figure 4.3. Kin-term map for American kinship terminology. Upward arrows represent the result of taking kin-term products with the kin term Parent. Downward arrows represent the result of taking kin-term products with the kin term Child. The equal sign represents the result of taking kin-term products with the kin term Spouse. The nodes labeled "Etc." indicate that the map continues using the same pattern as displayed in the immediately preceding nodes.

falsifiable because we can quite easily draw a structure that cannot be generated in this way. On the other hand, success in generating the structure argues strongly for the claim that the terminology structure is the locus of cultural concepts about kin relations because were this not the case, it is unlikely that the terminology structure would be logically consistent.

The generative approach to analysis of kinship terminology structure is formally related to the conceptual basis for the genealogical grid in the following way. Recall that the genealogical grid is formally based upon (1) a set of symbols, (2) the concatenation operation on symbol strings, and (3) certain equations that give the genealogical grid its particular structure. For the genealogical grid the set of symbols includes a special symbol, *ego,* that acts as a right-identity element with respect to the concatenation operation; the other symbols are interpreted as kin types. To generate the genealogical grid, we must determine the equations needed to ensure that the distinct symbol strings in the formal model will have one-to-one correspondence with the distinct kin-type products represented in the grid. To generate the terminological space, we change the procedure in the following ways. First, we note that the concatenation operation for the genealogical grid is a binary product on the set G of symbol strings that begin with the symbol *ego.* That is, given a symbol string that we denote by x, and a second symbol string that we denote by y, we can think of the concatenation operation as acting on the two symbol strings denoted by x and y to form the new symbol string xy, which is also a member of the set G. Thus, if we let $\circ$ represent the concatenation operation, then we have $x \circ y = xy$ and $\circ$ maps a pair of symbols from G to a symbol in G (more formally, $\circ: G \times G \to G$). For the terminological space, instead of the concatenation operation and a set of symbol strings G that begin with the symbol *ego,* we now only assume we have a set of symbols, S, and a binary operation, $\circ$, defined over S so that $\circ$ maps any pair of symbols from S to a symbol in S. The interpretation of $\circ$ with respect to kin terms will be the kin-term product. We can think of the kin-term product, then, as based on the idea of a binary product. The idea of a binary product is already used with kin-type products, but the binary product for kin terms differs by replacing the the binary product defined as the concatenation operation on symbol strings with a binary product defined over the symbols in the set S. In this respect, the kin-term product further abstracts the idea of recursively applying genealogical father and genealogical mother (or of genetic father and genetic mother) to compute kin relations. Second, we do not specify in advance what set of symbols should be used as generating elements, but derive these from the kin-term map via identification of kin terms that are atomic; that is, those that cannot be expressed as the kin-term product of other kin terms. No universal set of atomic terms is postulated and the atomic terms will be terminology specific. For example, the atomic kin terms in the AKT are found to be Self, Parent, Child, and Spouse (Read 1984; 1998), whereas the atomic kin terms in the Shipibo terminology (Behrens 1984:139–47) are found to be *Ea* ("Self"), *Papa* ("Father"), *Tita* ("Mother"), *Bakë* ("Child"), *Ahuiín* ("Wife") and *Bënë* ("Husband") (Read and Behrens 1990; Read 1998). Nor must the atomic consanguineal kin terms correspond to one of the terms Parent, Child, Mother, Daughter, Father or Son; the atomic terms for the Trobriand terminology, for example, are *Tama* ("Father") and *Tuwa* ("Elder Brother") (Read and Behrens 1990; Read 1998).[13] Further, no assumption is made that a terminology will have a term for Self, and some terminologies, such as the Trobriand terminology, lack such a term. Thus, whereas the symbols used in generating the genealogical grid are based on the structure shown in figure 4.2, the structural properties for the symbols used in generating the terminological space are not specified a priori (i.e., the structure shown in figure 4.2) but instead are specified terminologically. Third, the structural equations giving the generated structure its particular form depend upon the structural properties of the terminology as displayed in the kin-term map and will be terminology specific rather than universal, as is assumed for the equations underlying the structure of the genealogical grid. For the AKT, the relevant equations are as follows:

Parent of Child = Self (consanguineal structure)   (eq. 10)

Spouse of Spouse = Self   (eq. 11)

Spouse of Parent = Parent and reciprocally
    Child of Spouse = Child   (eq. 12)

Parent of Parent of Spouse = o[14] and reciprocally
    Spouse of Child of Child = o   (eq. 13)

Parent of Spouse of Child = o   (eq. 14)

Spouse of (Child of Parent) = (Child of Parent)
    of Spouse.   (eq. 15)

For example, equation 10 means that if ego refers to $alter_1$ as Child, and $alter_1$ refers to $alter_2$ as Parent, and if ego, $alter_1$, and $alter_2$ are consanguineally related, then $alter_2$ must be ego and so ego refers to $alter_2$ (= ego) by the term Self, hence Parent of Child = Self.

These equations, along with a rule for assigning sex marking of symbols based on whether or not products with the Spouse term yield kin terms in the algebraic model, and a rule for equating Cousin symbols so that an "*I*th Cousin *J* Times Removed" is a self-reciprocal kin term, suffice to generate a symbolic (algebraic) structure isomorphic to the kin-term map for the AKT (Read 1984; 1998, see figure 4.4). The fact that a structure is generated also makes it possible to identify structural properties arising from the logic of the structure's generation as opposed to these properties originating for reasons extrinsic to the logic of the structure.

One such property for the AKT is the lack of the "-in-law" suffix and the use of Uncle and Aunt for Spouse of Aunt and Spouse of Uncle, respectively. Schneider (1980 [1968]: 107n.7) asserted that "it is *clearly inconsistent* for them [husband of aunt and wife of uncle] to be uncle and aunt when cousin's spouse is not cousin and son's spouse is not daughter," and he suggested as an explanation that "uncle's wife is accorded aunt *as a form of respect,* aunt's husband is accorded uncle *as a form of respect*" (emphasis added). However,

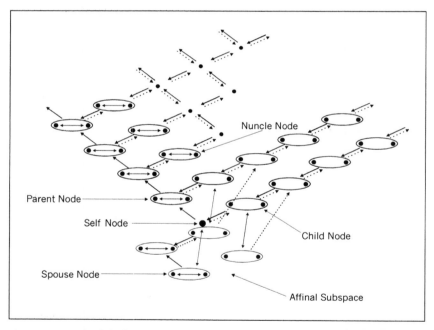

Figure 4.4. Graph of algebraic structure isomorphic to kin-term map for AKT. The nodes for the generating symbols Self, Parent, Child, and Spouse are indicated with arrows. The latter three nodes are bifurcated into two nodes due to the rule for sex marking of symbols. The double-headed arrows indicate taking products with the Spouse-generating symbol. The four circled pairs of nodes at the bottom of the graph form the affinal subspace and are precisely the nodes marked with an "-in-law" suffix when the algebraic structure is mapped to the kin-term map.

the algebraic model demonstrates the following: (1) that the equations Spouse of Aunt = Uncle and Spouse of Uncle = Aunt are a consequence of the logic of the structure (see figure 4.4, where the Nuncle node is bifurcated via the sex marking rule into the pair of nodes, Aunt and Uncle, and the arrows between these two nodes indicate that Spouse of Aunt = Uncle and Spouse of Uncle = Aunt); hence the lack of terms such as Aunt-in-law or Uncle-in-law demonstrates consistency between the logic of the structure and the semantic form of kin terms; (2) that the logic of the structure would preclude the kin-term product Spouse of Cousin from yielding a kin term, which is the case; and (3) that all of the terms marked with the -in-law suffix correspond precisely to those nodes in the structure introduced by taking products with the kin term Spouse.

Finally, the mappings Self → {*ego*}, Parent → {*m, f*} (and reciprocally, Child → {*d, s*}) and Spouse → {*w, h*} from the terminological structure to classes of primary kin types, in conjunction with the algebraic model for the kin-term structure, suffices to predict with complete accuracy the kin types included in the range of each kin term (see figure 4.5). (The prediction is verified empirically through mapping kin terms to the genealogical grid using Rivers's genealogical method.) Whereas the rewrite-rule analysis assumes that a mapping from kin types to kin terms links the genealogical grid with the set of kin terms, this result demonstrates the reverse, namely, that the mapping can be defined from the terminological space to the genealogical grid, and using kin terms as labels for classes of kin types derives from this mapping rather than serving as a basis for defining kin terms.

Conclusion

A comparison of the four structures that have been discussed is provided in table 4.2. As one goes across the table from left to right, each of the subsequent structures can be considered as produced by relaxation or abstraction of a property or properties of the previous structure. Thus the genealogical tree is more abstract than the genetic tree because *genealogical father* and *genealogical mother* are symbols with rules of instantiation that are not constrained by biological facts, whereas *genetic father* and *genetic mother* refer to persons with a specified biological relationship to the focal person.

Next, whereas the genealogical tree uses the more concrete notion of recursion as a way to construct an empirically based structure, the genealogical grid abstracts from recursion a binary product in the form of concatenated symbol strings (i.e., kin-type products), abstracts from *genealogical father* and *genealogical mother* the kin-type symbols *f* and *m,* and extends the

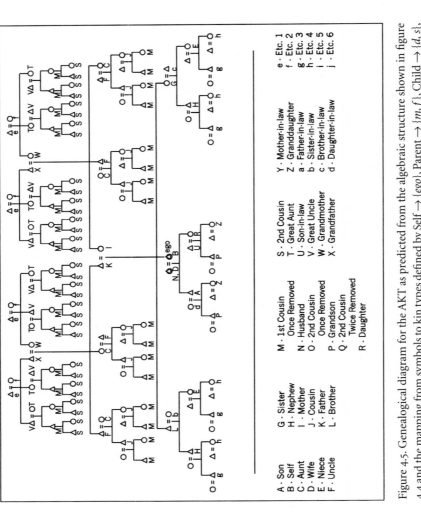

A - Son
B - Self
C - Aunt
D - Wife
E - Niece
F - Uncle

G - Sister
H - Nephew
I - Mother
J - Cousin
K - Father
L - Brother

M - 1st Cousin
      Once Removed
N - Husband
O - 2nd Cousin
      Once Removed
P - Grandson
Q - 2nd Cousin
      Twice Removed
R - Daughter

S - 2nd Cousin
T - Great Aunt
U - Son-in-law
V - Great Uncle
W - Grandmother
X - Grandfather

Y - Mother-in-law
Z - Granddaughter
a - Father-in-law
b - Sister-in-law
c - Brother-in-law
d - Daughter-in-law

e - Etc. 1
f - Etc. 2
g - Etc. 3
h - Etc. 4
i - Etc. 5
j - Etc. 6

Figure 4.5. Genealogical diagram for the AKT as predicted from the algebraic structure shown in figure 4.4 and the mapping from symbols to kin types defined by Self → {ego}, Parent → {m, f}, Child → {d, s}, and Spouse → {w, h}.

Table 4.2. Comparison of Four Types of Kinship Structure

	TYPE OF STRUCTURE		
Genetic Tree	Genealogical Tree	Genealogical Grid	Terminological Space
		STRUCTURAL ELEMENTS	
Empirical relation	Cultural relation	Abstract symbols: universal kin types	Abstract symbols: terminology-specific atomic kin types
Genetic father	Genealogical father	Ego	AKT
Genetic mother	Genealogical mother	Consanguineal	Self
	Spouse	f, m, s, d, b, z	Consanguineal
		Affinal	Parent, Child
		h, w	Affinal
			Spouse
			Shipibo
			Ea ("Self")
			Consanguineal
			Papa ("Father")
			Tita ("Mother")
			Bake ("Child")
			Affinal
			Bënë ("Husband")
			Ahuin ("Wife")
		STRUCTURAL OPERATION	
Recursion	Recursion	Binary product: concantenation	Binary product: kin-term product

Table 4.2. Con't.

	STRUCTURAL EQUATIONS		
Genetic father ≠ genetic mother	genealogical father ≠ genealogical mother	Universal equations: equations 2–9	Terminology-specific equations: AKT equations 10–14
		INSTANTIATION OF SYMBOLS	
Genetic father = male providing spermatozoon	Genealogical father = culturally prescribed male person	Ego = focal person	(1) AKT
Genetic mother = female providing ovum	Genealogical mother = culturally prescribed female person	f = genealogical father	Self = focal person
	Spouse = culturally defined person	m = genealogical mother	Parent = culturally prescribed person
		s = male person whose genealogical father or genealogical mother is ego	Child = reciprocal of parent
		d = female person whose genealogical father or genealogical mother is ego	Spouse = culturally prescribed person
		b = genealogical father's or genealogical mother's s	(2) AKT (genealogical)
		z = genealogical father's or genealogical mother's d	Self = {ego}
		w = female spouse	Parent = {m, f}
		h = male spouse	Child = {s, d}
			Spouse = {h, w}

latter to include the other elementary kin types via reciprocity and the definition of the kin-type symbols b and z. By shifting to the symbolic/ideational
level, these symbols, along with the concatenation operation and its equations, suffice to generate the genealogical grid. Unlike the genealogical tree
or the genetic tree, the form of the structure derives from the logic of its
generation and not from empirical events. The shift to abstract symbols also
requires that the rules of instantiation be more explicit. Finally, because the
terminological space does not require instantiation of the generating symbols in terms of genealogical father, genealogical mother, and so on, the structural elements of the terminological space become symbols whose identification and instantiation are culturally specific. Similarly, concatenation as the
binary operation is replaced by the kin-term product, which depends upon
cultural knowledge for its implementation. The equations giving the terminological space its particular structure are also culturally specific, and instantiation is generalized. While it is possible to map the abstract symbols used
to construct a generative model for the kin-term map to the genealogical grid
(see "(1) AKT" in table 4.2, right column, and figure 4.5), this is not necessary. Instead, the kin terms, taken as abstract symbols, can be instantiated by
cultural rules (see "(2) AKT" in table 4.2, right column, and figure 4.6), which
need not be identical to the way the kin terms might be mapped to the genealogical grid. For example, Parent in the AKT might include "adopted
parent" as part of its cultural specification.

Whereas the genealogical grid is supposedly universal and, hence, uses
concepts that are presumably shared by all cultures, the terminological space
has a priori specification only through general structural properties such as
(1) the structure must have a focal element, that is, a kin term from which
all other kin terms can be reached via kin-term products; and (2) the structure preserves reciprocity; that is, for each term there is a reciprocal term and
the reciprocal form of an equation is also valid in the structure. Whereas the
presumed universality of the genealogical grid determined by the elementary kin types and equations 2–9 has been challenged by Schneider as assumed
rather than demonstrated, the terminological space is consistent with his
concern that the anthropologist's first task is to "understand and formulate
the symbols and meanings and their configuration that a particular culture
consists of" (Schneider 1984:196). The algebraic analysis that I introduced
(Read 1984) and implemented in the form of a computer program (Read and
Behrens 1990; Read 1998) elucidates the symbols and their configuration. To
understand the meanings of kin terms, it is necessary to know the structure
in which the terms are embedded. But their meanings are more fully elaborated via the rules of instantiation; for example, who is a Parent in Ameri-

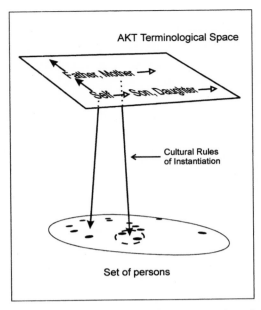

Figure 4.6. Diagram illustrating the mapping of AKT kin terms viewed as symbols onto a set of persons via cultural rules that specify how the symbols should be instantiated. The left arrow indicates that the kin term Self has been mapped to a person (ego), and the pair of symbols Mother and Father have been mapped to two persons circled with a dashed line. No a priori claim is made as to the genealogical relationship (if any) of the latter two persons to ego; e.g., the two persons might be the two persons ego calls Mother and Father by virtue of adoption.

can culture? Who is a Spouse? The answers are culturally constructed and are not fixed but changeable as illustrated by the way the answer to the first question has been revised since the introduction of surrogate mothers, artificial insemination, and the like. The answer to the second question may be revised through the debate on whether or not same-sex marriage should be legally recognized.

Meanings are not only changeable, but may also vary depending upon which structure (genealogical tree, genealogical grid, or terminological space) has cultural salience in a particular instance. While Schneider argued against the claim that the genealogical grid universally represents what constitutes kinship, this does not preclude the claim that the genealogical grid has cultural salience in some cultures. Nor does Schneider's argument against universality preclude the notion that the genealogical grid and the terminological space have cultural salience and serve as alternative conceptual structures that can be used to frame how persons are seen to be related to one another. It is evident that users of the American kinship terminology often use the genealogical grid to define a kin term, as when a parent explains to a child that an Uncle is a parent's brother. As discussed earlier, Schneider's argument against the universality of "kinship" is predicated upon his assertion that the genealogical grid is part of European culture (Schneider 1984:200); hence, it cannot be assumed to be a pancultural conceptual structure. Since kin terms determined via the terminological space can also be mapped onto the genealogical grid, they can be given definition via the genealogical grid even if the genealogical grid is irrelevant to how the terminological space is formulated.

Even when the genealogical grid does not have cultural salience, the genealogical tree, which only depends upon recursive use of the concepts of genealogical father and genealogical mother, may be an alternative way in which relations are conceived. The fact that the !Kung San use something like the kin-term product to determine whether or not ego and alter are kin does not preclude the possibility that in other contexts genealogical tracing may be the means for working out the relationship between ego and alter. Or, to put it another way, if genealogical tracing (as opposed to the genealogical grid) is universal, as some have suggested, the relation between ego and alter can be viewed either from the perspective of the terminological space and its attendant culturally defined rules of instantiation, or from the perspective of genealogical tracing. When the meaning of kin terms as determined through the terminological space is not based upon properties that can also be expressed via genealogical tracing, the two systems for how relations are perceived need not be congruent. Recognizing this fact provides a way to resolve the seeming native contradiction posed by Andrew J. Strathern. He notes that "at a Melpa exchange ceremony a ceremonial speech-maker declared 'I call you my sister's sons, my cross-cousins. I am your true cross-cousin, living close to you. My sisters' sons, my cross-cousin, you say you see big pigs, big shells, well, now I have given you large pigs.' . . . The speaker says he is a 'true' cross-cousin because he lives near to his kin and is their regular and generous exchange-partner" (Strathern 1973:32).

In terms of the framework presented in table 4.2, the speaker is making reference to the terminological space and how the abstract symbols are given instantiation. Yet at the same time, Strathern notes that in other contexts "speakers will say that 'X is not my true (i.e. immediate genealogical) cross-cousin, we call each other by this term only because we exchange pigs and shell valuables.' In the latter context the genealogical component is selected as indicating the 'true' relationship" (Strathern 1973:32). In terms of table 4.2, the speaker refers not to how abstract symbols of the terminological space are instantiated but to genealogical tracing. Once we recognize that genealogical tracing and the terminological space can both be culturally salient, yet need not be congruent when the means for giving the abstract terminological symbols instantiation do not relate to properties that can be expressed in terms of genealogical tracing, there is no conflict in the two seemingly contradictory statements to which Strathern refers, only a difference with regard to the context that makes one or the other framework more salient for the situation at hand. The interesting question then becomes one of understanding which conceptual framework is appropriate at any given time, not whether the genealogically framed reference is somehow more real and the terminologically framed reference is "metaphoric." As Schneider observed "One must take the native's own categories, the native's units, the native's organization, and articulation of those categories and follow their definition, their symbolic and meaningful divisions wherever they may lead" (1972:51). The notion that kin are specified by the rules that produce a culture-specific structure expressed in the culture's kinship terminology is a step in this direction.

Notes

1. The genealogical grid is defined more formally later. Roughly, it is the structure represented in the form of a standard genealogical chart and presumed to have indefinite extension.

2. This approach has much in common with Montague's suggestion (this volume) that kinship be viewed as a "multiple slotting system" of classification. However, whereas Montague is interested in the definitions of individual taxa, my concern is with the formal logical integration of the overall system.

3. That kin terms can be related to the genealogical grid is evident and is the basis of Rivers's genealogical method for eliciting kin terms. The algebraic modeling demonstrates something more, namely, that the terminological structure can be generated without reference to the genealogical grid and the mapping of kin terms onto the genealogical grid can then be predicted from the terminological structure. The prediction can be verified by Rivers's genealogical method. For the two terminologies where this has been tested, the predicted mapping of kin terms to the genealogical grid is in complete agreement with the empirically obtained mapping.

4. In accord with J. A. Barnes (1961) and Ira Buchler and Henry Selby (1968:33–35), the following distinctions will be made: (1) genetic father/mother—the person providing the spermatozoon/ovum, (2) genitor/genetrix—the culturally defined person(s) (if any) who

is (are) culturally recognized as, or asserted to be, the physical father/mother and (3) *pater/ mater*—the person(s) recognized as the social father/mother.

5. Although in some cultures genealogical tracing may be conducted on the basis of genitor/genetrix, the process requires only that a single male person and a single female person be associated with ego in such a manner that the association can be done recursively with respect to the two persons so identified. Whether or not the male person is genitor and the female person is genetrix is irrelevant from the viewpoint of the logic of genealogical tracing. One can also trace using a cultural specification such as the male person is the husband of mother. In this case the genealogical "tree" so identified would not be the pedigree of ego, but would be ego's culturally relevant genealogical tree structure.

6. Kin types are usually viewed as abstractions of genitor and genetrix, but genealogical tracing need not be based upon such notions. Yet it is evident that the genealogical grid, even if defined in terms of kin types based upon genitor and genetrix, is supposed to represent an idealized genealogy based upon the idea of genealogical tracing. To avoid inconsistency, then, the basis for genealogical tracing and the basis for the genealogical grid must be the same. Hence I am using genealogical father and genealogical mother as the common basis for genealogical tracing and the genealogical grid. Genealogical father and genealogical mother can, but need not, be genitor and genetrix, respectively. Identification of genealogical father and genealogical mother with genitor and genetrix depends upon cultural specification rather than an assumption that genitor and genetrix are universally recognized as the basis for genealogical tracing.

7. A binary operation such as the concatenation operation is associative when it is not necessary to use parentheses to indicate the order in which the binary operation takes place. Thus, if s, t and u are symbol strings, then the fact that $(st)u = s(tu) = stu$ implies that the concatenation operation is associative.

8. Equations 2 and 3 are the same as the "Half-Sibling Rule" used in rewrite rule analysis.

9. Equations 4–9 are considered axiomatic by Scheffler and Lounsbury: "It may be regarded as an axiom of all kinship systems we know of that, e.g., the parent of a sibling is a parent or step-parent, and conversely, the sibling of a child is a child or step-child. Similarly, the sibling of a sibling is regarded as a sibling" (Scheffler and Lounsbury 1971:128n).

10. From the perspective of genealogical tracing, ego's father's son could be ego if ego is male. However, the genealogical grid represented by the genealogical chart seems to assume that ego's father's son is ego's brother; that is, some tracing paths are not allowed in the genealogical grid.

11. In the algebraic modeling, kin terms begin with a capital letter in order to distinguish them from kin types for those cases where the kin term and the kin type use the same semantic form; e.g., Father (kin term) versus father (kin type).

12. Right to left notation is used for kin-term products, rather than the more common left to right notation, as a way to distinguish between kin-term products and kin-type products. In symbolic notation, the kin-term product Parent ∘ Child, for example, is read "Parent of Child," whereas the kin-type product pc is read "parent's child." The former expression refers to a kin term (namely the kin term ego uses for alter$_2$ when ego properly refers to alter$_1$ as Child and alter$_1$ properly refers to alter$_2$ as Parent in the AKT), where-

as the latter expression refers to a genealogical position (namely the alter who is ego's parent's child).

13. This is consistent with Montague's argument (this volume) that Trobriand Islanders do not define kin terms genealogically, and that the usual English glosses for Trobriand kin terms are fundamentally misconceived.

14. The "o" indicates that the kin-term product does not yield a kin term. The symbol "o" is added to the set of symbols to ensure that the kin-term product is closed over the set of symbols.

References Cited

Barnes, J. A. 1961. "Physical and Social Kinship." *Philosophy of Science* 28:296–99.

Behrens, Clifford. 1984. "Shipibo Ecology and Economy." Ph.D. dissertation, University of California at Los Angeles.

Buchler, Ira, and Henry Selby. 1968. *Kinship and Social Organization: An Introduction to Theory and Method.* New York: Macmillan.

D'Andrade, Roy. 1970. "Structure and Syntax in the Semantic Analysis of Kinship Terminologies." In *Cognition: A Multiple View.* Ed. Paul L. Garvin. 87–144. New York: Spartan Books.

Fortes, M. 1969. *Kinship and the Social Order.* London: Routledge and Kegan Paul.

Glasse, R. M. 1969. "Marriage in South Fore." In *Pigs, Pearl Shells, and Women.* Ed. M. J. Meggitt and R. M. Glasse. 16–37. Englewood Cliffs, N.J.: Prentice-Hall.

Goodale, Jane. 1994 [1971]. *Tiwi Wives.* Prospect Heights, Ill.: Waveland Press.

Goodenough, Ward. 1970. *Description and Comparison in Cultural Anthropology.* Chicago: Aldine.

Hirschfeld, Lawrence A. 1986. "Kinship and Cognition: Genealogy and the Meaning of Kinship Terms." *Current Anthropology* 27 (3): 217–29.

Holmberg, A. 1948. "The Sirionó." In *Handbook of South American Indians* (BAE *Bulletin* 3 [143]). Ed. Julian Steward. 455–63. Washington, D.C.: Bureau of American Ethnology.

———. 1950. *Nomads of the Long Bow: The Siriono of Eastern Bolivia.* Institute of Social Anthropology Publications, Vol. 10. Washington, D.C.: Smithsonian Institution. (Reprinted in 1969 by the Natural History Press, Garden City, N.Y.)

Keesing, R. M., and F. M. Keesing. 1971. *New Perspectives in Cultural Anthropology.* New York: Holt, Rinehart and Winston.

Kronenfeld, D. 1996. "Componential Analysis." In *Encyclopedia of Cultural Anthropology.* Vol. 2. Ed. D. Levinson and M. Ember. 224–28. New York: Henry Holt and Co.

Langness, L. L. 1964. "Some Problems in the Conceptualization of Highlands Social Structures." In *New Guinea: The Central Highlands.* Ed. J. B. Watson. 162–82. Special issue of *American Anthropologist* 66.

Leaf, Murray J. 1971. "The Punjabi Kinship Terminology as a Semantic System." *American Anthropologist* 73 (3): 545–54.

Lehman, F. K. 1992. "The Relationship between Genealogical and Terminological Structure in Kinship." *Journal of Quantitative Anthropology* 4 (2): 95–122.

———. n.d. "Aspects of a Formalist Theory of Kinship." Ms.

Lehman, F. K., and K. Witz. 1974. "Prolegomena to a Formal Theory of Kinship." In *Genealogical Mathematics*. Ed. Paul A. Ballonoff. 111–34. Paris: Mouton.

Lounsbury, Floyd G. 1964. "The Structural Analysis of Kinship Semantics." In *Proceedings of the Ninth International Congress of Linguists*. Ed. H. Hunt. 1073–93. The Hague: Mouton.

Lowman-Vayda, Cherry. 1971. "Maring Big Men." In *Politics in New Guinea*. Ed. P. Lawrence and R. M. Berndt. 317–61. Perth: University of Western Australia Press.

Marshall, Lorna. 1976. *The !Kung of Nyae Nyae*. Cambridge, Mass.: Harvard University Press.

Needham, R. 1971. "Introduction." In *Rethinking Kinship and Marriage*. Ed. R. Needham. xiii–cxvii. London: Tavistock.

Read, Dwight W. 1984. "An Algebraic Account of the American Kinship Terminology." *Current Anthropology* 25:417–49.

———. 1992. "The Utility of Mathematical Constructs in Building Archaeological Theory." In *Mathematics and Information Science in Archaeology: A Flexible Framework*. Ed. A. Voorips. 29–60. Bonn: Holos.

———. 1998. "The Kinship Algebra Expert System Software Program." Ms.

Read, Dwight W., and Clifford Behrens. 1990. "KAES: An Expert System for the Algebraic Analysis of Kinship Terminologies." *Journal of Quantitative Anthropology* 2:353–93.

Rivers, W. H. R. 1900. "A Genealogical Method of Collecting Social and Vital Statistics." *Journal of the Royal Anthropological Institute* 30:74–86.

———. 1968 [1924]. *Social Organization*. London: Dawsons of Pall Mall.

Scheffler, H. W., and F. G. Lounsbury. 1971. *A Study in Structural Semantics: The Siriono Kinship System*. Englewood Cliffs, N.J.: Prentice-Hall.

Schneider, David M. 1972. "What Is Kinship All About?" In *Kinship Studies in the Morgan Centennial Year*. Ed. Priscilla Reining. 32–63. Washington D.C.: Anthropological Society of Washington.

———. 1980 [1968]. *American Kinship: A Cultural Account*. Chicago: University of Chicago Press.

———. 1984. *A Critique of the Study of Kinship*. Ann Arbor: University of Michigan Press.

Strathern, A. J. 1973. "Kinship, Descent, and Locality: Some New Guinea Examples." In *The Character of Kinship*. Ed. J. Goody. 21–34. Cambridge: Cambridge University Press.

Vivelo, Frank Robert. 1978. *Cultural Anthropology Handbook*. New York: McGraw-Hill.

Woolford, Ellen. 1984. "Universals and Role Options in Kinship Terminology: A Synthesis of Three Formal Approaches." *American Ethnologist* 11:771–90.

5. Relativism in Kinship Analysis

MARTIN OTTENHEIMER

Schneider's Contribution to Anthropological Discourse

THE CRITICAL ANALYSIS of kinship by David Schneider is a quintessential example of cultural relativism. Although the phrase, "cultural relativism," has become imbued with a variety of meanings the term's central focus clearly applies to Schneider's work. Robert Redfield (1953:144) enunciated the core tenets of cultural relativism nearly a half-century ago: "Cultural relativism means that the values expressed in any culture are to be both understood and themselves valued only according to the way the people who carry that culture see things." Broadened over the years to include other aspects of culture beyond values, cultural relativism has broadly been accepted as the notion that the only proper study of a culture is in terms of the specific culture under analysis. This fundamental idea continues to be widely expressed today. Students are told in a basic cultural anthropology textbook, for example, that cultural relativism requires "understanding other cultures by their own categories, which are assumed to be valid and worthy of respect" (Bodley 2000:13). Defined in this way cultural relativism is a mainstay of anthropological discourse, an icon for many anthropologists, and a central part of Schneider's critique of kinship.

Schneider's cultural analysis of kinship has made an important contribution to anthropological studies. It has had an impact well beyond kinship. One example of this impact is in the area of gender studies. Jane Fishburne Collier and Sylvia Junko Yanagisako, for example, point out that Schneider's studies of kinship led them "to question the assumption that 'male' and 'female' are two natural categories of human being whose relations are everywhere structured by their biological difference" (1987:7). Furthermore, they point out: "Just as Schneider (1968) questioned, rather than took for granted, the meanings of blood, love, and sexual intercourse in American kinship and their influence on the construction of categories of relatives, so we have to question the meanings of genes, love, sexual intercourse, power, independence, and whatever else plays into the symbolic construction of categories of people in any particular society" (Collier and Yanagisako 1987:41). Schneider's work has also been cited as instrumental in the investigation into the developing community of social relationships among same-sex couples (see Weston 1991).

With the publication of *American Kinship: A Cultural Account* in 1968, Schneider became widely associated with the search for underlying cultural categorizations of human social relationships. His approach is one of the more important contributions that anthropology has made to the study of human behavior. When applied to cultures around the world, there is no doubt that the explication of a group's relationships in terms of their own categories rather than the biological notions from Western cultures can provide significant insights into human behavior (see Feinberg 1981, for example). But this approach can be misused. Cultural relativism, as well illustrated by Schneider, goes beyond simply exploring alternative views of a subject. It confers a differential weighting to these views and makes a judgment about their fundamental nature. This judgment raises pivotal theoretical issues about the analysis of human social relationships. Thus, Schneider's critique of kinship is important because it brings into sharp focus the fundamental weaknesses of the concept of cultural relativism. In this essay I will examine Schneider's approach to kinship, discuss the fundamental issues involved, point out the problems with cultural relativism, and question his conclusion that the concept of kinship has no analytical utility and must be discarded.

Schneider's Error: The Absolutism of Cultural Relativism

David Schneider believed that the traditional anthropological treatment of kinship was "simply wrong. It could not be applied to some, perhaps many, non-European cultures of which Yap was one example, and it contained assumptions and presuppositions that were wholly incorrect. 'Blood is thicker than water' is one of the most important of these. In short, the analytic scheme does not work" (Schneider 1992:629). Since the time of Lewis Henry Morgan, argued Schneider, kinship analysis had expressed a European model of biological relationships. It did not correspond to the models other cultures held for family and marriage relationships and was, therefore, inappropriate for understanding kinship in other cultures. In fact, "kinship," as an expression of an "ethnoepistemology of European culture" (1987 [1984]: 175), was, outside of European folk categories, a meaningless construct. As Schneider put it, "Robbed of its grounding in biology, kinship is nothing" (1987:112).

Schneider's antidote to a Eurocentric, biologically based mode of analysis was to use the "units which the particular culture itself marks off" (1987:184). While he recognized that the union of sperm and egg is a universal and essential part of human procreation, Schneider argued that the proper analysis of family and marriage systems could not assume that the biology of procreation was at the core of social relationships. The reason was that procreation did not have the same significance in every culture. Proper analysis required eliciting the meanings assigned to family and marriage relationships from the culture rather than assuming the biology of procreation. And if that were done, Schneider concluded that there would be no common referent for the term "kinship." Thus, the concept would be vacuous and without analytical utility (1987:175).

Schneider's conclusion that "kinship" has no analytical utility is wrong. It results from the application of a nonrelativistic framework to a situation that requires a relativistic approach. Though Schneider's cultural approach appears to be relativistic, I will show that it is not. One of my concerns with the Schneider critique of kinship arises from the recognition that a relativistic framework is necessary for successful anthropological research. Schneider does not offer one as a viable alternative to Eurocentric absolutism, however, but provides us with an absolutistic approach that is, in essence, not much different from the approach he so strongly criticized. Instead of being a cure for ethnocentrism, it is only another form of the disorder. It, too, inhibits the development of workable hypotheses about behavior in different cultures and the development of effective theories about human behavior. I will make my reasoning for this conclusion clear in the succeeding paragraphs, which are partially based upon a previous work (Ottenheimer 1995).

Schneider's description of kinship analyses as primarily based upon European conceptions of the biological nature of human relationships is, first of all, acceptable only if you categorize Americans in terms of their European cultural background. But, as I have pointed out elsewhere (Ottenheimer 1996), Americans and Europeans approach social relationships in significantly different ways. These differences have been clearly expressed in the laws governing marriage, particularly the marriage of cousins. Schneider overlooks this difference and, for the purposes of the argument here, I will also ignore this detail. Instead, I will begin in essential agreement with Schneider's basic contention that the traditional analysis of kinship rests upon a cultural foundation. Since no one, including anthropologists, stands outside culture, this is a simple point. Furthermore, since most of the kinship analyses were done by investigators of European cultural background, it should be no surprise that they are Eurocentric. The human condition simply does not allow for an objective (i.e., culture-free), absolute framework for kinship. Consequently, any field of investigation lies within the purview of a cultural context and is culturally biased. The fundamental theoretical issue here is not one involving the choice between an objective and a subjective basis for the investigation of human behavior. It ultimately entails a choice between cultural frameworks or perspectives. Furthermore, since cultural bias is a normal condition of human life, it, in itself, should not be considered an impediment to analytical inquiry. If it were, not only the Eurocentric bias in the study of kinship would be "without analytical utility"; so would any framework one chooses. This is not the case.

The fundamental point that Schneider addressed was that culturally derived symbolic interpretations of basic human social relationships based on notions of biological relationships between spouses and between parents and their children had been elevated to the status of an absolute truth. Kinship had been given a fundamental, absolute status by many investigators who founded their cross-cultural analysis of social relationships upon their notions of the biological conditions of human reproduction. They took these to be not simply universal but absolute factors of human life (see, e.g., Scheffler and Lounsbury 1971). When sexual intercourse and genealogical connections are assumed to be the universal cognitive basis of kinship because they involve "the basic facts of life" (Fox 1983 [1967]: 27), the problem of Eurocentric ideational imperialism exists. Schneider made this problem very clear by attacking the assumption that biology provides an absolute framework for analyzing kinship. He argued that the framework itself is a cultural product and must be treated as such. Schneider thus refuted the biological claim to absolute status by focusing on its cultural underpinnings. He pointed out that, because "blood" and coitus are recognized as fundamental and necessary elements of human social organization in one culture, it is incorrect to assume that all peoples share a belief in these "facts." Schneider plainly exposed the ethnocentric bias of the claim that biology is absolute and that biological processes play a universal role in the articulation of kinship. But we must be careful to distinguish between a claim that the biological processes of reproduction lay at the base of all cultural interpretations of kinship and the very different approach that takes application of these processes as a framework for analyzing social relationships in every culture. I will have more to say about this distinction later.

In an effort to provide an alternative to this absolutistic, ethnocentric approach to kinship studies, Schneider proposed a different approach that took culture into account. It focused on the culture of a group as the proper framework for analysis. In this approach, the investigator derives the concepts for the examination of social relationships from the symbols in which the relationships are embedded. At first glance this appears to be a relativistic antidote to an absolutistic, ethnocentric European biological model. But, under close examination, it is not. It simply substitutes one form of ethnocentrism for another. Schneider's approach is not relativistic, but one version of what I have called the "monistic approach" to kinship (Ottenheimer 1995). It is "monistic" because it calls for only one true framework for analyzing a set of data.

When someone chooses to analyze social behavior in terms derived from the culture under analysis, as Schneider suggests doing, one does not avoid ethnocentrism; one simply changes its location. The investigation, furthermore, if restricted to viewing the social data from the one perspective, is simply utilizing another form of absolutism. The analyst is being constrained to the one "true" way for analyzing the data, only it is from within rather than from without the culture being analyzed. If the claim is that there is only one true way to look at a culture, whether it is from within or without the culture, the approach is ethnocentric and absolutistic, not relativistic. Schneider has merely shifted the focus of the analysis; rather than being Eurocentric, his approach is localcentric.

Relativism, Genuine and Spurious: The Value of Multiple Approaches

The distinction I am drawing between a relativistic and an absolutistic approach to data may be made clearer by referring to a widely known distinction that has been made between the concepts "etic" and "emic." The words were invented in 1954 by Kenneth Pike (1967) and derived from the words "phonetic" and "phonemic" used in linguistics. To discriminate and describe the sounds of a language, the linguist can use the external framework of the vocal tract's points of articulation. Such a procedure is known as articulatory phonetics. The linguist can then use an internal framework to discover how the sounds are grouped to change meaning within the language. This procedure is known as phonemic analysis. This analysis requires an internal viewpoint. It necessitates knowing what meanings are assigned to the collection of sounds utilized by speakers of the language. No amount of investigation from the external viewpoint will provide this information. Pike extended the linguistic phonetic and phonemic approaches for more general purposes and coined the terms "etic" and "emic." These were meant to represent the external and internal viewpoints, respectively, in an investigation of human behavior. While Pike points out that "etic criteria may often be considered absolute" (Berry 1990:85), he undoubtedly saw one as being derived from the culture of the investigator and the other as being derived from the internal characteristics of the system under investigation. Both "are of value; neither is more important than the other" (Berry 1990:86). Furthermore, like stereoscopic vision, the two different approaches provide distinct images of the data that together provide a greater dimensionality to the overall picture than either can provide by itself (Pike 1967:41). Pike thus saw the external and internal approaches to analyzing human behavior in relativistic terms. Each represents a particular perspective and each has value for interpreting or describing data. Neither has greater ontological status than the other, so neither represents the one true way of analyzing or describing data.

Analytical concepts in kinship can be derived either from the culture under investigation or from the culture of the investigator. The former are, in Pike's terms, emic concepts, while the latter are etic concepts. Etic concepts have been used for cross-cultural comparisons while the emic concepts have been restricted to the investigation of the culture under analysis. Though etic analytical concepts have been granted a scientific or even an absolutistic status by some anthropologists as if they were objective and culture-free, Schneider knew that the notion of an objective, culture-free analysis is an illusion and recognized that what are called etic concepts are nothing more than the notions from the external analyst's culture. Thus, Schneider recognized that what is involved is two sets of emic concepts: those of the people of the culture under investigation and those of the investigator. But, instead of treating the etic and emic concepts in a relativistic manner, he denigrated the etic approach in kinship and conferred upon the internal viewpoint the greater ontological status, making it the one true approach. At this critical point, Schneider's critique of kinship fails. It fails because it does not provide a relativistic alternative to the Eurocentric, absolutistic work he so strongly decried. If anthropological analysis is to succeed in producing significant statements about kinship, or any aspect of human behavior, the anthropologist must stop thinking in terms of one "true" framework, whether it be Eurocentric or localcentric, and move beyond the ultimately unproductive argument over whether it is the culture of the investigator or the culture under investigation that has the "truth."

The problem with cultural relativism as a framework for the study of kinship may be made more apparent by returning again to the world of linguistic phenomena. Important contributions to the study of language have been made using articulatory phonetics. In this approach to language, sounds made by humans are investigated by reference to the physical makeup of the vocal tract. The sound /p/, for example, is described as the brief stopping of air pushed up from the lungs by pressing the lips together. We can readily see that this approach is as Eurocentric as the biological models for studying kinship. Suppose now that an ethnographer discovers a group of people who describe human speech to be the result of small, invisible spirits located in the vocal tract of each person. This culture provides us with a different, non-Eurocentric view of language. Do we now declare phonetics to be a vacuous concept without analytical utility since it is derived from a Eurocentric view of the way sounds are created by humans? Isn't that what David Schneider has asked us to do in the case of kinship? That articulatory phonetics has been developed within a particular culture should not mean that it has no analytical utility. Nor does the fact that this framework for analyzing human speech has been developed within a particular culture confine it to an investigation of only the language of that culture. Nor does its source make it incapable of describing universal characteristics of language. We can recognize that it is both a framework developed within a cultural tradition and a framework that can provide useful insights into the characteristics of language across cultures. As Pike recognized, it provides a means for describing universal characteristics of language while neither being an absolute framework nor one which pretends to describe some absolute reality. Likewise, the study of kinship from a Eurocentric perspective can provide a means for analyzing behavior across cultures. It need not be abandoned merely because the analytical framework is derived from a particular cultural tradition.

Schneider's localcentric approach is different from a Eurocentric approach to kinship in two major ways: (1) It does not assume that biological relationships are the basis of the social world, and (2) it does not claim that the local framework has universal applicability. In fact, in regard to the second point, it is just the opposite. It claims that the concepts of social behavior are a cultural matter and that the cultural framework of the people from the society under investigation is the only appropriate one for the data. These differences, however, are of little consequence. The significant point for the argument over whether the approach is relativistic or not is that if the approach claims to be the one "true" framework for analysis of the data, it is not a relativistic approach. Whether the "true" framework is localcentric or Eurocentric, cultural or biological, internal or external, does not matter. If either framework is claimed to be the only appropriate one, it is not relativistic. In Schneider's attempt to provide an alternative to the Eurocentric analyses of kinship, he has simply shifted the conceptions, categories, and values of analysis from one culture to another. We are still told the one, proper way of analyzing the data. Thus, in spite of appearing so from its name, cultural relativism is not truly relativistic.

Lacking this characteristic, cultural relativism fails to provide a method for making any scientific use of the data derived from cultural analysis. It cannot be generalized. If we are limited to the examination of each culture in the terms of its own categories and values, how is one to compare the categories derived from different cultures? How does one construct a framework with universal application for analyzing kinship? Achieving the level of generalization necessary for an adequate analysis of human social relationships requires comparison of the different categories or units derived from the particular culture. In other words, once investigators have uncovered the categories or units from various cultures, what categories or units does one use to compare these? Obviously, units of comparison will have to be selected from some particular culture and applied to others. Thus, the problem of ethnocentric bias reappears at higher levels of analysis, and cultural relativism is unable to solve it. It provides no mechanism for comparing data cross-culturally. If the Eurocentric concept of kinship is meaningless because it does not provide the local interpretation of social relationships, the local-centric conception of social relationships is powerless because it is restricted to a singular cultural perspective regarding social relationships. If the Eurocentric conception of kinship is vacuous, the cultural relativistic conception is impotent.

The concept, "kinship," which appears vacuous to Schneider as a category for comparative analysis because it is based upon notions of biological relationships derived from European culture, isn't meaningless. It is meaningful in terms of the European analysts' culture from which it is derived. There is no reason to suppose that it could not be used to analyze European social relationships. Schneider's concern that the concept "kinship" is vacuous because it is Eurocentric is ill founded. Nor is it necessary to deny that a Eurocentric framework be used for comparative purposes to analyze social relationships in other cultures. Such a framework does provide a means for making comparisons, even though it is based on a single perspective. The problem with kinship analysis does not arise from the use of a culturally derived concept. This should not be the basis for evaluating the usefulness or vacuousness of an analytical framework. The fundamental issue is whether it is possible to undertake analyses that will facilitate meaningful interpretations of social behavior and also be able to provide valid cross-cultural comparisons.

Schneider's critique of kinship places us on the horns of a dilemma: One is caught between a Eurocentric framework with claims to absolute factuality and a localcentric framework restricted to a specific cultural context. The Eurocentric approach provides a universally applicable framework with a claim to cross-cultural validity by reference to the biological mechanisms of human reproduction. It makes no attempt to elicit the meaning of social relationships from cultures under investigation, since it presumes to have an absolute standard of measurement. This standard is supposedly sufficient for an understanding of kinship. But, instead of being an absolute measure, the concepts of the Eurocentric approach are, in fact, the expressions of a particular culture and are not universally shared by other cultures. The localcentric approach, on the other hand, claims specific validity within a culture but does not provide a framework for comparative analysis. For those who seek meaningful interpretations of social relationships and who want to construct sound generalizations that they can apply to more than one culture, neither approach is satisfactory.

There is an alternative approach to kinship, however, one that recognizes, as Schneider did, that a value-free, objective, or nonethnocentric analysis of data is impossible. The notion of an objective observer in some areas of anthropology may still have some utility, just as the ancient geocentric view of the earth's place in the cosmos is useful for celestial navigation even though understanding of the earth's relationship to other astronomical bodies has shifted. In kinship studies, however, the notions of absolutes and objective scientific analysis must be replaced by a new approach, one that, unlike cultural relativism, enables cross-cultural comparison without imposing any absolute framework. This can be accomplished through a truly relativistic approach. Such a model for kinship analysis could be used to analyze meaningful categories from inside cultures and, at the same time, provide a basis for productive cross-cultural comparisons.

A relativistic approach implies that two or more frameworks can each be used to provide productive results for analyzing data. Thus, for example, it could be possible to analyze the same set of social relationships in a meaningful way from both a Eurocentric framework based on notions of human biological relationships, and a localcentric framework based on notions derived from the culture under investigation. Here, the focus of discourse shifts. In looking at a system of kinship terminology, for example, one no longer asks, "What does a kinship term really mean?" Instead, one asks, "What meaningful statements can be made about the local culture when we examine the usage of kinship terminology from the perspective of a given framework?" Note that although results may be contradictory, all may be true. A relativistic approach does not recognize an absolute framework of analysis and does not insist that there is one proper framework for examining cultural data. Consequently, what may be "true" in the purview of one framework may not be from another.

In a genuinely relativistic approach, the scientific investigator must recognize that any framework is ultimately culturally derived and so objectivity is impossible. What is demanded in this situation is awareness and honesty on the part of the investigator rather than objectivity. Awareness requires the investigator to understand that a framework of investigation is culturally derived and to be cognizant of the major assumptions of that framework. Honesty requires that the investigator remain fully committed to the framework in recording and comparing data within and across cultures. Only then can the investigation be trusted and its results provide adequate solutions to questions being investigated. Evaluation of the results based on criteria such as predictability and coherence can be used to accept, modify, or reject a framework. Since no framework is absolute, each must be tested against the data, and the results of analysis based upon the different frameworks compared to see whether one or another meets the criteria of evaluation. The same criteria must be applied to each framework before any conclusion can be drawn about the utility of any one, and the success of a particular framework is always relative to the set of criteria used to evaluate it.

A relativistic framework avoids the restriction to a particular culture, which is characteristic of cultural relativism. While it recognizes that a framework upon which analysis is based is ultimately derived from the concepts of a culture, it also recognizes that there is no requirement for an objective, absolute basis in order to apply an analytic framework universally. For example, a biological model based upon the precepts of European culture, such as the necessity of sexual intercourse for ordinary humans to produce children, can be used to investigate cross-cultural data. If using this model leads to the discovery that people in all cultures utilize sexual intercourse to produce children even in spite of some, such as the Trobriand Islanders, who deny that coitus is responsible for the birth of children, the results must still be considered a universal characteristic in reference to the Eurocentric framework from which it is derived. It should not be elevated to the status of an absolute truth about the nature of kinship. Today, the introduction and widespread use of new reproductive technologies clearly emphasize the point. Using these technologies to produce offspring makes sexual intercourse unnecessary.

With a relativistic approach to kinship, filial relationships can be used in an analytical framework without assuming that the filial relationships are intrinsically defined by biology. As argued by Murray J. Leaf (this volume) and Dwight W. Read (this volume), we can use the well-known kinship diagrams to analyze parent-child links around the world without assuming that these links are based upon genetic relationships in every culture under investigation. We can examine the systematic ways that filial relationships are dealt with in cultures with matrilineal, patrilineal, or other descent principles. We can inquire about the meanings of these links without assuming that the definitions are the same across cultures or that there is a "true," "natural," or "real" meaning of the kinship relationships. The important practice is to hold the framework constant across cultures for comparative purposes and make no assumption that the framework is objective or that the analysis is somehow derived from the "facts" of nature. We can, thus, analyze kinship without the illusion of objectivity, but with cross-cultural applicability.

Having no objective framework in a relativistic approach implies that no one model can provide a complete view of kinship data. A model, from whatever culture it is derived, provides a means for looking at the universe that furnishes some insights into the way the world operates but will always leave some aspects unexplained. Thus, the analysis of kinship data in terms of a framework derived from either the culture of the participants or another culture will provide insights into the data, but neither will provide a total picture of the system of social relationships. While neither framework provides an objective point of view, each can be discredited, disproven, and discarded from within the framework, or from the viewpoint of some other framework that provides better insights into the way the data operate. Each may also contribute something of value to the understanding of kinship behavior. Rather than seeking the *one* framework for kinship analysis, future investigations must learn to benefit from multiple perspectives achieved through the use of multiple frameworks.

Conclusion: Toward a Synthetic Approach to the Study of Kinship

The philosopher-physicist Niels Bohr (1938) noticed similarities between anthropological inquiry and research into the nature of atomic structure. He recognized that in the investigation of subatomic particles, as in cultural analysis, a relativistic framework is necessary to make sense of the data. In both quantum physics and social anthropology, objectivity is impossible and a degree of uncertainty always remains due to the intimate interaction between the observer and the observed. He also noticed that both fields of study exhibit complementarity. Both the interactions among subatomic particles and the social interrelationships of humans demonstrate a duality that emerges from the interplay between data and the investigator. Quantum physicists recognize a complementarity in the nature of light, which manifests two distinct natures under different experiments. Sometimes it acts as if it were made up of particles, and sometimes it acts as if it were made up of electromagnetic waves. Bohr and others have recognized that these seemingly contradictory behaviors result from the interaction between the nature of light itself and the specific type of experimental apparatus used. The experiment or framework one utilizes in examining the nature of light will partially determine what the results will be. The different results are equally true: Light is considered to be fundamentally both particlelike and wavelike. In a similar way, the study of kinship reveals the complementarity in the nature of social relationships (Bohr 1938). Such relationships reflect the interaction between both biological and cultural aspects. Like experiments with the nature of light, the biological and cultural frameworks used in the investigation of kinship reveal distinct natures within its dual aspect. Again, like investigations into the nature of light, an interplay exists in social research between the investigation of the observer and the phenomena observed. The physical and cultural attributes of human beings represent the two natures of the complementarity of social interaction. We do the complexity of human nature an injustice if we assume that either one or the other represents the one true foundation of kinship.

Today, the newly emerging kinship relations, in which a child may have only one parent, two male parents, two female parents, many parents, or even no parents, emphasize the need for a new theoretical framework to analyze basic social relationships. To understand these phenomena plus the traditional relationships, and to develop an understanding of the basis of human social behavior, we must learn to recognize that the positions of both cultural relativism and biological reductionism represent inadequate, absolutistic approaches. We must learn how to move beyond the traditional conflict between nature (biology) and culture (meaning) that frames the argument for David Schneider's approach to kinship. We can build upon Schneider's insight that culture plays an important role in human behavior. As new reproductive technologies continue to be developed, genetic mechanisms become better understood, and the ability to control genetic forces grows, the interlinkages between human biology and culture are becoming even more apparent. But we ultimately gain little by affirming the importance of culture in the study of kinship while, at the same time, denying the import of a biological framework for analysis. If anthropology is to continue to contribute to the understanding of human behavior in the twenty-first century, it must move out of the absolutistic frameworks of the past. Anthropologists must reject Schneider's conclusions about the nature of kinship, advance beyond both cultural relativism and biological reductionism, and develop a truly relativistic framework for analysis.

References Cited

Berry, John W. 1990. "Imposed Etics, Emics, and Derived Etics: Their Conceptual and Operational Status in Cross-Cultural Psychology." In *Emics and Etics: The Insider/Outsider Debate*. Ed. Thomas N. Headland, Kenneth L. Pike, and Marvin Harris. 84–89. Newbury Park, Calif.: Sage Publications.

Bodley, John H. 2000. *Cultural Anthropology*. Mountain View, Calif.: Mayfield Publishing.

Bohr, Niels. 1938. *Natural Philosophy and Human Cultures*. Copenhagen: Comptes Rendus du Congrès International de Science, Anthropologie et Ethnologie. (Also published in Nature 143 [1939]: 268–72.)

Collier, Jane Fishburne, and Sylvia Junko Yanagisako. 1987. "Introduction." In *Gender and Kinship: Essays toward a Unified Analysis*. Ed. Jane Fishburne Collier and Sylvia Junko Yanagisako. 1–13. Stanford, Calif.: Stanford University Press.

———, eds. 1987. *Gender and Kinship: Essays toward a Unified Analysis*. Stanford, Calif.: Stanford University Press.

Feinberg, Richard. 1981. "The Meaning of 'Sibling' on Anuta Island." In *Siblingship in Oceania: Studies in the Meaning of Kin Relations*. Ed. Mac Marshall. 105–48. ASAO Monograph No. 8. Ann Arbor: University of Michigan Press.

Fox, Robin. 1983 [1967]. *Kinship and Marriage*. 2d ed. Cambridge: Cambridge University Press.

Headland, Thomas N., Kenneth L. Pike, and Marvin Harris, eds. 1990. *Emics and Etics: The Insider/Outsider Debate*. Newbury Park, Calif.: Sage Publications.

Marshall, Mac, ed. 1981. *Siblingship in Oceania: Studies in the Meaning of Kin Relations*. ASAO Monograph No. 8. Ann Arbor: University of Michigan Press.

Ottenheimer, Martin. 1995. "Why Is There No Kinship, Daddy?" *Human Mosaic* 28 (2): 65–72.

———. 1996. *Forbidden Relatives: The American Myth of Cousin Marriage*. Urbana: University of Illinois Press.

Pike, Kenneth L. 1967 [1954]. *Language in Relation to a Unified Theory of the Structure of Human Behavior*. The Hague: Mouton.

Redfield, Robert. 1953. *The Primitive World and Its Transformations*. Ithaca, N.Y.: Cornell University Press.

Scheffler, Harold W., and Floyd G. Lounsbury. 1971. *A Study in Structural Semantics: The Sirionó Kinship System*. Englewood Cliffs, N.J.: Prentice-Hall.

Schneider, David M. 1968. *American Kinship: A Cultural Account*. Englewood Cliffs, N.J.: Prentice-Hall.

———. 1972. "What Is Kinship All About?" In *Kinship Studies in the Morgan Centennial Year*. Ed. Priscilla Reining. 32–63. Washington, D.C.: Anthropological Society of Washington.

———. 1987 [1984]. *A Critique of the Study of Kinship*. Ann Arbor: University of Michigan Press.

———. 1992. "Ethnocentrism and the Notion of Kinship." *Man* 27 (3): 629–31.

Weston, Kath. 1991. *Families We Choose*. New York: Columbia University Press.

6. The Philosophy of Kinship: A Reply to Schneider's *Critique of the Study of Kinship*

ROBERT McKINLEY

Three Opinions on Kinship

In my view, "kinship" is like totemism, matriarchy, and the "matrilineal complex." It is a non-subject. It exists in the minds of anthropologists but not in the cultures they study. (Schneider 1972:51)

Many thanks for sending me "What is kinship all about?" While I agree with you on most points I would not go so far as to say that kinship is a "non-subject." I would define it as a way of classifying people and defining their rights and duties in accordance with past marriages and in prevision of future ones. This is very clumsy because nothing is more difficult than to phrase a definition in a foreign language, but I am sure that you will grasp my point, namely, that kinship has to do with marriage, and that marriage prohibitions, preferences, or prescriptions are not a "non-subject." (Lévi-Strauss to Schneider, February 10, 1971)

It [the kinship term "grandfather"] is not only applied to human persons but to spiritual beings who are persons of a category other than human. In fact, when the collective plural "our grandfathers" is used, the reference is primarily to persons of the latter class. Thus if we study Ojibwa social organization in the usual manner, we take account of only one set of grandfathers. When we study their religion we discover other grandfathers. But if we adopt a world view perspective no dichotomization appears. . . . A child is always given a name by an old man, i.e., a terminological grandfather. . . . This name carries with it a special blessing because it has reference to a dream of the human grandfather in which he obtained power from one or more of the other than human grandfathers. In other words, the relation between a human child and a human grandfather is functionally patterned in the same way as the relation between human beings and grandfathers of the other than human class. (Hallowell 1960:21–22)

In the above exchange between David Schneider and Claude Lévi-Strauss, we see that Schneider's one-man campaign to do for kinship what Lévi-Strauss (1962) had already done for totemism was flawed from the start. For, in respectfully disagreeing with Schneider, Lévi-Strauss, who clearly knows a nonsubject when he meets it, does not bite. Instead, he politely points out that declaring kinship a nonsubject requires ignoring a great many social phenomena of real importance, such as people's conventionally assigned rights and duties and the rules and social sanctions regulating marriage. Other social phenomena such as moral beliefs, gender identities, and "native" social theories of the relations between self and social milieu could also be added to Lévi-Strauss's list. These matters are not, and perhaps never could be, nonsubjects. Rights and duties, marriage rules, moral beliefs, gender notions, and theories of self in relation to concrete social milieu all bear upon what we loosely refer to as kinship, and kinship as culturally constituted bears upon them.[1]

Anthropologists before and after Schneider have been correct in their view that kinship is a subject worthy of inquiry. But to make such inquiry productive, I will argue that kinship must first be identified and respected as a philosophy in its own right. It is a philosophy possessing analytical power as well as having moral and ethical content. It enters into every known culture's analysis and shaping of degrees of social relatedness between people and even between humans and other than human persons. In other words, this philosophy often embraces the spiritual as well as the human world. Thus we meet the many supernatural Grandfathers and Grandmothers of Native American religions, God our Father in Christianity, and Our Nephew Hare the Trickster and Bringer of Mortality and Immortality among Central Algonkian peoples.

With the very rare exception of Hallowell in his statement on "Ojibwa Ontology" quoted above, most anthropologists have viewed such religious references as "metaphoric extensions" of human kinship. However, the approach taken here follows Hallowell's lead and warns that such a view seriously underestimates both the power and scope of the philosophy of kinship. The supernatural kin are no more metaphoric than the human ones. They may be "more intangible," but they are not more metaphoric. All kinship involves metaphor right from the start or it could not have any moral and ethical content at all. Mothers and fathers would just be, as our common fixed expressions would have it, "machines for making babies" and "sperm donors." So the philosophy of kinship requires that all kinship terms be metaphors to some degree. Even where procreative models of kin relatedness prevail, as in the West, this metaphoric quality of all kinship should be obvious.

Furthermore, we see how little escapes the philosophy of kinship when we turn to the cosmological concept and moral notion of the witch, for it is a cross-cultural commonplace that the image of a good kinsperson is aligned against that of the malevolent witch, each as a powerful inversion of the other. We can see in this that the philosophy of kinship has often, in contexts where such beliefs prevail, completed itself by comprehending the problems of good and evil as well. It thereby leaves little or nothing out of the moral notion of social relatedness. This all adds up to no small accomplishment.

The philosophy of kinship is one of the great masterpieces of human so-ciological imagination, and as such it has a very special relation to the mod-ern world's attempt to fashion a science of society and culture. As C. Wright Mills (Mills 1959) declared four decades ago, anthropology and its sister so-cial and human sciences are engaged in the task of contributing to modern consciousness a new form of sociological imagination, one that will offer penetrating perspectives on the complexities of contemporary social life both now and in the future. It is my contention that in pursuing this goal, these sciences risk a serious impoverishment of themselves should they neglect the older formulations of an analogous perspective already present in the phi-losophy of kinship.

Anthropology's Study of Kinship

Every society has a subset of words and phrases for talking about the rules of marriage and a vocabulary for populating social reality with people to whom one is related through past marriages, births, and orderings of "kin" relationships. These orderings that bind people together are logically analo-gous to those apparently genealogical relationships produced out of past marriages. Words to populate social reality with categories of relatives oc-cupying culturally typified social roles are as universal as the use of names, personal pronouns, and all other social status terms. In some societies almost the entire social field is mapped by these categories. Beyond these "kin and marriage" categories, only the category of "stranger" applies. Because such word sets are known to be systematic, to have a "genealogical resonance" (Fortes 1969:53), to have a greater or lesser fit with behavioral expectations, and yet to vary cross-culturally they have attracted the interest of many gen-erations of anthropologists. Such inquiries have been central to what the study of kinship is all about.

From 1871, when Lewis Henry Morgan's monumental *Systems of Consan-guinity and Affinity of the Human Family* was first published, to 1949, which saw the publication of both George Peter Murdock's *Social Structure,* with its statistically based tests of hypotheses regarding kinship, and Lévi-Strauss's *Les Structures Élémentaires de la Parenté,* with its revolutionary emphasis on marriage possibilities and impossibilities as structuring patterns of exchange, the study of kinship had been anthropology's most fruitful area for the development of social theory. This continued to be the case until the late 1960s or the early 1970s, when most of the received paradigms for research on kinship seem to have reached a point of exhaustion.[2] With perhaps the two exceptions of highly specialized formal analyses of kinship vocabularies and of very particularistic cultural analyses of kinship, nothing really new was happening. And as important as these two refinements were, they did not command the interest of the field of anthropology as a whole. New generations of graduate students began turning their attention to other interests: gender, power, personhood, the body, medical anthropology, development studies, historical ethnographies, and the subjective side of ethnography itself.[3] By the late seventies, kinship studies had been virtually abandoned, a situation that lasted through the anthropologically introspective and often harshly self-critical eighties. David Schneider's deconstructive polemic *A Critique of the Study of Kinship,* which came out in 1984, made this rejection of kinship studies explicit, forceful, and total.

Before examining Schnieder's argument, I would like to report that kinship as a focus of anthropological research has survived his attack. Indeed, from the late 1980s to the present, we have witnessed a considerable revival of kinship studies. This renewal of interest was sparked in part by rising concerns, both political and theoretical, over issues of gender and sexual orientation as they relate to aspects of kinship and family life. And in part it came as a response to newly available choices created by breakthroughs in reproductive technology (see Collier and Yanagisako 1987; Strathern 1992; and Yanagisako and Delany 1995). These new choices have not only raised many ethical and legal questions, but they have also brought to the surface many deeply held cultural assumptions regarding the meaning of kinship and related matters such as procreation, personhood, filiation, descent, genealogy, sex, mating, biological surrogacy, incest, and marriage.

In Western societies, the new reproductive and lifestyle choices now available to individuals and to couples are so much at the heart of popular discussions of kinship that anything about kinship not subject to autonomous choice is lamented. I offer the example of American journalist Susan Scarf Merrell's 1995 book on sibling relationships, which bears the very telling title, *The Accidental Bond.* Merrell informs us that whether experienced as a blessing or a curse, siblings are a sort of lifelong obstacle to a true development and awareness of the self. They are the chance source of an early attachment so formative and conflictual that they preempt one's psychological autonomy. Merrell goes on to suggest that as adults we can better cope with our siblings' denial of our personal freedom by realizing that our culture only minimally obligates us toward them. Thus, "we can make the rules" ourselves and finally arrive at the mature stance that enables us to deal with our accidental relatives any way we please (17).[4] Dare we go on to cousins?

As an ethnographer of Malay society, where siblingship represents the epitome of all human obligation and the very reason for the existence of extended kin bonds across a broad personal kindred (McKinley 1981), I find this diminished sense of sibling obligation in the contemporary American case emblematic of many other reductions in the sphere of kinship as it now exists in parts of Western society. Despite the once-meaningful adage that "blood is thicker than water," attachment keeps giving way to autonomy right at the core of Western kinship. No doubt there has always been some scope for personal choice in developing or not developing the ties available within a personal kindred. But Merrell's insistent assertion of autonomy over attachment with regard to siblings goes well beyond that.

As with practically everything else in our consumer culture, we are now confronted by new brands of designer kinship. Indeed, Marilyn Strathern (1992) has drawn anthropological attention to just how far choice has already been extended into matters of family and kinship. She finds that we are creating a new form of "enterprise kinship." The context for her argument is the debate surrounding passage of the British Human Fertilization and Embryology Act of 1990, which aims to protect the lives and rights of embryos created through in vitro fertilizations and supported through surrogacy gestations. Strathern's most telling point with regard to Euro-American responses to the new reproductive technology is that the cultural emphasis on connections between the natural and the social in the area of kinship has shifted away from concerns about assigning parenthood and toward those of asserting personhood. Thus it is reasoned that the "physical individuality" of an "artificially" conceived human embryo is socially prior to the question of its parenthood, whether social or biological. The cultural view here is that the biological basis of unique individuality in the embryo has a stronger basis in what is naturally "real" than does parenthood. Strathern notes that in the "dialogue conducted with respect to the being not yet born, the emergence of personhood itself was taken to be a natural process, the outcome of biological development rather than the person's own moral [or even physical] standing or participation in relationships with other persons" (23). The force of the statute is to declare the embryo a person, not just a human organism in transition. And why is it so declared? Not because it comes from or will later belong in relationships to others, but because it is, itself, genetically and physically unique. I concur with Strathern's observation that "it is of some moment, I think, to imagine the reproduction of persons in a nonrelational way" (23).[5]

The nonrelational reproduction of a person is an arresting thought, to say the least; and it is a thought that is already being realized both technologically and morally. With all these issues under renewed popular discussion, it is no wonder that anthropologists have decided to give kinship a second look.

I mention these points because it was a fundamental tenet of Schneider's final understanding of kinship studies that Western society, which inevitably gave its definition of kinship to anthropology, was in a very strict sense the only society that ever had kinship at all. Even though Schneider was careful to restrict this claim to the uniqueness of the symbolic configuration surrounding the Western concept of kinship, I still find this conclusion doubly at odds with what we know cross-culturally: first, because many non-Western societies do seem to rely heavily on what looks like kinship even if what defines these relationships does not correspond to the Western definition; and second, because the West seems to be almost unique in its undervaluing and structural dislocation of kinship. Elsewhere kinship seems to go public; in the West it has been made into a reflex of folk biology, a matter of civil law, and an aspect of individual life alone.

This same objection to Schneider's views has been effectively presented by Michael Peletz (1995:343–72) in an article for *Annual Reviews, Anthropology* that takes stock of kinship studies in the late twentieth century. Peletz points out that Schneider's claims have "negative implications for the comparative study of social relatedness." He continues: "Rather than insist that no one else has kinship as we do, and that kinship as we understand it is a non-subject, we should perhaps first examine the systems of social relatedness others do have" (348). Examining the systems of social relatedness others do have is exactly the direction taken in most recent studies of kinship.

The point that one culture's categories should not be forced upon another's in doing a cultural analysis is, of course, very well taken (but see Martin Ottenheimer's cautions, this volume). However, I regard Schneider's conclusion that only the West has kinship at all to be one of the most misleading comparative statements ever made. In what follows I will try to show why. At this point, however, let me say that the present return to kinship has not been unaffected by the criticisms Schneider raised in his unreneging, if flawed, attack upon kinship studies as he knew them. I believe his influence has been, on balance, positive. Writers on kinship now have to be more careful than ever to avoid smuggling Western categories into other people's concepts of how to identify and relate to "relatives." In Southeast Asian studies, the area I know best, I can point to three very successful ethnographies that take these matters into account: Michael Peletz's own (1988) *A Share of the Harvest,* Susan McKinnon's (1991) *From a Shattered Sun,* and Janet Carsten's (1997) *The Heat of the Hearth.* Each of these gives close attention to the broader cosmological understandings that enter into the cultural construction of both the gender and kinship systems under investigation and each pays close attention to the historical enactments that shape and reshape the meaning of kin relationships. Few a priori assumptions about kinship were made other than that the ethnographies produced had to reflect the importance that participants themselves gave to a varied array of close relationships. Schneider (1991) himself gave his dust-jacket blessing to McKinnon's study calling it "a brilliant analysis." Using the same measure I would happily extend this acclaim to the other two named.

A Personal Note

Having been a publisher's reviewer for David's *Critique,* I was in a position to challenge much of his argument before it came out in print. This led to some very useful discussions between us. I must say that I was pleasantly surprised by the sincerity with which David accepted the challenge of my objections. He addressed many but not all of these objections in the rewriting of his book (see Schneider 1984:viii). Though we fundamentally disagreed on kinship's viability as a subject for cross-cultural analysis, our exchanges on kinship created an avuncular friendship that became part of the genealogy binding together the anthropology departments of the University of Michigan, the University of Chicago, and Michigan State University at that time.[6]

Despite our basic disagreement, David always urged me to convert my manuscript rebutting his argument into a book to answer his, and to introduce my own argument for what I had called "the philosophy of kinship." This chapter has the double burden of offering my critique of Schneider's *A Critique of the Study of Kinship* and of presenting a sketch of what I mean by the philosophy of kinship. In it I will also re-examine the place kinship terminologies have in cultural analyses, and I will consider the comparative relevance of the philosophy of kinship in different social and cultural systems. On this front I will claim that, in addition to comparing varieties of kinship systems, it is important to compare kinship as social theory with other social theories across cultures. In particular I will argue that the philosophy of kinship has been for many nonstate societies what a well informed sociological imagination should be, but so far is not, for "modern" state and market-organized societies. It is from this standpoint that I would reverse Schneider's contention that kinship only exists in Western culture.

Treating kinship as an overarching philosophy of moral obligation, I would say that Western culture has no effective equivalent to kinship. What is taken for kinship in the West is merely a penumbra of bonds surrounding individual social life, with the value of individual autonomy always pushing such attachments very near to their vanishing point. Strathern's assessment (1992:12) of the "hyper-individualism" voiced with regard to embryos in the British human fertilization and embryology debates suggests that this attitude is rapidly becoming far more prevalent than ever before. What was being argued for in those debates was more like blood Thatcherism than kinship. Society was being told to put the natural individuality of the embryo above any moral or even physical relationships it might have with its probable or potential parents. Put more cynically, an embryo understood in that way would have no encumbering moral bonds such as filiation to intervene in its eventual direct entrance into the free-market society. In my view, the many reductions of the scope of kinship within Euro-American society are not simply a case of atrophy due to other institutions having taken over the functions of kinship in a complex society. The fact is there has been no adequate replacement for kinship, and for better or worse we live in that vacuum.

Situating Schneider's Critique

The 1980s can be remembered as a decade of deep professional self-doubt within anthropology. Fear of "othering" and of essentializing others came to impede ethnography. And with ethnography itself in question, commentary on cultural differences that made a difference started to fall silent. That decade nonetheless produced two very clear and opposing views of the long-term importance to anthropology of kinship studies. Contrasting them will prove instructive. The first was Schneider's *A Critique of the Study of Kinship* (1984) and the second was Thomas R. Trautmann's *Lewis Henry Morgan and The Invention of Kinship* (1987). Schneider took the negative view, claiming that all anthropological studies of kinship, from Morgan on, and including even his own previous contributions, were fatally flawed as one-way translations of culture. Everything that had been said about kinship was "simply wrong" because no such phenomenon existed cross-culturally. Trautmann, on the other hand, found that the most original aspect of much of Morgan's scientific work on kinship was the way it broke through the bonds of Morgan's own ethnocentrism at significant points to create a comparative framework for the awareness of scientifically important differences among social and cultural systems. This awareness was to become the corner stone not only of kinship studies, but of all anthropological understanding. Driven by direct fieldwork encounters that led to "broader comparative studies," Morgan's "works document the successive attempts [on his part] to rationalize by generalizing the original intense, meaningful, and baffling encounter with the cultural other" (Trautmann 1987:10). The most famous illustration of this was Morgan's identification of "classificatory" as opposed to "descriptive" kinship terminologies. Because the Seneca classified "mother" and "mother's sister" under a single term, *noh-yeh*, and English people did not, it appeared that the Seneca had created a whole class of "mothers" whereas in English there is only a single person whom one can properly and exclusively identify as mother. Neither the Seneca nor Anglo-Americans by themselves had to think of this difference as special. The Seneca and other users of classificatory terminologies had been getting along just fine, thank you, not knowing that they had a classificatory relationship system. Conversely, Anglo-Americans had no compelling reasons to categorize their own system as descriptive or to learn about and ponder over what might be implied by the existence of systems so basically different from their own. Only curiosity of a comparative sort made the classificatory system a special category worthy of investigation, and Morgan had that kind of comparative curiosity. Classificatory as opposed to descriptive terminology systems were neither Seneca facts nor English facts; they were anthropological facts. Morgan laid them out as such and then made several attempts to explain this cultural difference.

The difference was real, but the reasons for it were not obvious. Figuring out what this difference and many others like it could mean or imply became the central project of the anthropological study of kinship. Morgan launched this study at the level of anthropological facts. That his own explanations were soon to be questioned does not diminish his original discovery of a new set of problems that could only be understood through some new and powerfully cross-cultural mode of understanding. We call this mode anthropology.[7] Like all science, anthropology is about the significance of differences that make a difference, and Morgan started the project of thinking that systematic variations in kinship were among the differences that make a difference for human societies.

Yet differences in kinship always seemed to be tethered to constants in biology: the facts of reproduction, maternal-infant bonding, inherent differences in the degrees of biological relatedness among individuals, and so on. Even the genealogical grid, against which we plot how different cultures and languages vary in their verbal classifications of kin, depended in the last analysis upon a biological grounding of "the universal facts" of kinship. Terms like "social" versus "physical or biological" kinship began to crop up to distinguish two different levels of kinship meanings. But the predominant view was the common Western idea that biology is somehow at the bottom of kinship no matter how subject to cultural reshaping. Morgan himself read biology back into classificatory kinship by hypothesizing that it had originally derived from group marriages between sets of brothers with sets of sisters. He did this in spite of his own frequent insistence on the "artificial" and "arbitrary" nature of the classificatory systems.

Culture, in the domain of kinship, never seemed to be working on its own. Until Schneider, no one had taken a resolute stand on culture versus biology in the realm of kinship. Many had come close, but always with some confusion. Usually genealogy in the biological sense was brought back into the analysis as primary. For example kin terminologies were always translated and ordered according to the meanings they would have if applied to the nearest known genealogical positions like parent, child, spouse, parent of spouse, male sibling, and so forth. Later I will return to this issue of what Meyer Fortes called "the genealogical resonance" of kin terminologies (1969:53). It is important to note that this issue will not go away, but it is also important to have a cultural theory of its relevance. I will present such a theory below.

In his critique of kinship studies, Schneider rather boldly rejected this whole business. The important thing for anthropologists to study was culture. And culture consisted of symbols and meanings, not blood lines and matings. Thus, claiming that a system of relationships was based on biology, either directly or indirectly, was unacceptable. In his own words:

> Anthropology, then, is the study of particular cultures. *The first task of anthropology,* **prerequisite to all others,** *is to understand and formulate the symbols and meanings and their configuration that a particular culture consists of.*
>
> My difficulty with the study of kinship can be summed up simply: the assumptions and presuppositions which the anthropologist brings to the process of understanding the particular culture he is studying are imposed on the situation blindly and with unflagging loyalty to those assumptions and little flexible appreciation of how the other culture is constituted, and with it a rigid refusal to attempt to understand what may be going on between them. (1984:196, emphasis and bold in original.)

He further suggested that if these biases could ever be dropped and an empirical investigation be done regarding the comparative validity of European models of kinship, then at long last the very limited applicability of these biologically based models might be realized. At that point, he muses, "kinship might then become a special custom distinctive of European culture, an interesting oddity at worst, like the Toda bow ceremony" (201).[8]

Interestingly, this final verdict of Schneider's came after a period of advocating "cultural analyses" of kinship. These were aimed at getting at the native point of view on how important relationships, whether we want to call them kinship or not, were defined, symbolized, and codified regarding the behavioral expectations assigned to them. The chapter by Susan Montague in this present volume illustrates well the ethnographic depth of this approach. These cultural analyses were to be done with as little projection of Western kinship beliefs as possible. But it was still the study of kinship. While at the University of Chicago in the 1960s and 1970s, Schneider trained several generations of students to pursue this approach. The ethnographic standard of their work was very high, and it appeared for a while that Schneider had created a kind of school of cultural analysis that would win the day and make him famous. To a significant degree, that is what happened. Then things changed.

Schneider's Critique of Kinship Studies

Some ambivalence about kinship studies in anthropology has always been present. On the one hand, Robin Fox tells us in a textbook called *Kinship and Marriage* that "kinship is to anthropology what logic is to philosophy or the nude is to art: it is the basic discipline of the subject" (1968:10). That certainly sounds central, and so Morgan lives. But on the other hand, Thomas Beidelman warns us that for a time American anthropology seemed to be overspecializing on kinship at the expense of other things, among which was social reality in the larger sense. As he put it: "That parochial mandarin of American academe, the 'kinship expert,' is certainly the product of this viewpoint." Speaking with disdain, Beidelman urges us to put aside the "dreary obsession with kinship terminologies" and the like (1970:505).

Schneider was no "parochial mandarin" by any means, but he was regarded as an expert on kinship at a time when this was one of the few areas in which anthropology could claim any real expertise of its own on anything. His final insistence on disowning kinship and drowning it in an even more dreary discourse of ethnographic solipsism did much to undercut the ground on which he had built his own career. Perhaps the Parsonsian notion of culture upon which he based his analytical style succumbed finally to Boasian epistemological relativism. In any case, Schneider left a strange legacy to his students and fellow anthropologists.

What led Schneider to dismiss kinship was his obsession with culture. As

I have already indicated, our common folk notion that the social side of kinship is tethered to the biological side makes it an ambivalent vehicle for ethnographic inquiry. We can often see that the analytical model of kinship used by many anthropologists imposes Western thinking on non-Western cultures. Schneider correctly perceived that the trend toward formal semantic analyses of kin terminologies exacerbated this bias by enshrining it in method. And if grasping the meaning of life in other cultures from the inside was to remain the goal of ethnography, then the study of kinship was in trouble because it had so often short-circuited this process by smuggling Western categories into the analysis. The West's emic was being made into a universal etic: a kind of kinship Esperanto of the genealogical grid. So the best recommendation was to do away with kinship studies altogether. For this reason, beginning in 1972 Schneider (1972:51) declared kinship a "non-subject."

Nonetheless, Schneider's subsidiary conclusion that only Western society has anything close to anthropology's concept of kinship while other cultures apparently do not flies in the face of ethnographic facts. First, it ignores the diminishing importance of kinship in Western culture, where it has virtually vanished. Kinship so competes with individualism in the West that one sociologist (Luckmann 1970:94) has projected hypothetically that with just a few more de-socializations of the Western individual's life-world, autism could become the ideal, if seldom reachable, goal of the Western social self. Put in less dramatic terms, Western valuing of kinship, though often strong in personal life, is both circumscribed and intermittent. Second, despite our situation in the West, most other cultures still highly value kin ties.

In the sections that follow, I will reformulate kinship in a manner capable of rectifying these two serious discrepancies in Schneider's view.

Kinship as a Philosophy That Counts

As Murray J. Leaf and Martin Ottenheimer have argued in this volume, it often seems that anthropology's insistence on an "epistemological cultural relativism" is on a collision course with its quest for a science of culture. In the area of kinship studies, Schneider has pushed things to their logical limit and made the collision acute. In the end he even abandons the cultural analyses of kinship that he used to advocate, thereby extinguishing kinship in an act of ethnographic solipsism.

As a thought experiment, Schneider's treatise makes many valid points. But, as Richard Feinberg and Martin Ottenheimer point out (this volume), he leaves nowhere to go from his deconstructive onslaught. Comparison ends. Here I think he not only missed some opportunities, but basically failed to recognize overwhelming evidence for the importance of kinship, not as tied to biology, but kinship as a philosophy. It is a philosophy about how a person can feel categorically obligated to a series of other persons. The concrete natural symbolism for categorizing such a series of persons and for placing them in relationships with each other may or may not be "biological" in the Western sense, but it does convey the idea of there being some social locus of unquestioned obligation. As to the universality of the philosophy of kinship, this remains an open question. On this score, kinship philosophy seems to resemble religion. There may be cultures existing without either religion or the philosophy of kinship, but so far, under the definitions commonly used, there are no known cultures that clearly lack either.

To indicate what I mean by the philosophy of kinship I can do no better than offer the following quote from Clyde Kluckhohn and Dorothea Leighton on Navajo kinship. They say that "the worst thing that one may say of another person is 'He acts as if he didn't have any relatives.' Conversely, the ideal of behavior often enunciated by headmen is, 'Act as if everybody were related to you'" (Kluckhohn and Leighton 1946:100). This, to me, expresses the philosophy of kinship most succinctly. Kinship is the philosophy many cultures hold about what completes a person socially, psychologically, and morally, and how that completeness comes about through a responsible sense of attachment and obligation to others. Receiving the support of kin also adds to one's completeness as an effective actor in society. Kinship puts both the bureaucratized concept of "human resources" and the pop psychology notion of "support groups" to shame. I say this because the reciprocal rights and duties shared among kin and affines often have such strong obligatory force that to deny them is to deny or negate oneself. Within this sphere of obligations, there can be further differentiations such as those of the anthropologically famous joking and avoidance relationships that sharply define and multiply the performative contents of differing kinship obligations.

The framework for rights and duties among kin and affines is expandable in two important ways. It is expandable in time by making persons of different generations feel mutually implicated in each other's lives as each other's most categorical, if not most significant, social predecessors and successors. And it is expandable in social space through marriage which turns some social contemporaries, whether kin or nonkin depending on the rules of marriage, into more immediate and mutually obligated consociates as specific rather than merely potential affines. It does this in a manner parallel to that distinguished by Alfred Schutz (1967:176–214), who argued that the social phenomenology of any actor's life-world includes "We-relationships" of "varying degrees of concreteness and intimacy" (176).

Conventional studies of kinship treat these two expansions of the frame-work of kinship obligation genealogically, in terms of widening the scope of descent and alliance. By approaching kinship as a philosophy and applying Schutz's ideas, these two dimensions get broadened from the start. The tem-poral and spatial range of kinship obligations is seen not just as the expan-sion of narrow genealogical attachments but also as ways of carving out from much broader social experience specific types of social predecessors, succes-sors, contemporaries, and consociates. The philosophy of kinship narrows at the same time it broadens one's obligations. Neither the narrowing nor the broadening is primary. The philosophy of kinship is designed to do both.

Determining which social predecessors will be treated as most significant can be manipulated, as is illustrated by Laura Zimmer-Tamakoshi's chapter (this volume) describing "ancestral gerrymandering" or lineage hopping for land claims among the Gende people of Papua New Guinea. What remains central even in this example, however, is the idea of establishing categorical-ly significant social predecessors. And with marriage it is always an open question of who among marriageable contemporaries will finally be convert-ed into a new or renewed set of more closely consociated affines.

These two hallmark expansions and contractions of the scope of kinship, usually referred to as descent and alliance, are at the very heart of its success as an institution and as a social philosophy. Kinship founds obligations and then provides the mechanisms for spreading and restricting them over so-cial time and space. Indeed, for preliterate societies the construction of so-cial time and space is almost inconceivable in the absence of the philosophy of kinship.

What makes people kin will be specified very differently in different cul-tures, but the moral, temporal, and spatial implications of this philosophy are not difficult to recognize. Nor, I must add, does the vocabulary for spec-ifying kin stray very far from that which would specify the relationships de-riving from "past marriages" as Lévi-Strauss puts it in his letter to Schnei-der. Past marriages are a perfect shorthand for indicating the combined effects of the two important expansions of kinship obligation just pointed out. Reference to past marriages in kin classifications means that the overlap be-tween social and physical kinship is spoken for in most cultures. Putting to-gether the points that kinship is a philosophy and that there is always a lan-guage for describing the relational set that culturally maps kinship over social time and space in ways that obviously contain some genealogical symbolism, we have the study of kinship still very much in tact. Schneider's critique leaves this philosophy and its application completely unscathed.

Janet Carsten (1995) has examined Malay kinship in light of Schneider's critique. Avoiding a universal procreative model of kinship, she finds that the Malay notion of *satu darah, satu daging,* that is, being of "one blood and one flesh," is as much based on cooking, feeding, and house composition as it is on procreative ideas. This is because Malays see blood and flesh as coming from cooked food and nurturant activity. So the basics are, as Carsten puts it, "the heat of the hearth" and not blood or flesh. She points out that the form of social relatedness viewed as kinship, *saudara,* among Malays is thus always in process and is in a sense never complete. Yet, as I know from first-hand observation, it is always important. The creation of kinship is the creation of attachment, trust, and loyalty for Malays, and the master of the hearth, where kinship is formed, is primarily a currently or at least once-married woman.

In the foregoing example, we can see that Malay kinship can be viewed as a combination of what I am calling the philosophy of kinship and what Lévi-Strauss has singled out in his letter to Schneider as the specification of social relatedness in terms of past marriages. In this case the two are fused as kinship.

Attention to such points cross-culturally re-opens the matter of kinship in a way that incorporates Schneider's critique without abandoning the topic. What I wish to stress here is the importance of continuing such studies along many innovative new lines. The new direction that I am advocating insists that the question of what to compare in cross-cultural studies is not always obvious. With respect to kinship I find that the philosophy of kinship as it exists in most prestate societies compares not so directly with what Americans take to be kinship in their own lives, but rather with something Americans do not have at all, namely, a coherent sociological imagination. Here I refer to C. Wright Mills's (1959) once-famous notion of a sociological imagination capable of tracing the links between personal troubles (or joys) and institutional or societal issues.

My reason for going back to Mills is that I see an important parallel between his ideas about sociology and those of Meyer Fortes on kinship. In particular, I find that Fortes's (1969) reappraisal of kinship already laid the grounds for seeing kinship not as a given entity or single domain of social life, in and of itself, but rather as a framework that linked such domains. He emphasized kinship as linking the domestic or personal domain with the public or politico-jural domain. The parallel between Fortes on kinship as a bridge between domestic and political domains and Mills on the sociological imagination as a bridge between a circumscribed personal sphere and a broader public and societal sphere has not, to my knowledge, ever been explored before. I think it holds promise in reacquainting us with the power

and relevance of the philosophy of kinship in its proper, by which I mean
prestate, context. It also presents a more demanding mirror in which to reflect
back on tendencies within our own society.

The discovery of a larger role for kinship in prestate societies was a product of nineteenth-century anthropology's preoccupation with the primitive.
In his last book, comprising interviews with Richard Handler and published
in 1995, Schneider claims that the old way of studying kinship had already
been used up by the 1960s. In fact, he offers an odd but rather amusing speculation as to the source of anthropology's original fascination with kinship.
He says it had to do with what he calls the Victorian period's preoccupation
with sex (195–97). Kinship was pointed to as the institution for containing
the untrammeled sexual drives of early humans. From this standpoint, the
old evolutionists saw something a bit titillating in kinship. Bride capture,
primitive promiscuity, group marriage, and the like could be fascinating
possibilities, allowing ancient humanity to have sewn a good few wild oats
before civilization and monogamy set in. This put some much-needed spice
into the overly sober narrative of progress that occupied nineteenth century
evolutionists. Schneider claims that, after Freud, sex was at last taken in stride
and there was really no more point to all this; so the study of kinship just
moved along on its own momentum, having already become entrenched in
academic anthropology (195–97). From this standpoint anthropology's de-
votion to kinship studies had been a false project all along.

Schneider came into the field in the late forties, and he took Murdock's
course on kinship at Yale. He did not like it; nonetheless, he wound up studying kinship in Yap for his dissertation at Harvard. His speculations about sex
and kinship and how everything on the topic after Freud became an empty
pursuit is a clever ploy. It insinuates that Murdock, A. R. Radcliffe-Brown,
Fred Eggan, Fortes, Edmund R. Leach, Rodney Needham, Jack Goody, and
even Lévi-Strauss were already intellectual carrion for having devoted so
much of their major work to the topic. However, he would not permanently
fall to the lure of kinship. Like a snake, he would eventually shed the dry skin
of kinship studies to re-emerge as the immortal father of cultural analyses.

It is ironic, in light of the fact that Kluckhohn and Leighton provide such
a succinct articulation of the Navajo appreciation of the philosophy of kinship, that Kluckhohn himself should have become Schneider's patron and
advisor through the completion of his dissertation at Harvard. Doubly ironic
is Schneider's comment that Kluckhohn "didn't know beans about kinship"
and didn't like kinship (1995:21), yet he backed Schneider against criticisms
from Murdock on Yapese terminology. According to Schneider, Kluckhohn

remarked, "'Kinship terminology—who gives a shit!'" (22). Whether Kluck-hohn, then, or Schneider himself, later on, liked it or not, a great many peoples are like the Navajo in that they really do care a great deal about kinship. It is for them their most important social philosophy.

A Reply to Schneider

Schneider begins his critique of kinship with a critique of his own ethnography of kinship on the Micronesian island of Yap. He believed that the major fault with his early account of Yap was that it assumed what kinship was about and then, by way of a fairly standardized typology, proceeded to give a kind of shorthand military debriefing on the culture—or rather that part of the culture that seemed to connect with "kinship." For example, the *tabinau* was a land holding patrilineage and a patrilocal compromise kin group. Meanwhile the *genung* was a dispersed matrilineal clan, thus making the Yapese kinship system one of double descent. In Schneider's view, a better cultural understanding of how Yapese actually view their own social world was produced by David Labby (1977) in his monograph *The Demystification of Yap.*

Some definitions are needed to catch the difference here. The *tabinau* can be thought of as a line of men straight through fathers and sons along with their sisters and daughters. The latter leave the land at marriage. The *genung* can be thought of as a line of women straight through mothers and daughters along with their brothers and sons. Everyone belongs to both a *tabinau* and a *genung* in both descriptions, but since women move at marriage and Labby's analysis focuses on land, the *genung* seems to move relative to land holdings and the *tabinau* seems to stay in place. A *genung* is on a site for two generations: one for a woman's marriage and one for her son's succession to his father's place on the land. The *tabinau,* on the other hand, appears to have a perpetual hold on the land that goes back to ancestral claims. Labby finds that the perpetuity of *tabinau* land rights is only an appearance and that the reality is a chain of transactions between the separate *genung* lines that precede and succeed each other on the land.

Labby found that the Yapese viewed land as being worked and cared for by members of a *genung* (which he renders as *ganong*) who had married into a particular *tabinau.* They would then pass that land on into the care of the next *genung* to marry into the same *tabinau.* The system was about the exchange of and obligations to land and to the *tabinau* ancestors of the land; it was a malleable set of relations between separate *genung* who had succeeded each other in the upkeep of the garden and other lands they had come to occupy and care for as a result of women moving onto their husbands' lands at marriage. There was a special term, *mafen*, to describe the relation between a *genung* earning its right in a particular *tabinau's* land and the *genung* which had acquired this right in the previous generation but was now involved with a new *tabinau*. This was not easily described by the notion of double descent; it was only specifiable by the Yapese notion of doing things with the land and then passing that duty and privilege on to the next supporters of the land. Who these might be in each generation was an open question and not assimilable to an idea of descent, filiation, or even marital alliance. In genealogical terms a man, the man's sister, and her children represented the *genung* leaving his and her *tabinau* land for another's, while his wife and his children represented the new *genung* in the process of earning its favor with the *tabinau* ancestors. The former were *mafen* to the latter. Culturally the *mafen* held a kind of moral authority over the land they no longer worked.

Schneider accepted Labby's subsequent account as culturally more accurate than his own. The success of Labby's account is that it broke with the goal of trying to describe Yapese cultural understandings by translating them into a cross-culturally valid notion of kinship. In Schneider's account, kinship was predefined in terms of birth, ancestry, marriage, procreation and the like. Formal organizations such as descent groups could then be constructed out of the cultural recognition of these various universal genealogical features. None of this captured the pivotal sense of obligations to and through land that mattered to the Yapese. So Schneider had a powerful point to make. Having found fault with his own account of kinship on Yap, he presented a serious challenge to all of anthropology: namely, that to live up to its long-avowed goal of being faithful to native points of view it would have to abandon the field of study that had been its very trademark among the social sciences, the study of kinship. But a closer inspection shows that this conclusion does not follow, since there is nothing in Labby's account or in Schneider's interpretation of it to allow for the inference that the Yapese do not have a philosophy of kinship in terms of which they meet important social obligations. Indeed Labby's (1976:35–44) discussion of honoring *mafen* relationships implies that they do.

Just as with the Malay example cited above, we see that this Yapese example, which Schneider relied upon to demolish kinship, pivots around the moral philosophy of kinship and the specification of existing social relatedness in terms of past marriages. Once again the fusing of these two constitutes kinship. Having now glanced at three non-Western cultures—Navajo, Malay, and Yapese—with the result being Kinship 3 and Schneider 0, I daresay that a longer tally would continue this trend.

In Defense of Kinship

If the main objection to the study of kinship is that "it assumes kinship" and, therefore, "converts native cultural constructs into those of kinship," then I would give the following defense of the conventional wisdom. We must keep in mind that "assuming kinship" and assuming what kinship is or means in any given case are two different things. The only important assumption regarding kinship so far as I can see is the simple sociological proposition that it is almost universally important for individual members of a society to have relatives. We should assume no more than this in "assuming kinship." Schneider spends a great deal of time on the accusation that anthropologists from Morgan to Lévi-Strauss have, in fact, assumed much more than this by assuming kinship. They have assumed that it is defined by genealogical connection, that it automatically causes a "blood is thicker than water" set of social priorities, and that there are simpler societies which are "kin based."

I would agree that these additional assumptions do reflect an ethnocentric bias. Schneider did a masterful job of exposing these biases, but he then made the fatal mistake of discarding everything. His skepticism led him to deny (or at least fail to recognize) a very important truth, namely, that wherever one journeys it pays not only to know some people, but to know some of their relatives as well. Eventually one may discover that other things are of greater importance, but the simple truth is that no matter how people count their relatives, relative always count. If this is not so then why are the mythologies of peoples all over the world filled with such figures as pathetic orphans, incestuous mates, exotic spouses, heroic twins, fraternal strife, and supernatural in-laws? Such mythic images always assume and elaborate the philosophy of kinship. Furthermore, it is the virtually universal recognition of the moral force of the philosophy of kinship that makes so many political and social movements want to call themselves sisterhoods and brotherhoods. In short, there is overwhelming evidence to suggest that a general notion of kinship is an important philosophy, and because kinship is not a matter of indifference, it cannot be a "non-subject."

For ethnographers, the near universal importance of kinship has always had practical as well as theoretical relevance. Kinship has often been an advantageous point of entry into another cultural system. From there the larger field of native meanings can be explored, both literally and figuratively. For who could deny the value of coming to know the relatives of one's informants and friends in the course of fieldwork? Nonetheless, I would agree with Schneider that each time we enter another culture using the idea of kinship, we may quickly find that native meanings begin to knock the ground from under our feet. But I would hasten to point out that this dislocation seldom totally obliterates all that is familiar. The better ethnographies show that adjustments can be made. True, the ethnographer's meanings are not the participant's meanings. But the move from the ethnographer's meanings to the participant's and back has to start somewhere. And kinship, partly because it contains the promise of trust and partly because it is valued in a general sense cross-culturally, is at least as good a place as any other to start the process of discerning ethnographic facts. On top of all of this, of course, is Lévi-Strauss's all important point that it is by kinship that certain constraints are placed upon marriage.[9] Although it may be our own model, as Schneider claims, kinship is a model in keeping with the ethnographic spirit of wanting to know and establish a bond with others, of wanting to share in their humanity. And it is in this flexible spirit that the model of kinship should be applied to the initial steps of a cultural analysis.

A second defense of the conventional wisdom on kinship has to do with the ideas of "a kin-based society" and of "the idiom of kinship." Schneider has many objections to these notions. His strongest objection to the idea of kinship as an idiom for other social purposes is aimed at its unquestioned assumption that in simpler societies kinship is a "privileged system" upon which all else depends (1984:57–63). This makes the kinship-based society idea and the kinship idiom idea rather "akin" to each other, though they disagree on the uniqueness or irreducibility of the content of kinship. A further argument against kinship as an idiom is offered by Fortes (1969:56–57), who contends that kinship has some recognizable and irreducible content of its own. Such content includes an element of genealogical meaning in its main social categories along with the all important "axiom of amity" behind the sanctioned expectations for conduct between relatives. The trick, he warns is to avoid falling into "the genealogical fallacy" of thinking that the "genealogical resonance" of kinship terms is somehow their primary and most intended social and jural meaning (1969:50). Fortes also points out that the "total social universe of what have been clumsily called kinship-based social systems" had been overlooked in functional as well as structural anthropology (72). In his book, *Kinship and the Social Order* (1969), he sought to rectify this failure, something he, in my opinion, accomplished quite admirably. Leach has also commented on kinship as an idiom in a remarkable essay (1967) on the nonkinship metaphors in the language of Kachin kinship nomenclature, where he insists that there is often a metaphoric dependence of "kinship" upon other meanings as the idiom for itself. The example he gives shows many plant and gift references in the etymologies of Kachin kin terms.

So semantic borrowing in the language of kinship is much more reciprocal than we have so far been given to realize.

Although I accept these objections of Schneider and others to the ideas of the kin-based society and of kinship as the dominant idiom for other things in nonstate societies, I would argue that these ideas are more in need of revision than of elimination. The revision I advocate is that kinship be regarded as a philosophy. It is a cultural answer to the question "How is it possible for one human being to be morally obligated to any other despite conflicts of interest?" Schneider would have recognized in this our own culture's code of conduct "enjoining diffuse enduring solidarity" between relatives (1984:53). Fortes's notion of an "axiom of amity" or of "prescriptive altruism" also fits here (1969:110, 219–49, 232). But whereas Schneider warns that these ideas are strictly our own culture's creations and should not be assumed for other cultures, I am willing to risk this much culture-boundness in beginning the analysis of other cultures. The important point is to treat the *idea* that relatives are important, and are perhaps universally so viewed, as a philosophy belonging to many cultures, and not as an empirical fact of group formation or of observable patterns of interaction. Here Schneider's critique is paradoxical: he is emphatic in his attacks upon the force of Western folk beliefs about the biological basis for kinship, but in abandoning the study of kinship, he leaves the field open for a theoretical takeover by sociobiology, which treats kin-related behavior as a highly specified biological fact. Fortunately, the recent return to kinship by cultural anthropologists seems to have rectified this situation. A new awareness of cultural differences surrounding kinship poses a clear alternative to the claims of sociobiology.

Implications

The recommendation to treat kinship as a philosophy, indeed as a major plane of "native" social theorizing equivalent in significant ways to the social sciences in the West, has already been made by Lévi-Strauss (1968).[10] Adopting this view has implications that help to resolve many of the problems raised by Schneider. For example it forces us to situate kinship in the context of native cosmology as a whole and to look at the larger field of cultural meanings entering into each culture's view of what this philosophy is all about. It also leads us toward an appreciation of native versions of this philosophy as in their own way analytical and able to penetrate the phenomenon of how actors in a society comprehend their own social world. So treating kinship as philosophy leads straight to the issues of meaning and context which Schneider urges us to take into consideration when he says: "the first problem of any ethnographic account is to comprehend the conceptions, ideas, beliefs, images, [and] meanings of a culture and that this is the material which must be the substance of any statement of 'the ethnographic facts'" (1984:6).

Of course, being a philosophy concerned with human obligations, kinship does lead back to the problem of action as well. In studying kinship one cannot yield to American anthropology's temptation to follow Parsons only a third of the way in his three-way division of social life into its analytically separable cultural, social, and personality systems. Since we are dealing with a product of the social construction of reality, it is important to recognize that every meaning has social as well cultural implications. The separation which Schneider relied upon here has always seemed a mystification to me, but I will not enter into that territory here.[11]

Another important result of treating kinship as philosophy (and I must admit, I find it difficult to imagine what else it could be) is that this forces a change in the way we do comparative studies of kinship. The conventional typologies that Schneider so heartily lambastes quickly get bracketed because the significant comparisons no longer require a uniform grid; the comparisons must be contextualized. Instead of asking whether one society does with agnates what another does with affines, we come up against the more challenging question, "What in any one society is really comparable to the philosophy of kinship in another?" And here is where the attacks on the notions of the kinship-based society and the idiom of kinship in simpler societies can be seen in a new light. For kinship thinking in tribal societies is a way of transcending the difference between the personal or domestic sphere and the public or political sphere. Kinship resides not at one or the other of these levels, but rather ranges across both. An illustration of this would be kin vengeance. Revenge is often given as the reason for war in tribal societies. If we translate this into the idea of seeking private justice in our own society we miss the point that kin vengeance in a nonstate society is very public and political. Even the suitable target for retaliation need not be the actual perpetrator of the offense being avenged. Under a notion of collective guilt, any member of the enemy group is substitutable for any other. Each homicide between rival groups is more an assassination than a common murder, and where warfare exists each assassination translates into an act of war. In the "blood feud," kinship goes public.

Let me now indicate where these points are leading by showing how Fortes's formulation of kinship in most nonstate societies corresponds less with kinship in the West than it does with other more expansive and totalizing views of society, such as those formulated by social theorists.

Locating Bridges between Domains of Social Life

As indicated earlier, I have been struck by the parallel between Fortes's view of kinship as a bridging framework linking the circumscribed domestic domain with the larger politico-jural domain in tribal societies and C. Wright Mills's formulation of the sociological imagination. Mills's concern is the comparative theory of all societies, but especially of complex and differentiated modern societies. For Mills the sociological imagination "is the capacity to shift from one perspective to another—from the political to the psychological; from examination of a single family to comparative assessments of the national budgets of the world. . . . It is the capacity to range from the most impersonal and remote transformations to the most intimate features of the human self—and to see the relations between the two." Personal troubles or joys are to be seen in relation to public issues and institutions. With a sociological imagination people could understand what was "happening in themselves as minute points of the intersection of biography and history within society" (1959:7).

Now compare this with Fortes's attempt to go beyond Radcliffe-Brown's treatment of kinship in terms of structural principles. For all their elegance, Fortes contends that these principles left kinship as a one-dimensional reality. Kinship for Radcliffe-Brown manifested principles of structure such as the unity of the lineage group or the structural equivalence of siblings, but it did so only at the level of the ordering of familial and more or less extended familial relationships. As Radcliffe-Brown studied it, kinship was an abstract and homogeneous level of tribal social realities. Fortes felt that Radcliffe-Brown, in most of his writing, had not dealt with the political dimensions of kinship as they related to a wider social universe or polity. In struggling to tease out these points he states that "the major advance in kinship theory since Radcliffe-Brown, but growing directly out of his work, has been the analytical separation of the politico-jural from the domestic domain within the total social universe of what have been clumsily called kinship-based social systems" (1969:72). An articulation between clans or interclan communities as polities and among household groups as the domestic units within them was provided by the notion that kinship touched and ordered both levels. It did so by providing homologous segmentary models that keyed the two levels to each other. More directly it allowed actors to be so connected through kinship as to exert influence at both levels. What is most important to understand, if not always easy to follow in Fortes's argument, is that this separation between domains did not lodge "kinship" in either the domestic domain or the politico-jural domain. Rather, the virtue of kinship was that it provided nonstate societies with a practical theory of the bridge between these domains. Within this perspective Fortes finds that variations in kinship systems are best approached neither in terms of the universals of biology, which explain no variations, nor in terms of family make-up, nor even in terms of prime movers like economic production or reciprocity, but rather in terms of how social systems differ at higher levels, where the make-up of the wider social order and its politico-jural domain comes to bear upon the bridging conundrum which is kinship. Thus the complex visions of both Mills and Fortes are parallel. We could even say that kinship as Fortes has recast it is the most common kind of sociological imagination found in non-state societies, the ones we have so facilely called kin-based societies.

Mills hoped that the sociological imagination would allow men and women in modern mass societies to trace out the larger institutional causes of their personal troubles and so make the centers of power in their societies more accountable in improving their lot. Thus, institutions of power would be less opaque to ordinary consciousness. The actions of elites would be more readily known and more forcefully challenged because the sociological imagination would penetrate the ideological masks of power.

The moral tone of Mills's ideal has its parallel in the moral tone of the philosophy of kinship as the bridge between domestic and political domains in tribal systems. Since the axiom of amity is part of this philosophy, it validates certain appeals for higher levels of cooperation, the rectification of wrongs, and the demand for social accountability within tribal societies. Such appeals can span social domains, and when they fail, they can take a darker turn in the leveling of accusations of witchcraft. Indeed, there is an under-explored possibility that witchcraft accusations in tribal socieites are the final resort when actors have determined that the axiom of amity has either failed or does not apply. I suspect there is an elective affinity between the pervading values of the philosophy of kinship and witchcraft beliefs. The former may in certain circumstances give rise to the latter. In being a very positive doctrine, the philosophy of kinship requires an antithesis of itself to account for negative social outcomes—which witchcraft provides.

Raymond Kelly's (1993) analysis of "the hierarchy of virtue" in certain Melanesian societies offers support for this view. The pervading values of kinship set the standard for the virtuous person, while their negation describes the witch. Given that kinship completes the person and also lays down a standard of altruistic behavior, then a hierarchy of virtue applying to the character of individuals as social persons is not hard to imagine. As Kelly suggests, a hierarchy of moral standing and one of prestige versus stigma can very readily be constructed with regard to people's performance of kinship duties and their upholding of other related values through displays of generosity and the like (1993:15). In my view, the strong influence of the philosophy of kinship is indicated by the fact that, almost universally, the persons at the very bottom of such a hierarchy of virtue are fellow humans, kin or not, who are believed to be witches. As Kelly argues, "the witch represents the lowest category in the moral hierarchy" (15) and is the prototype of the most stigmatized social person. Witches are imagined as the perfect antithesis and inverse of an ideal—or even just a passable—kinsperson. I take this as indirect evidence for the widespread importance of the philosophy of kinship, for in supplying the primary content of hierarchies of virtue, this philosophy also provides the cultural foil against which nearly every society draws its image of evil in the witch.[12] One could say that the philosophy of kinship has been so unrelenting in most tribal societies that it has often produced its own theory of evil as well as good. On either side the main doctrine is one of complete social accountability.

Returning to Mills, though he hoped that the sociological imagination would allow people in modern societies to move back and forth between their personal troubles and public issues, he never claimed that the great day had arrived. As he put it: "Its acquisition by individuals and by the cultural community at large is often slow and fumbling; many social scientists themselves are quite unaware of it" (Mills 1959:14). For Mills the sociological imagination remained only a promise. But it was the promise about something important, something that would allow everyone the possibility of an accurate and powerfully critical perspective on all of social life. With the sociological imagination at work, one could be located anywhere in the social fabric and yet be able to bring one's just claims to bear upon relevant parts of the system as a whole.

The power of the state and now global economic powers affect the lives of all people on earth. Yet the internal workings of power and the actions of those wielding it remain remote and distant from ordinary people. Information itself is not freely or readily available to all. Mills's sociological imagination was to become a way of seeing through screens of secrecy and behind the masks of power to the sources of prevailing forms of oppression, exploitation, inequality, and injustice. Optimists suggest that an inherent democratization of access to information and opinion through information age technology and communications may provide a new means to attain that about which Mills could only dream. Of course, this remains to be seen. To date, computer hackers seem more bent on self indulgent mischief or electronic extortion than on imaginative analysis. Internet skills could eventually help, but the sociological imagination's main goal is a form of consciousness that seeks to trace with accuracy the connections between personal and much wider levels of social life.

It is indicative of our current situation that there are many false versions of this form of modern consciousness. Mass media images can give one only a vicarious sense of relating through celebrities and media events to the more distant power centers of the wider social milieu. People may think they have the answers to the issues of the day, but the dominant ideologies of modern life have already prevented them from even knowing any of the questions. If our sociological imaginations often seem feeble and immature, we get no comfort in being able to fall back on the philosophy of kinship. For, as we have seen, that too is very stunted in modern society. So the parallels between Mills's hopes for the sociological imagination in complex societies and Fortes's claims for the philosophy of kinship in tribal societies are of no avail to us. To our detriment, the sociological imagination which could someday become for global and national social life what kinship philosophy has been for tribal social life remains something beyond our reach and for which we must yet strive.

Resituating Kinship Terminology

In my opening remarks I referred to kinship vocabularies as being among the words that serve to populate social reality. Dwight W. Read's chapter in this volume, and the writings of many other anthropologists on kinship terminologies, give ample testimony to the almost palpable structure of these vocabulary sets. The special value of Read's chapter is in showing that the relative product associations of the terms in these word sets can be described and applied to particular people, namely, the relatives of a particular ego, without making any immediate reference to genealogical meanings. An overlap between the terminological and the genealogical placements of people as relatives seems in all cases to be present, but according to Read this does not make the genealogical meanings or mappings of relatives or of the terms for relatives primary. The overlap is not a coincidence, but neither is it the fundamental essence of kinship, as I will soon show.

Since the days of Morgan, studying kinship vocabularies has involved use of a genealogical framework that is applied as though it were cross-culturally neutral. Schneider condemns this as the false doctrine of "The Genealogical Unity of Mankind" (1984:156, 188–89, 195). Its methodological advantage is often defended by saying that it can be applied in a way that actually brings out significant cultural differences while helping to control the data that make up different terminology systems. Unlike Schneider, I am willing to concede this point. Without adroit use of the genealogical reduction of kinship terminologies we would not have a clear sense of the technical differences between such seemingly similar terminology systems as Dravidian and Iroquois (Lounsbury 1964; Scheffler and Lounsbury 1971; and Trautmann 1981). Our awareness of significant differences among kinship terminology systems has come about primarily through the application of the same genealogical grid to all cases. But I agree that many writers go one step too far and read this method into the data of kinship. They wind up treating the terminology systems as taxonomies of genealogical kin types rather than as symbols for highly relational social categories. As Fortes has warned (1969:53), this forgets Morgan's insistence that kinship terms were primarily ways of "calling" people, an alternative to names and personal pronouns.

Schneider did not buy the idea that the words for relatives in all cultures have a primary genealogical meaning and that the rest is extension. I agree with this. We have only begun to study the nongenealogical and nonkinship meanings of the terms that make up kinship vocabularies. Still, in advocating a view of kinship as a philosophy I am not able to escape concern over the meanings of kinship words. Nor does the genealogical element of their meanings disappear. But it does get repositioned. The genealogical element of the meanings appears more as a borrowing from nature of a model of linkability among social positions and categories than it does as a set of literal term-for-term references to positions of biological relatedness, or to the nodes on a genealogical chart. If anything, the physical side of genealogical meanings is drawn upon in kinship vocabularies as a way of saying that a natural model exists for the embodiment of relational qualities in the self who is a kinsperson. All kin terms relate more to each other than they do to the physical and genealogical elements of their referential meanings. In a very important sense all kinship terms are metaphors right from the start. The terms "mother" and "child" are much more about mothers and children being in a relation analogous to that between a biological genetrix and her offspring than they are about mothers being in fact or in name the bearers of children or children being in fact or in name the biological offspring of any particular female. This point seems to have escaped most treatments of the genealogical elements of kinship semantics. The lexical items have been interpreted in terms of a cognitive literalism that totally ignores the essentially metaphoric qualities of all kinship terms.

Embodiment has become a major theme in recent anthropological assessments of the concept of personhood. But kinship also involves embodiment. In representing social relationships as being like or parallel to the physical relations of genealogical linkage, kinship has been about the embodiment of relational qualities right from the start. Such is the imagery used in the domain of kinship. It has the effect of being a concrete native theory of social psychology: people will exist socially as embodiments of their social relations with others. It comes with the territory. That is the symbolism behind the genealogical resonance of kinship terminologies.

The relational quality of the terms has been apparent to anthropologists ever since Morgan. But the tendency has been to pseudo-literalize the meanings of the terms and to see the differentiations they make as a matter of imposing a taxonomy on genealogical positions or "kin types." This notion is similar to viewing clan totemism entirely as matter of the relation between each "clan" and its "totem" rather than looking at the series of relational differences supplied by the contrasting totems to the social series of an otherwise underdifferentiated set of clans. As Lévi-Strauss convincingly relocated the problem of totemism from a symbolist or nominalist question to a relationalist set of questions (1962), I think the study of kinship terminologies is due for a similar re-orientation. There needs to be a move from denotationalist and conotationalist analyses to a more strictly relationalist analysis. In such a procedure the fact that the terms permute and yield relative products is more important than the fact that each term can be assigned a nearest possible genealogical referent or set of referents, with other meanings fanning out from there. This allows the relational quality of linkability as a feature of the set of kin terms to come into the foreground. Read's chapter illustrates this point very well. I believe this feature of pure linkability is what has the most social relevance.

So, in trying to provide recognition of the genealogical content in kinship terminologies and yet not wanting to treat genealogy as the primary point of reference, here is what I propose. The genealogical content of kinship terminology has a metaphoric appropriateness to social kinship in that it uses biological relatedness among relatives as suitable bricolage for modeling the linkability of categories of persons as required by the philosophy of kinship. It is not that a father, even in a descriptive system, is first thought of as being the physical sire of his son or daughter, and that this is then given a congruent social meaning. It is rather that as a sire is seen as being in one kind of relationship to his offspring, so categories of persons can be see as relatable to each other in a similar way. Father in relation to child and child in relation to father already incorporates the relational quality of the "biological" fact as a metaphor for a social relationship and not as the literal sense of the relationship so named. Culturally, as we all know, there can be and often is a concern that "father" also be physical genitor. But if that were the primary meaning of the term "father," then the result would be a partialization of the metaphoric value of the relational meaning of the term "father" through overliteralizing the metaphor itself. Father would be reduced to sperm donor, and the implication of there being an ongoing and future relationship between genitor and offspring would be weakened. Going too literal on the biology of kinship kills the metaphor. That is why genealogy is much more the idiom than the substance of kinship terminologies. I believe this is what Fortes was driving at when he declared that kinship terms always have a genealogical resonance but that in our studies of kinship we should not become too literal and fall into the "genealogical fallacy."

It is the model of linkability and relative products that counts most. Biological kinship always overlaps with social kinship but it is never taken literally as being what kinship is all about. To think that the primary meaning of English "father" is genitor or sperm donor gives the term "father" and all other kin terms a literalness that they necessarily lack. It is like assuming that people who speak of Mother Earth really believe they will someday see babies emerging out of the ground. No such literalism is intended. In all cases the metaphoric appropriation of genealogy begins in the first instance, not just in the extensions from primary, literal, "real" examples.

Schneider raises the question, "If kinship and genealogical expressions are an idiom for social relations, why must it always be kinship?" Why not numbers or letters or tree branches? There is a good answer to this. The reason genealogy seems to work best is not a worldwide obsession with the rootedness of social kinship in biology. Rather, the tangible model of linkability provided by biology is not just present and available but also comes linked bodily to persons. Other models, numbers, tree branches, and so forth, are only secondarily related to actual persons. But birth, copulation, genealogical proximity, age, and sex all start out attached bodily to persons and to interpersonal bonds and oppositions. Therefore, they provide a model that is semantically redundant in the right direction: toward persons and interrelations among persons. These physical features of genealogy furnish an idiom that can be iconic of as well as metaphoric for the connections that the philosophy of kinship assumes can be possible between persons in social networks.

In short, the genealogical resonance of kinship terms is overdetermined. Furthermore, the philosophy of kinship and the genealogical idiom in which it is expressed provide an exceptionally apt model for movement in thought from self to both near or distant social others and back. Given the problem of representing social networks involving past marriages, genealogical imagery has more to offer than most other models. The choice of genealogy does not occur in a vacuum. Since kinship itself is a theory and not an entity, there is all the more reason for there to be a high degree of selectivity with respect to the aptness of the natural symbols chosen as its representation. But the culturally important point is to find a model of linkability, not just slotting people or terms onto a grid. Fortes was right: we can have the genealogical resonance without falling into the genealogical fallacy. The meaning of kinship terms can never be reduced to their genealogical or "kin-type" referents. Supplying those referents serves only as a methodological device for making comparatively useful descriptions of such terminological systems.

Chapters by Read and Ward Goodenough (this volume) deal impressively with the values and limitations of this methodological practice. My point is only to clarify that even this limited methodological success owes its productivity not directly to the universals of biology, but rather to the fact that what we call genealogy is good to think when it comes to representing pure sociological linkability. Without that linkability, the philosophy of kinship would be amorphous and would dissipate culturally. In the case of our own society, this is exactly what is already happening, although it is happening for other and almost opposite reasons. We have become too narrow and too literal about kinship and its genealogical components. We have wrung the metaphoric value out of the meaning of our kin categories. By reading them too close to biology we strip them of their power to have a strong social message. We took the symbols of the old sociological imagination, kinship, much too literally and lost the moral scope of its model for linkability. As for the new sociological imagination, the horizon of its dawning still seems a long way off.

Anthropology, more than any of the other social sciences, bears a heavy responsibility for passing the baton of effective social theory from the old sociological imagination to the new. For it is in the pages of Morgan's work and of some of his contemporaries that we see anthropology being built on the study of kinship in tribal cultures. Whatever else may be said and done about the study of kinship, its prominence in anthropology from Morgan's day to the present speaks eloquently as a metacommentary on the attempt of Western culture to fill the gap left within itself after the fragmentation of the old philosophy of kinship with something new called the science of man. That science and its sister human and social sciences still aspire to complete the sociological imagination once called for by Mills.

Conclusion

If I have been correct in positing a parallel between the philosophy of kinship in nonstate societies and the absent but vitally needed sociological imagination in complex societies, then we have every reason not to listen to Schneider's call for the abandonment of the study of kinship. We should even have a sense of urgency about rethinking and continuing Morgan's project. But this will be done along many new lines, and it will be done in a way that has been vitally informed by David's trenchant critique.

In a review of David's last book, *Schneider on Schneider: The Conversion of the Jews and Other Anthropological Stories,* Aram Yengoyan (1997) notes that the embattled career of David M. Schneider had many twists and turns, triumphs and defeats. Never a parochial kinship mandarin, always an intellectual gadfly who refused to be dismissed, someone who raised other people's standards of ethnographic reporting while demeaning ethnography as against theory, David was infuriating to both friend and foe. Yengoyan searched for a note on which to end his rough tribute to Schneider, concluding that, "if you haven't been infuriated by David, then you've never really been infuriated." I would add in light of personal encounters, anthropological folklore, some cheap psychologizing of my own, and David's autobiographical interviews, that one of those who must have experienced some of the worst of this infuriation was the man himself. Perhaps that is why he chose to end his academic career on so many negative notes, brashly confessing himself to be an inauthentic ethnographer and self-hating kinship expert.

Peace, David. We *will* keep studying culture—and kinship.

Notes

1. It is under the question of theories of self in relation to concrete social milieu that I would put the matter of sexual identity or what I can only hesitatingly refer to as gender, taking the latter term in its usual sense as referring to culturally constructed notions of sexual identities and categories. The complex relationship between gender and kinship must be reserved for a separate paper.

2. For convenience, I would set the terminal date for the exhaustion of earlier paradigms at 1971. John Barnes's *Three Styles in the Study of Kinship* (1971) reflects this exhaustion, as does the ASA monograph *Rethinking Kinship and Marriage* (1971), edited by Rodney Needham. The Morgan centennial volume edited by Priscilla Reining (1972) also became a sort of inadvertent epitaph on the study of kinship. Schneider's provocative paper, "What Is Kinship All About?" in which he declared kinship a "non-subject," appeared in that volume.

With the exception of a few sterling ethnographic papers, the retrospective stock-taking in these volumes did more to close the books on old ways of studying kinship than it did to rally anthropology to new ways of approaching its hallmark subject. Later on, the tide of gender-oriented research would draw many anthropologists back to kinship but more as an interpretive means than as a scientific end. So the continuity with older schools is less than might be expected given the sizable investment of prior anthropological thought on the topic.

3. For additional comment on these historical issues, see essays in this volume by Feinberg, Fogelson, DeMallie, and Goodenough.

4. Why siblings are more accidental as relatives than are one's parents Merrell does not clearly explain. Apparently the ideal human state for Merrell would be one in which all God's children were only children. The ideal content of siblingship, in turn, would be a condition whereby every family with more than one child learned to treat them all as multiple only children. Radcliffe-Brown, creator of the structural principle of the "unity of the sibling group," and its corollary, "the equivalence of siblings," must be turning in his grave over Merrell's attempted rectification of the accident of siblingship.

5. Strathern makes many other important observations in her book. For example she notes that the drift toward the diminishing social importance of kinship in Britain and America was already present in the emphasis on the naturalness of kin ties. If the facts of life at the bottom of kinship are culturally perceived as being "birth, copulation, and death" then these "are not about society. Rather they chart the individual person's movement 'through' it" (Strathern 1992:106). So individualism in the wake of the new reproductive technology just narrows the social relevance of kinship for self and society even more. Some other implications of what has already been present in the Anglo-American emphasis on the naturalness of kin ties will be examined in the section of this chapter dealing with kinship terminology.

Strathern's discussion of conflict between the surrogate and the legal parents of a child (1992:178), or what I call fragmented filiation, is also revealing. Children are sometimes taught to call one woman their birth mother and another their actual mother. As for conception parents versus social or legal parents, I have so far not heard of children using these terms. Our ways of talking about fragmented filiation finally vindicate Morgan's original choice of the term "descriptive" to talk about our own terminology system. A classificatory terminology is not even available to us now, when we actually do have more than one mother or father to recognize. We have to differentiate not only between lineal and collateral relatives, but between one kind of lineal and another. I also regard it as very revealing that surrogate mothers are called by that term and not by the term "surrogate wives." That surrogate father's are merely called "sperm donors" reflects the "non-relational" thinking about the reproduction of persons that Strathern highlights in her discussion of the legal debates surrounding clinical interventions in the reproductive process.

Furthermore, Strathern's discussion of the individuality of embryos as having taken on social, cultural, and legal significance has obvious implications for debates concerning the ethics of abortion. Opponents of a woman's right to abortion have already latched onto this same reading of biology. As Strathern points out, the relation between the individual embryo and "society" is coming to be seen as superseding the relation between that same embryo and its parents. Ironically, the new reproductive technology seems to support the anti-abortion movement because it has helped support their notion that the personhood of a fetus (or even stored sperms and ova) begins biologically, at conception. Ontogeny is coming to outweigh phylogeny in the cultural interpretation of "nature." Because no product of human ovulation or spermatogenesis is likely ever to develop into an elephant, giraffe, or even a chimpanzee, it is already and especially after fertilization considered to be human. But in what sense it is human is an age old debate within and between cultures.

One last point about enterprise kinship and culture. If it is our current fate, as Strathern observes, to be made to feel that "one has no choice not to make a choice" in every area of life and all of the time (1992:37), then it is time that anthropology develops a more serious understanding of the structure of human volition than is now provided by the various "models for decision making" currently available in the social sciences. At a time when anthropologists are trying to write agency into every breath of life and every moment of history, the absence of any powerful anthropological models of human volition is a glaring deficiency. The area of volitional aspects of kinship may yet prove a good place to start making up for this deficiency.

6. David and I had already had some favorable exchanges prior to the work on his *Critique.* We first met in 1969, having been introduced by Aram Yengoyan, who had sent him a manuscript copy of my paper on Crow and Omaha kinship (McKinley 1971a, 1971b). David liked this paper for its criticisms of prior approaches to Crow and Omaha, and for the broader cultural and ideological meanings that I suggested were at work in making these terminologies attractive to a fair number of prestate societies. He later used this paper as a reading in his course on kinship. David also commented on my paper dealing with Malay sibling relationships in the ASAO volume *Siblingship in Oceania* (Schneider 1981; McKinley 1981) edited by Mac Marshall (1981). We had frequent discussions on many matters during my 1982 stay in Chicago. I am pleased to say that David was a fine host and that our friendship endured until his death.

7. The notion that anthropology is a unique and irreducible form of knowledge is an extremely important one, but most anthropologists seem to miss the point. In a separate paper (McKinley n.d.), I argue for a very special relation between anthropology, science, and other modes of knowing. Morgan also argued that cultural differences produce a new order of facts and knowledge. In his argument, Morgan (1871) usefully contrasted the classificatory and descriptive systems. He characterized the classificatory system as "artificial" and "arbitrary" even though systematic and coherent, and the descriptive as simply "descriptive." He clearly placed the burden of anomaly, or departure from nature, on the classificatory side, which he contended had to have come about for social and cultural reasons. But this having been established, Morgan then made the even more radical inference that the same would also have to be true for the descriptive system. It too would have to be made after culture not nature. But since descriptive systems distinguished "true" direct blood lines rather than merging lineal and collateral relatives, it would be harder to reveal the social and cultural factors behind this closer correspondence to what could be seen in nature alone. So Morgan's typology emphasized that attention to the details and systematics of cultural otherness unmasked the supposed naturalness of cultural sameness, showing it to be an outcome of the social as well. Thus, in Morgan's evolutionary theory, it was not more accurate biological understanding that led to the "overthrow" of the classificatory system and the rise of the descriptive one; rather it was civilized hu-

manity's obsession with private property. The transmission of private as opposed to communal property required descent to be cut fine.

So despite his group marriage hypotheses and his tendency to read biology back into the kin term equations of the classificatory system, Morgan's comparative thinking was remarkable for sustaining an operational insistence that cultural differences are irreducible to anything but other cultural, social, and historical differences. This realm of knowledge and knowing stood on its own. Morgan's argument is all the more amazing when one considers Trautmann's convincing demonstration that Morgan's epistemology was heavily guided by the Scottish common sense philosophers. That epistemology might have suggested to him that language classifications would follow human consciousness in combining or distinguishing things in terms of their salience in direct social experience. But it would not have suggested that the phenomenon of purely cultural differences throughout all of humanity had an irreducible quality of its own. Yet that is exactly where Morgan's reasoning is at its creative best. And in my view this is the epistemological locus of all anthropological understanding.

8. Schneider's allusion to the Toda bow ceremony here refers to a textbook favorite of mid-twentieth-century anthropologists. The Todas of South India had polyandry and the paternity of a child among the multiple husbands of a wife was supposed to have been assigned according to which husband had performed this ceremony at the time of the pregnancy. To make this comparison puts Western kinship in the Ripley's "Believe it or not" category.

9. In a fuller treatment of the philosophy of kinship it would be necessary to bring together the kinship theories of Lévi-Strauss and of Fortes. The axiom of amity insists that kinship relations be valued or honored. But as Lévi-Strauss has pointed out (1963:202–28), incest would be an overvaluing of kinship. Therefore, sexual and marriage prohibitions set a limit to the conduct that is allowed under the axiom of amity. It excludes sex and marriage with certain relatives. Thus, as anthropologists since Tylor have insisted, marrying out broadens the range of kinship and in a sense, following Fortes, this means that marriage is enlisted in the mission of kinship to bridge the familial and the politico-jural domains. In essence I am arguing for a "marriage" between what have simplistically been polarized as "descent" and "alliance" theories of kinship.

10. Lévi-Strauss's views on this crucial point are given in a thoughtful and moving set of comments he made at the 1968 conference on *Man the Hunter*. His lesson is so important that I quote him in full: "Hiatt has suggested two possible explanations for the discrepancy between model and reality in Australian society; however, there is also a third worth considering—that at one time, all this completed theory was clearly conceived and invented by native sociologists or philosophers. Thus what we are doing is not building a theory with which to interpret the facts, but rather trying to get back to an older native theory at the origin of the facts we are trying to explain" (1968:350). He goes on to speculate that "mankind should not have waited until recent times to produce minds of the caliber of a Plato or an Einstein. Already over two or three hundred thousand years ago, there were probably men [and women] of similar capacity, who were of course not applying their intelligence to the solution of the same problems as these more recent thinkers; instead, they were probably more interested in kinship!" (351).

In particular, he suspects that the refinement in the conceptual shorthand of many classificatory kinship systems, which we recognize as the cross and parallel distinction with respect to siblings and cousins, was originally a product of such early theorizing. These insights, I believe, rank with Morgan's "invention" of kinship and with Fortes's profound rethinking of the relation between kinship and the social order. If a Nobel Prize were to be given in anthropology, it would be for developing *and sustaining* insights such as these.

11. In his book *Culture: The Anthropologists' Account*, Adam Kuper (1999) provides an excellent account of Schneider's links to Parsons's project. Kuper's chapter on Schneider explains the intellectual grounds for Schneider's supreme indifference to the sociological implications of his cultural analyses, and it also suggests biographical motives for his final dismantling of kinship. Kuper is convincing on all counts.

12. That the image of the witch is a near perfect inversion of the image of a good kinsperson is true along many dimensions. Needham (1978:23–50) points out that anthropologists have examined the social tensions that may be addressed by witchcraft beliefs but have neglected the details of the image of the witch. Details such as animal companionship, animal transformation, being able to fly, feeding off of the life force of fellow humans, hidden nightly predations from a distance and so forth are all perfect opposites of the definitions of a kinsperson. Kinspeople are morally bound in exclusive ways to certain human others, not animals; they are rooted to substance and place, not flying about; they are nurturant toward, not devouring of, others, and they are openly generous, not exploitative and predatory.

References Cited

Barnes, J. A. 1971. *Three Styles in the Study of Kinship*. Berkeley: University of California Press.

Beidelman, Thomas O. 1970. "Some Sociological Implications of Culture." In *Theoretical Sociology, Perspectives and Developments*. Ed. John C. McKinney and Edward A. Tiryakian. 499–527. New York: Meredith Corp.

Carsten, Janet. 1995. "The Substance of Kinship and the Heat of the Hearth: Feeding Personhood, and Relatedness among Malays in Pulau Langkawi." *American Ethnologist* 22:223–41.

———. 1996. *The Heat of the Hearth: The Process of Kinship in a Malay Fishing Community*. Oxford: Clarendon Press.

Collier, Jane Fishburne, and Sylvia Junko Yanagisako. 1987. "Toward a Unified Analysis of Gender and Kinship." In *Gender and Kinship: Essays toward a Unified Analysis*. Ed. Jane Fishburne Collier and Sylvia Junko Yanagisako. 14–50. Stanford, Calif.: Stanford University Press.

Fortes, Meyer. 1969. *Kinship and the Social Order: The Legacy of Lewis Henry Morgan*. Chicago: Aldine.

Fox, Robin. 1967. *Kinship and Marriage: An Anthropological Perspective*. Harmondsworth, U.K.: Pelican Books.

Goodenough, Ward H. 1956. "Componential Analysis and the Study of Meaning." *Language* 32:195–216.

Hallowell, A. Irving. 1960. "Ojibwa Ontology, Behavior, and World View." In *Culture in History: Essays in Honor of Paul Radin.* Ed. Stanley Diamond. 19–52. New York: Columbia University Press.

Kelly, Raymond. 1993. *Constructing Inequality: The Fabrication of a Hierarchy of Virtue among the Etoro.* Ann Arbor: University of Michigan Press.

Kluckhohn, Clyde, and Dorothea Leighton. 1946. *The Navaho.* Cambridge, Mass.: Harvard University Press.

Kuper, Adam. 1999. *Culture: The Anthropologists' Account.* Cambridge, Mass.: Harvard University Press.

Labby, David. 1976. *The Demystification of Yap: Dialectics of Culture on a Micronesian Island.* Chicago: University of Chicago Press.

Leach, Edmund R. 1967. "The Language of Kachin Kinship: Reflections on a Tikopian Model." In *Social Organization.* Ed. M. Freedman. 125–52. London: Cass.

Lévi-Strauss, Claude. 1962. *Totemism.* Boston: Beacon Press.

———. 1963. *Structural Anthropology.* New York: Basic Books.

———. 1968. "The Concept of Primitiveness." In *Man the Hunter.* Ed. Richard B. Lee and Irven Devore. 349–52. Chicago: Aldine.

———. 1969 [1949]. *The Elementary Structures of Kinship.* Trans. James Harle Bell and John Richard von Sturmer. Ed. Rodney Needham. Boston: Beacon Press.

———. 1971. Letter to David M. Schneider (in the author's possession, courtesy of the recipient).

Lounsbury, Floyd G. 1964. "The Structural Analysis of Kinship Semantics." In *Proceedings of the Ninth International Congress of Linguists.* Ed. Horace G. Hunt. 1073–93. The Hague: Mouton.

Luckmann, Thomas. 1970. "On the Boundaries of the Social World." In *Phenomenology and Social Reality: Essays in Memory of Alfred Schutz.* Ed. Maurice Natanson. 73–100. The Hague: Martinis Nijhoff

Marshall, Mac, ed. 1981. *Siblingship in Oceania: Studies in the Meaning of Kin Relations.* ASAO Monograph No. 8. Ann Arbor: University of Michigan Press.

McKinley, Robert. 1971a. "A Critique of the Reflectionist Theory of Kinship Terminology: The Crow-Omaha Case." *Man* 6:228–47.

———. 1971b. "Why Do Crow and Omaha Kinship Terminologies Exist?: A Sociology of Knowledge Interpretation." *Man* 6:408–26.

———. 1981. "Cain and Abel on the Malay Peninsula." In *Siblingship in Oceania: Studies in the Meaning of Kin Relations.* Ed. Mac Marshall. 335–87. ASAO Monograph No. 8. Ann Arbor: University of Michigan Press.

———. n.d. "Fourth Doorway to Knowledge: The Irreducible Structures of Anthropological Knowledge." Ms.

McKinnon, Susan. 1991. *From a Shattered Sun: Hierarchy, Gender, and Alliance in the Tanimbar Islands.* Madison: University of Wisconsin Press.

Merrell, Susan Scarf. 1995. *The Accidental Bond: How Sibling Connections Influence Adult Relationships.* New York: Ballantine Books.

Mills, C. Wright. 1959. *The Sociological Imagination.* London: Oxford University Press.

Morgan, Lewis Henry. 1871. *Systems of Consanguinity and Affinity of the Human Family.*

Smithsonian Contributions to Knowledge Vol. 17. Washington, D.C.: Smithsonian Institution.

Murdock, George Peter. 1949. *Social Structure*. New York: Macmillan.

Needham, Rodney, ed. 1971. *Rethinking Kinship and Marriage*. London: Tavistock Publications.

———. 1978. *Primordial Characters*. Charlottesville: University Press of Virginia.

Peletz, Michael Gates. 1988. *A Share of the Harvest: Kinship, Property, and Social History among the Malays of Rembau*. Berkeley: University of California Press.

———. 1995. "Kinship Studies in Late Twentieth-Century Anthropology." In *Annual Reviews of Anthropology* 24:343–72.

Reining, Priscilla, ed. 1972. *Kinship in the Morgan Centennial Year*. Washington, D.C.: Anthropological Society of Washington.

Scheffler, Harold W. 1971. "Dravidian-Iroquois: The Melanesian Evidence." In *Anthropology in Oceania: Essays in Honor of H. I. Hogbin*. Ed. C. Jayawardena and R. L. Hiatt. 231–54. Sydney: Angus Robertson.

———. 1972. "Systems of Kin Classification: A Structural Typology." In *Kinship Studies in the Morgan Centennial Year*. Ed. Priscilla Reining. 113–33. Washington, D.C.: Anthropological Society of Washington.

Scheffler, Harold W., and Floyd G. Lounsbury. 1971. *A Study in Structural Semantics: The Sirionó Kinship System*. Englewood Cliffs, N.J.: Prentice-Hall.

Schneider, David M. 1972. "What Is Kinship All About?" In *Kinship Studies in the Morgan Centennial Year*. Ed. Priscilla Reining. 32–63. Washington, D.C.: Anthropological Society of Washington.

———. 1980 [1968]. *American Kinship: A Cultural Account*. Chicago: University of Chicago Press.

———. "Conclusions." In *Siblingship in Oceania: Studies in the Meaning of Kin Relation*. Ed. Mac Marshall. 389–404. ASAO Monograph No. 8. Ann Arbor: University of Michigan Press.

———. 1984. *A Critique of the Study of Kinship*. Ann Arbor: University of Michigan Press.

———. 1995. *Schneider on Schneider: The Conversion of the Jews and Other Anthropological Stories, as Told to Richard Handler*. Ed. Richard Handler. Durham, N.C.: Duke University Press.

Schutz, Alfred. 1967. *The Phenomenology of the Social World*. Evanston, Ill.: Northwestern University Press.

Strathern, Marilyn. 1992. *Reproducing the Future: Anthropology, Kinship, and the New Reproductive Technologies*. New York: Routledge.

Trautmann, Thomas R. 1981. *Dravidian Kinship*. Cambridge: Cambridge University Press.

———. 1987. *Lewis Henry Morgan and the Invention of Kinship*. Berkeley: University of California Press.

Yanagisako, Sylvia, and Carol Delaney, eds. 1995. *Naturalizing Power: Essays in Feminist Cultural Analysis*. London: Routledge.

Yengoyan, Aram. 1997. "Yengoyan on Handler's Schneider on Schneider." *American Ethnologist* 24 (1): 208–10.

7. The Trobriand Kinship Classification and Schneider's Cultural Relativism

SUSAN P. MONTAGUE

As a new graduate student at the University of Chicago, I was required to take "Systems," the anthropology department's basic cultural anthropology course. That year it was taught by David Schneider. One of the points he made insistently is that while all kinship classifications slot people into categories of relatives, the definitional criteria for, or as he said, the "distinctive features" of, those categories need not be the same as the ones used in the American kinship system. Indeed, he went so far as to indicate that, in his opinion, most of what was wrong with kinship studies to date was that anthropologists had made the ethnocentric mistake of assuming that foreigners use variation(s) on the same definitional criteria as do Americans.

I took these observations with me when I went to the Trobriand Islands to conduct doctoral and subsequent fieldwork, and I found that they were borne out in the Trobriand instance.[1] But my field data pushed Schneider's observations a step further. It turns out that the Trobriand kinship system does not have a ready equivalent to the Western concept "relative." That is, whatever the Trobriand kinship system is about, it is not about relationships between people who very properly fit definitions of the English language term "relative." Additionally, it turns out that much of what is wrong with the traditional anthropological picture of Trobriand social organization rests on the ethnocentric projection of the Western concept of the "relative" onto a cultural arrangement which does not use it.

In this chapter, I briefly present the Trobriand kinship classification (summarized in table 7.1), and then look at why it is difficult to apply the Western concept "relative" to it. Then I offer a brief discussion of problems which have arisen from the attempt to apply that concept to the Trobriand kinship sys-

Table 7.1. Types of Exchange Associated with First- and Second-Tier Terms

First-Tier Term	Exchange Type	Second-Tier Terms
veyotatu	sharing	*ina, kada, tuwa, bwada, nuta, natu*
veyo	one-ended	*keyawa*
tabu	sales and purchases	*tama, yawa, yavata, lubou, natu*

Note: The term *natu* is the reciprocal for both *ina* and *tama*. The *ina/natu* relationship is of the sharing type, and the *tamu/natu* relationship is of the sales and purchase type. I do not include the term *tabu* as a second-tier term, although Malinowski did. In the context of the second tier of Trobriand kinship relations the term *tabu* is used to denote someone with whom ego has none.

tem. I close by considering in what sense, if any, we can legitimately say that Trobriand Islanders have a kinship system. After all, if, as Schneider (1968) indicates, kinship is about relatives, and if, in the Trobriand case, it is difficult to apply the concept "relative," then we must face this last issue. I will argue that they do have a kinship system insofar as all of the systems that anthropologists have termed "kinship systems," including the Trobriand system, are anchored in multiple-slotting classifications. In short, while their content may differ even to the extent that they are not about "relatives," they all manifest a single classificatory structure.

The Trobriand Kinship Classification: The First Tier

The Trobriand kinship classification is two-tiered. The first tier sorts all Trobrianders into relational categories on a dietary basis. The categories are *veyotatu, veyo,* and *tabu.*[2] Ego's *veyotatu* are people who avoid consuming the same *manua* ("bird") as does ego and who also avoid consuming the same *kawenu* ("plant foods of the air") as does he. Plant foods of the air consist of leaves, fruit, and seeds. Ego's *veyo* are people who avoid consuming the same bird as does ego, but who avoid consuming different plant foods of the air than does he. Ego's *tabu* are people who avoid consuming different birds than does he.[3] It does not matter whether or not they avoid consuming the same plant foods of the air.

The first-tier categories in the Trobriand kinship classification have to do with the ability to perform wind magic. Wind magic is viewed as very important by Trobrianders because it controls the weather, which in turn controls crop production. As Chief Katubai put it, "By controlling the wind, you can control rain, cloud cover, which affects the heat of the earth, and insect activity."

There are four seasonal winds, each of which has an associated bird whose flesh is thought to consist of condensed energy drawn from that wind. If a person who wants to magically affect the flow of a given seasonal wind has consumed that wind's associated bird, the magic will not work. It fails because the bird's flesh has become incorporated into that person's flesh and, as the magic originates in the person's mind and passes outwards through his body, it travels through his flesh and meets its target there. Then the magic just dissipates and never gets out to the external wind.

As Trobriand neonates are nursed, they all consume the flesh of three of the four birds related to the seasonal winds. This is because mother's milk contains traces of every foodstuff mother ever consumed (including things contained in *her* mother's breast milk). As it happens, all Trobriand women have consumed three out of four of the seasonal wind–related birds. Because eating the bird stops the magic, each living Trobriander can magically alter the flow of only one of the four seasonal winds. However, though individuals differ in terms of which of the four birds they have avoided consuming, the Trobriand population as a whole can possibly use magic to manipulate all four seasonal winds.[4]

I say "possibly" because an individual's ability to actually perform magic to manipulate any seasonal wind is contingent upon more than just dietary avoidance of that wind's associated bird. It is also contingent upon the individual's gender, possession of requisite knowledge, and upon his (because the gender criterion rules out females) dietary avoidance of various types of plant foods of the air. The first-tier categories in the kinship classification ignore the gender and knowledge criteria. But they do include the plant foods of the air criterion.

Trobrianders hold that some, but not all, plant foods of the air thicken the body's substance when humans eat them, making it harder for magic to pass successfully outward through the body. As Toinabuena told me, "Kidamwa bakam kawenua gaga, wowogu bibubutu agu miegava. Mapela gala betei yagina" (If I were to eat the wrong plant-food-of-the-air, my body would blunt my magic. Therefore it would not cut into the wind). Moreover, diet affects the body in a series of gradations. The more kinds of bodily substance–thickening plant foods of the air an individual has consumed, the thicker his bodily substance will be, and the less effective his magic. The fewer kinds of substance-thickening plant foods of the air an individual has consumed, the thinner his bodily substance will be, and the more effective his magic. The result is that the best magicians are the people who have consumed the fewest kinds of the bodily substance–thickening plant foods of the air. The worst are those who have consumed so many kinds of bodily substance–thickening plant foods that they really cannot perform effective magic at all, even if they are the right gender and possess the requisite knowledge.[5]

Trobriand neonates obtain their initial plant foods of the air from mother's milk, just as they do their initial seasonal wind–related birds. This is because, again, mother's milk contains traces of every foodstuff mother has ever consumed.

To summarize, the first tier of kinship categories divides people into *veyotatu,* those who, on the basis of bird consumption avoidance, can magically address the same seasonal wind as can ego and who also, on the basis of not eating plant foods of the air, can affect the flow of that seasonal wind to the same extent as can he; *veyo,* those who, on the basis of not eating certain birds can magically address the same seasonal wind as can ego, but who, on the basis of not eating plant foods of the air, can affect the flow of that wind to a greater or lesser extent than can he; and *tabu,* people who, on the basis of not eating certain birds, cannot magically address the same seasonal wind as can ego. The question whether or not those people can magically affect the flow of their various respective seasonal winds more or less than he can magically affect the flow of his is not covered under the Trobriand kinship classification. Neither are the questions whether or not any people, including ego, are the right gender and/or actually possess the requisite knowledge to perform wind magic.[6]

The Trobriand Kinship Classification: The Second Tier

The second tier of the Trobriand kinship classification sorts people into relational categories based on exchange arrangements. The second-tier kin terms are *mwana, kwava, tama, ina, natu, tuwa, bwada, nuta, kada, keyawa, yawa, yavata,* and *lubou.*

Mwana and *kwava,* Bronislaw Malinowski's "husband" and "wife" (1929: 516), are a man and woman who enter into an exchange arrangement wherein the man agrees to provide the woman with all the raw staple food necessary to keep her alive and healthy. In return, the woman agrees to prepare both the staple food and nonstaple foods which she provides and to serve both of them to the man and to any other members of their household whose presence is agreed upon by both of them.[7] *Tama,* Malinowski's "father" (516), is a man who agrees to provide staple food to a dependent child throughout the child's minority. The child, or *natu,* Malinowski's "child" (516), agrees in return to reimburse the man with all the staple food he grows after he reaches majority.[8] *Ina,* Malinowski's "mother" (515), is a woman who agrees to provide a dependent child with prepared staple and nonstaple foods as the child agrees to provide her with either raw staple food (if the child is a boy) or prepared staple and nonstaple foods (if the child is a girl) during her old age. The reciprocal to *ina* is *natu,* just as it is with *tama.*[9]

Tuwa and *bwada,* Malinowski's "older and younger same sex siblings"

(1929:516), are people of the same sex as ego who owe their minority food debts to the same man as does he and who enter with him into a mutual assistance pact to help one another meet those debts. As Boyomu put it to me, "Bogwa basagali doba. Tuwagu bipilasigu. Teta tama nani" (Soon I will give skirts at a mortuary ceremony. My *tuwa* will help me. Just [because we have] one *tama*). *Nuta,* Malinowski's "opposite sex sibling" (515), is the reciprocal term for a man and a woman who participate in an exchange relationship under which the man provides the woman's death vengeance coverage (to keep her safe from would-be killers) and she, in return, monitors his hearth to ensure that his wife does not serve him any dietarily inappropriate nonstaple foodstuffs.[10] *Kada,* Malinowski's "mother's brother" (516), is the reciprocal term for men who are party to an exchange wherein one confers capital property on the other and the other makes reciprocal payment under a specialized format known as *pokala.*[11] *Keyawa* is the reciprocal term for two men who enter into an arrangement wherein the survivor exacts death vengeance for the one who dies first. *Keyawa* are usually picked from among ego's *veyo.* As Katubai told me, "Veyotatumi bikatumatimu. Gala buena bukudoki keyawamu. Tabumi sena ituwali. Gala bineinei tokatumati. Veyomi gala bikatumatimu. Bineinei tokatumati. Buena bukudoki keyawamu" (Your *veyotatu* will kill you. [So it is] not good to make [a veyotatu] your *keyawa.* Your *tabu* is too different. [So] he will not hunt for [your] killer. Your *veyo* will not kill you. He will hunt for [your] killer. [So] it is good to make [a veyo] your *keyawa*).[12] *Yawa,* Malinowski's "father-in-law" and "mother-in-law" (516), *yavata,* Malinowski's "husband's sister" and "brother's wife" (516), and *lubou,* Malinowski's "wife's brother" and "sister's husband" (516), are people with whom ego has no direct exchange relationship, but people who can significantly affect ego's exchange relationships with either his spouse or his "siblings" because these are people with whom his spouse and siblings have very significant direct exchange relationships. Trobrianders lump these three second-tier terms together as terms for *vevai,* literally "actively marrieds," more colloquially "in-laws."[13]

Relating the First- and Second-Tier Terms

As indicated, the second-tier terms in the Trobriand kinship classification all denote partners to various exchange relationships. Trobrianders sort these (and all other) exchange relationships into three basic types; sharing, one-ended exchanges, and sales and purchase. A sharing exchange is one wherein two people agree to provide one another with something upon demand if they have it to spare.[14] A one-ended exchange is one wherein two people agree to provide one another with something, but only one of them will ever actually receive it from the other. In the kinship instance, the "something" is death vengeance, provided by the survivor to the deceased. A sales and purchase exchange is an arrangement wherein one person agrees to provide the other with a given commodity at a given time and in a given amount, and the other person agrees to reciprocate with another commodity, also at a given time and in a given amount.[15] Additionally, Trobrianders hold that each type of exchange is basically suitable to transactions between people who are related under only one of the three first-tier kinship categories. *Veyotatu* should basically interact through sharing exchanges. *Veyo* should basically interact through one-ended exchanges.[16] And *tabu* should basically interact through sales and purchase exchanges.

As *ina, kada, tuwa,* and *bwada* are all essentially recruited from among ego's *veyotatu,* their exchange relationships all fall into the sharing category. As *keyawa* is always recruited from among ego's *veyo,* their exchange relationship falls into the one-ended exchange category. And as *tama* is recruited from among ego's *tabu,* their exchange relationship falls into the sales and purchase category.

However, there are exceptions. When, as now and then happens, ego's *tama*'s *tama* is one of ego's *veyotatu,* he nonetheless participates with ego in the *tama-natu* arrangement, which is a sales and purchase type of exchange, the type which is basically held to be suitable between first-tier *tabu.* Additionally, ego's *kada*'s wife, who is virtually always one of ego's *tabu,* routinely participates with ego in the *ina-natu* arrangement, which is a sharing type of exchange basically suitable to interactions between *veyotatu.*

The Concept "Relative" and the Trobriand Kinship Classification

This overview of the Trobriand kinship classification is very brief and incomplete, but it does suffice for our present purpose, which is to look at why it is difficult to apply the Western concept, "relative," to the Trobriand kinship system. As we try to apply that concept, we run into two sets of major problems. The first set has to do with the nature of the kinship relationships themselves. The second set has to do with discrepancies between the first- and second-tier relationships. Let us take these in turn.

The First Set of Problems: The Nature of the Kin Relationships

As David Schneider (1968) pointed out in his ethnography of the American kinship system, a "relative" is someone to whom ego is related either by shared bodily substance (traditionally characterized as blood, more recently as biogenetic substance) or marriage. The second-tier Trobriand kinship terms *mwana* and *kwava* do specify partners to an exchange relationship which we can well gloss as "marriage," and, as the terms *yawa, lubou,* and *yavata* specify partners to exchange relationships which flow through marriage, we can also say that they are terms for in-laws. So thus far we do not have any problem applying either the term or the concept of the "relative" to the Trobriand kinship system. But what do we do about the fact that none of the Trobriand kinship terms are constructed around the idea that people share bodily substance? Indeed, what do we do about the fact that Trobrianders explicitly *deny* that people share bodily substance? At this point there is a very significant divergence between the Trobriand and the American kinship systems. It also is the point where using the term "relative" becomes not only inaccurate, but misleading.

Early on in my doctoral fieldwork I caused a group of women to roll on the ground laughing when I suggested that Westerners think that people are related because they share blood. (I did not know any way to couch the words "biogenetic substance" in the Trobriand language, so I had to fall back on tradition.) Finally, one of the women recovered herself enough to gasp out, "No! People are related through mother's milk!" The obviousness of this was sufficient to set the women all off again into another round of, literally, rolling on the ground in laughter.

When they finally managed to calm down, I said, "But Malinowski says that a human fetus is built out of a woman's menstrual blood. So, doesn't it have the same blood as its genetrix?" They explained that it does not because a woman's menstrual blood differs compositionally from her bodily blood. Her menstrual blood is composed solely out of digestively transformed *kanua* "plant foods of the ground" (certain roots, tubers, and corms), while her bodily blood is composed out of every foodstuff she has ever eaten. So the new body which she grows in her womb does not have the same kind of bodily blood as does she. Moreover, while her bodily blood is unique to her because, throughout her lifetime, she has consumed a unique personal diet, the bodily blood of her newborn child is exactly like that of every other newborn child. It only becomes differentiated when the child begins to eat.

The first food that any newborn child routinely ingests is mother's milk. Because mother's milk contains traces of everything that mother has ever consumed, and because, through digestion, mother's milk enters into the newborn child's blood, the newborn child's blood becomes compositionally identical to that of the woman whose breast milk it consumes. The result is that this woman becomes its *veyotatu,* a person who has avoided consuming the same seasonal wind–related bird and same plant foods of the air as has ego. Likewise, all of her *veyotatu, veyo,* and *tabu* also become the child's *veyotatu, veyo,* and *tabu.* In addition, this woman becomes the child's *ina,* someone who provides processed foodstuffs to a dependent child. So now she and the child are related both as *veyotatu* and as *ina* and *natu.*

As we look at this picture and we consider the applicability of the term "relative" to the Trobriand kinship system, we find ourselves saying, "Okay, so Trobrianders don't literally think that mothers and children share bodily blood, but since, through this somewhat more convoluted dietary procedure, mother and child wind up possessing identical bodily blood and are viewed as being related because their bodily substance is the same, why can't we just go ahead and characterize them as 'relatives'?" There are four reasons why we cannot.

First, the newly born child may not be nursed by its genetrix, but by some other woman instead. Then, as the child ingests the other woman's breast milk, the composition of its bodily substance becomes identical to hers, rather than to that of its genetrix. This other woman becomes its *veyotatu,* and her, rather than its genetrix's, *veyotatu, veyo,* and *tabu* become the child's *veyotatu, veyo,* and *tabu.*

Second, even if the newly born child is nursed by its genetrix, it still has a host of *veyotatu* residing on the face of the earth who are not, in our sense, its blood relatives. In part this is due to the fact that, as neonate adoption is not uncommon in the Trobriands, numerous of its *veyotatu* became its *veyotatu* by virtue of its being put to nurse at the breasts of women who were not their genetrixes. In part too, and, indeed, more significantly, it is due to something else: the fact that, ultimately speaking, *veyotatu* do not actually have to have identical bodily substance. The distinctive feature of *veyotatu* really is that they possess the dietarily derived potential to perform seasonal-wind magic on the same wind with the same degree of effectiveness. And this can be the case despite dietary differences between them. Put it this way: while all of ego's *veyotatu* must literally have avoided consuming the same kind of seasonal wind–related bird as he, they do not literally have to have avoided the same combination of plant foods of the air as he. They only have to have avoided a combination which produces human flesh which is of the same thickness or density as his. A number of different combinations will do this. Thus, while the mirthful woman gasped out, "Not blood, milk!" ego's *veyotatu* do not actually even have to have come from his same milk line—a line that, overlooking neonate adoption, we could otherwise equate with our own idea of a genealogical lineage, that is, a line of relatives.

Third, the substantial identity between any two *veyotatu,* including nurse and neonate, is mutable. Either one of them can at any time consume some foodstuff which alters his bodily substance such that is it no longer sufficiently the same as that of the other for them to still be one another's *veyotatu*.[17]

Fourth, while the first-tier Trobriand kinship terms do at least deal in some sorts of physical similarities and differences among people, the second-tier terms do not do that at all. They deal entirely in exchange relationships. Thus we confront the fact that, for example, even if ego's *ina* (Malinowski's "mother") *is* ego's genetrix, she is not ego's *ina* by virtue of *being* ego's genetrix. She is ego's *ina* by virtue of *deciding* to provide the child with processed staple and nonstaple foods. If ego's genetrix never provides ego with processed foods, she never becomes ego's *ina*. Moreover, if, having provided ego with processed foods, she decides to stop doing that at any time during ego's minority, she ceases to be ego's *ina*. As Bosiwosi put the matter, "Gala ina. Besa bogwa aokuva" (Not *ina*. This is already over).[18]

The Second Set of Problems: Discrepancies between the First- and Second-Tier Relationships

The second set of problems has to do with discrepancies between the first and second tiers of kinship categories. Let us suppose that, despite the objections I have already raised, we go ahead and do as Trobriand anthropologists have previously done, and, in terms of the first-tier categories, gloss *veyotatu* as meaning "close relative" or "blood relative," *veyo* as meaning "relative," and *tabu* as meaning "nonrelative." Now let us try and reconcile the two tiers.

At first glance the second-tier terms *ina, kada, tuwa, bwada,* and *nuta* (which Malinowski respectively translated as "mother," "mother's brother," "older same-sex sibling," "younger same-sex sibling," and "opposite-sex sibling"), all appear to be terms for various of ego's *veyotatu,* that is, "close relatives" or "blood relatives." But at second glance this breaks down. Ego's *ina* routinely include father's brother's wife and mother's brother's wife. While father's brother's wife can be one of ego's *veyotatu,* usually she is not. And, of course, mother's brother's wife is never one of ego's *veyotatu.* Ego's *kada* also routinely include men other than mother's brothers, men who usually are not ego's *veyotatu.* This is because men do not just confine capital property transactions utilizing the *pokala* exchange arrangement to interactions between themselves and *veyotatu.* Also, routinely included among ego's *tuwa, bwada,* and *nuta,* are father's brother's children, as well as own siblings and mother's sister's children. While these can be ego's *veyotatu,* usually they are not. So, as we look at these second-tier terms, terms which initially appear to be labels for various kinds of *veyotatu,* that is, "close relatives" or "blood relatives," we find that they also incorporate people who are not in those positions.

If we move on through the list, we encounter other anomalies. Various people are routinely given the second-tier label *tabu*. Included are father's sister, father's mother, mother's mother, and mother's father. Informants all say that, in the second-tier context, the label *tabu* means "someone with whom ego has no kinship relationship." So now we confront the assertion that ego's mother's mother, a first-tier *veyotatu*, that is, "close relative" or "blood relative" is a second-tier "nonrelative."

Then there is *tama* (Malinowski's "father"). At first glance *tama* appears to be a second-tier label for a particular sort of first-tier "nonrelative," since ego's father is virtually always one of ego's first-tier *tabu*. But, again, at second glance, this does not hold up. Ego's paternal grandfather is also labeled *tama* (contrary to Malinowski's report that he was labeled *tabu* along with ego's other grandparents). While usually ego's paternal grandfather is not one of ego's *veyotatu*, he can be, and when he is, he still is labeled *tama*. So now we confront an instance where a second-tier term for a "nonrelative" is also used as a term for a "close relative" or "blood relative."

To summarize, what we have is a considerable mismatch between the first and second tiers if we try to superimpose our ideas about the "relative" onto the Trobriand classification. Some first-tier "close relatives" or "blood relatives" are also what we can call second-tier "close relatives" or "blood relatives." But some are not; witness mother's mother, who is labeled as someone to whom ego has no second-tier kinship relationship. Additionally, some first-tier "nonrelatives" are incorporated under second-tier terms that presumably label "close relatives" or "blood relatives," for example, mother's brother's wife, father's brother's wife, and father's brother's children. And then, one "close relative" or "blood relative," namely paternal grandfather, is classed under a second-tier term that presumably labels a particular sort of first-tier "nonrelative." Thus, as we try to match up the two tiers using the Western idea of the "relative," we create a mishmash. Indeed, we have such a mishmash that we might as well go ahead and call it a mess.

Problems That Have Arisen from Trying to Apply the Term "Relative" to the Trobriand Kinship System

Trobriand anthropologists have always made the a priori assumption that Trobriand kinship is about relatives. And, as they have done this, they have fallen into the ethnocentric trap that David Schneider insistently urged his "Systems" students to avoid, even though Schneider himself did not push his urgings quite so far as to question whether or not it is the case that all kinship systems are about relatives. And that trap has seriously hampered anthropological efforts to comprehend Trobriand social organization.

Our basic picture, from Malinowski on down, is that Trobrianders possess what he called an "exclusively matrilineal" kinship system (1929:4). They possess this kind of kinship system because, not recognizing that semen enters into the construction of the fetus, they think that people are only biologically related through women. The Trobriand father, who Malinowski says should better be construed as "mother's husband," is not one of ego's blood relatives at all. Ego's true male blood relative is ego's mother's brother, and, because of the incest taboos that prevent brother and sister from personal interaction, a man pays his sister's husband to stand in for him as a father figure during ego's minority. Nonetheless, he, and not father, is ego's true authority figure. The pay is Malinowski's famous *uligubu*.

All of this would be fine if any of it were true. But none of it is. First, the kinship classification indicates that, whatever kind of kinship system Trobrianders have, it is not *exclusively* matrilineal. If it were, the classification would uniformly distinguish between matrilineal relatives and others, and it does not do that.[19] Second, whatever form of kinship system Trobrianders have, it is not based on a belief that only women are biologically related to their children. As we have seen, Trobrianders do not base their kinship system at all on the idea of biological relationships. Third, while Trobrianders, when asked to define the term *tama,* do sometimes respond with "*ina*'s husband," when asked to define the term *ina,* they equally often respond with "*tama*'s wife." Fourth, even initial fieldwork, both my own and Annette Weiner's (personal communication), revealed that mother's brother never has any authority over ego, and that, instead, ego's prime authority figure is father. It also revealed that the incest taboos are essentially designed to keep adolescent siblings apart and are relaxed once people marry, such that brother and sister are quite free to interact sufficiently frequently and closely that, if this were a system wherein mother's brother was ego's prime authority figure, mother's brother could directly handle that role. Fifth, my fieldwork revealed that, whatever *uligubu* exchanges are about, they are not about mother's brother paying mother's husband to stand in for him as the child's overseer.[20]

Conclusions

All of these distortions derive from one basic mistake: the attempt to project the Western idea of the relative onto the Trobriand kinship system. And they have basically held up because it was not just Malinowski who engaged in that attempt. Every subsequent Trobriand anthropologist (including Weiner, although to her credit, she does indicate in her writings that father plays as important a role in most people's lives as do matrilineal relatives) has done the same thing (Weiner 1976:21, 154). Indeed, the only reason I did not make the standard assumptions is that I took "Systems" from David Schneider. He went on so about the ethnocentric projection occurring in anthropological kinship studies that, even though he did not question whether or not foreign kinship systems are about relatives, he moved me to wonder about that. And, through Schneider's influence, the results of my Trobriand fieldwork, as set out in my forthcoming book about the Trobriand kinship system, should help to set matters straight—or at least a lot straighter than they have been in the past.

Of course, there are those who have been put off by Schneider's cultural relativism because they see it as threatening anthropology's scientific goal of producing cross-cultural generalizations. It is easy to understand their concern just by looking at this paper. After all, if I am right that kinship systems are about relatives and the Trobriand system that I am describing is not about relatives, on what grounds do I characterize the Trobriand system as a kinship system? And, if it is not a kinship system, how can we compare it with other kinship systems in order to draw cross-cultural generalizations about such systems?

Years ago Edward LiPuma (personal communication) pointed out to me that all of the systems that anthropologists have traditionally characterized as kinship systems have one significant feature in common: they are all arise out of multiple-slotting classifications. That is, they are all centered in relational classifications wherein ego routinely occupies more than one position in relation to others in the system. For instance, under what all Americans, and not just anthropologists, call the American kinship classification, a male ego can simultaneously occupy the slots or positions of son, father, grandson, grandfather, brother, uncle, nephew, cousin, husband, son-in-law, father-in-law, and brother-in-law. Thus that classification is a multiple-slotting classification. And under the Trobriand classification, a male ego can simultaneously occupy the slots *veyotatu, veyo, tabu, natu, tama, tuwa, bwada, nuta, kada, mwana, yawa, lubo,* and *yavata.* So it, too, is a multiple-slotting classification. Given that it is, I have called it the "Trobriand kinship classification." And, using the same logic, I have also called the larger system which centers in it the "Trobriand kinship system."[21]

I am suggesting that the use of different definitional criteria by different cultures to recruit people to relational positions under multiple-slotting classifications is not the crucial point in determining whether or not kinship systems should be said to exist cross-culturally. The crucial point is that every culture we know of does possess (at least) one multiple-slotting classification for relating people, and, in every instance, that classification appears to be at least as central to the organization of social life as the one which we American natives call the "American kinship classification."

If we look at it this way, we certainly formulate cross-cultural generalizations about kinship systems. For instance, we can say immediately that they are a cross-cultural universal. But if we look at it this way, we also confront a series of questions which, to my knowledge, anthropology has not to date addressed. For example, when I put all of the above to my colleague Richard Feinberg, he alertly responded (personal communication), "You seem to say that the Trobriands have a multiple-slotting system, and that this is what differentiates kinship in the Trobriands. But is every multiple-slotting system in the Trobriands (or elsewhere) necessarily a kinship system?" My answer is that, so far as I have been able to determine, this point is moot in terms of both Trobriand and American culture, because both of them seem to contain only one multiple-slotting classification. In American culture it is the one we natives call the "American kinship classification," and in Trobriand culture it is the one that I call the "Trobriand kinship classification." Moreover, none of the cross-cultural ethnographic accounts that I have read have indicated the existence of more than one multiple-slotting classification in any culture. That does not entail that there may not be some cultures in which more than one does exist. This is a point which remains to be determined. Only if exploration reveals that there are cultures which possess more than one do we need to concern ourselves with the question whether or not each should be considered to be a kinship classification (such that we might find ourselves in the novel position of characterizing a given culture as containing more than one kinship system), and the corresponding question, if not, on what grounds is it not?

In the meantime, what my studies of both American and Trobriand culture indicate is that, while both of them seem to contain but one multiple-slotting classification, both contain numerous single-slotting classifications. Indeed, in the American instance, the single-slotting classifications are far too numerous to enumerate as everything from religious to governmental to educational to business establishments are organized through them. In the Trobriand instance, single-slotting classifications are not so numerous, simply because the population is so much smaller than that of America. There are not enough people to set up anything like as many establishments. Nonetheless, single-slotting classifications far outnumber that one multiple-slotting classification and are central to the organization of everything from villages to trade to funerals to the famous Kula.

To me, these facts raise some interesting questions. If, as indicated by the prevalence of their numbers, single-slotting classifications are so widely useful for organizing social life, why do we and Trobrianders each have the one multiple-slotting classification? Why is not the entirety of our social existence just organized through single-slotting classifications? Why, too, is the one multiple-slotting classification as central to our social organization as it is, given that it is far outnumbered by the others? And, finally, how does it interdigitate with the others? My readers were probably not surprised at my assertion that single-slotting classifications far outnumber the one multiple-slotting classification in American culture, but they may have been surprised at my assertion that the same is true in Trobriand culture, because, to date, anthropological accounts of Trobriand culture have basically made it sound like everything is simply organized through the kinship classification. This is a common assertion in ethnographic accounts of nonindustrial cultures in general; but, in the Trobriand case at least, it is not accurate. The Trobriand case is like our own in that a number of single-slotting classifications play a significant organizational role and, as they do, they and their role must somehow interdigitate with the multiple-slotting classification and its role.

In summary, then, I feel fortunate that Schneider advocated relativism in kinship studies in his graduate "Systems" course at the University of Chicago. My subsequent research in the Trobriand Islands was shaped by Schneider's relativism. It also led me to the conclusion that, if anything, his relativism did not go quite far enough.

Notes

I am grateful to the National Institute of Mental Health, the National Endowment for the Humanities, and the Dean's Fund at Northern Illinois University for funding my Trobriand research. I also am grateful to the residents of Kaduwaga Village, the Trobriand Islands, and to all of the other Trobriand Islanders who assisted me in learning their culture. In this essay, all Trobriand words are presented in Kaduwagan dialect because Kaduwagans asked that this be the case in all of my Trobriand writings.

1. Zimmer-Tamakoshi (this volume) makes similar observations with respect to the Gende of highland New Guinea.

2. Malinowski (1929:495–96) and Harry Powell (1953:46) both substitute *kakaveyo*, which they translate as "spurious" or "pseudo-kin," for *veyo*. My informants disagree with this substitution, saying that *kakaveyo* does not allude to *veyo*, but instead alludes to people who, for some reason, are being interactionally construed as if they were *veyotatu*, although they actually are not.

Malinowski (1929:5) and Weiner (1976:53) substitute *tomakava*, which Malinowski defines as "outsider" or "stranger" and Weiner defines as "non-clansperson," for *tabu*. The stem *makava* means "to exist alone," and my informants say that *tomakava* alludes to persons who reside in a village wherein they have no *veyotatu*. They "exists alone" in the sense of not existing alongside of any *veyotatu*. It is usually persons of this sort who are transformed into someone's *kakaveyo*, a person whom someone is treating as if he or she were one of their *veyotatu* even though that is not actually the case.

3. Following Malinowski, there is a tendency for anthropologists to construe the Trobriand kinship system as basically involving three kinds of people: clan members, lineage members, and nonrelatives. Thus the tendency has been to anthropologically construe *veyo* as fellow clan members, *veyotatu* as fellow lineage members, and *tabu* as nonrelatives. However, the first-tier kin terms do not quite sort this way because informants all insist that the category *veyo* does not include *veyotatu*. They say that one's *veyo* are one's *veyo* and one's *veyotatu* are one's *veyotatu*, and that one's *veyo* are different people from one's *veyotatu*.

To make matters worse for the field anthropologist, Trobrianders very commonly elide words in the course of everyday conversation, and they routinely shorten *veyotatu* into *veyo*. Indeed, they do this so commonly that we only came into possession of the term *veyotatu* after its discovery by Annette Weiner. Both Malinowski and Powell before her seem to have missed it, as, so far as I know, did all of her contemporary anthropological fieldworkers, myself included. But, again, questioning reveals that the elision is not intended to incorporate *veyotatu* into the category *veyo*. It is just that most daily conversation is carried out among people who know both one another's *veyo* and *veyotatu*, so that the elision does not cause any categorical confusion on the part of the listener.

4. Trobrianders characterize things they should avoid eating because doing so would negatively alter their bodily makeup as things which are *boma* to them. Thus, Kunuvania, speaking about the birds related to the seasonal winds, said, "Ibomagu bakam ulo manua. Kidamwa bakam gala bigodegu bamigai ulo yagina" (My bird is *boma* to me. If I were to eat [my bird] it would not be possible for me to magically affect my wind).

5. While seasonal wind magic can only be performed by men, this is not true of all forms of Trobriand magic. Many can be performed by adults of either sex. It depends on the intensity of the energy that is mentally created and sent out through the creator's body. Men's bodies are held to be *kasai*, "hard" or "rigid," while women's bodies are held to be *pwapwasa*, "soft" or "squishy"; and strong energy beams are thought likely to disorganize soft or squishy bodily substance as they pass through it, causing either sickness or death. Women do not even like to be in close physical proximity to a man who is performing seasonal wind magic. They are afraid that some of the energy he is emitting will inadvertently pass through their bodies and injure them. Note that the issue of hardness/rigidity versus softness/squishiness is an issue that stands apart from that of the thickness of the individual's bodily substance. Both men's and women's bodily substance varies equally in terms of thickness in accordance with how many bodily substance–thickening plant foods of the air they have either consumed or avoided consuming.

6. Additionally, I have not included a discussion of the terms *dala* (Malinowski's "subclan" or "matrilineage") and *kumila* (Malinowski's "clan"), although it might be thought that they should be included somehow among the first-tier kin terms. The problem is that neither is actually a kinship term at all, nor is either the term for a type of corporate group. *Dala* means "a person's current complete range of mental abilities," and *kumila* means "a person's ability to transform either substance into nonsubstance or nonsubstance into substance." It can be applied to describe a person's ability to use wind magic to grow food (substance) out of seeds (by comparison, nonsubstance).

Trobrianders frequently characterize both *veyotatu* and *veyo* as having the same *dala,* meaning that, owing to dietary bird avoidances, they have the potential mental ability to perform seasonal wind magic to influence the flow of the same seasonal wind. But note that the usage is not literal—it only refers to their having a single mental ability in common, and not that they share their total current ranges of mental abilities. Informants all say that this is fine, because the characterization of any two living people as having "same *dala*" can never be literal, since no two living people possess exactly the same current range of mental abilities. But here we encounter something else as well. In daily conversation, Trobrianders routinely characterize people as having "same *dala*" whenever they are pointing out any mental commonality between them, whether or not it is the wind magic commonality that is treated under the first tier of Trobriand kinship terms and which is the commonality possessed by *veyotatu.* Thus my hostess once said to me, "Susan, you and I have same *dala.* We both know how to swim well."

The term *kumila* is more obscure. I do not mean that its meaning is obscure, but that it is very rarely used conversationally. Indeed, it is used so rarely that I am surprised that Malinowski happened to come up with it at all, much less happened to transform it into his word for "clan." The problem with it is that its direct transformational denotation too overtly alludes to the use of magic, making it dangerous either to speak about an individual's *kumila* or to characterize two or more people as possessing the same *kumila.*

It may seem strange that there is a great deal of danger in speaking too directly about people's magical prowess when the first tier of Trobriand kinship terms all squarely involve discriminations in magical abilities. But indeed the danger is so great that it cannot be overstressed. Note that, as I indicated in the text, the first-tier kinship terms only involve dietary discriminations, such that they only, even implicitly, say that a person could *possibly* perform magic. They omit the knowledge discriminations which would pin down whether or not a person can *actually* perform magic. However, if you stand up and announce that someone has *kumila,* i.e., the ability either to transform substance into nonsubstance or nonsubstance into substance, you implicitly also say that the person can perform magic, because there is no other way that a person can do either of these things. Therefore, no one ever talks about other people in terms of *kumila.* Even if they did, they would not talk about *veyo* as a group of people who possess same *kumila,* because *veyo* are a collection of people who run the gamut on plant foods of the air variation, which means that, while some of them have the same potential magical abilities, others among them do not.

Finally, note that, as Malinowski translated *kumila* as "clan" and *dala* as "sub-clan" or "matrilineage," anthropologists have viewed *kumila* as the more inclusive of the two terms. Actually the reverse is the case. *Dala* denotes a person's complete current range of mental abilities, while *kumila* focuses on a specific one among them.

7. While, in the West, marriage legitimizes sexual relations between the couple, it does not do that in the Trobriands. As Malinowski indicated long ago, premarital sex is the approved norm there. Malinowski also indicated that divorce is easy to obtain in the Trobriands, but he did not say how it is done. To obtain a divorce one or the other of the marital partners goes to the hearth, picks up the pots, pans, and dishes, and throws them out the front door of the connubial house. As they land in the street, notice is served to one and all that the partner who threw them is no longer going to abide by the food and cooking agreement that constitutes marriage. So the marriage is over.

8. Female children agree to reimburse with all of the *doba* ("fiber skirts") and *nunuga* ("fiber bundles"), they manufacture after they reach majority. However this repayment is forgiven once a woman undergoes pregnancy. As most women undergo at least one pregnancy, the most frequent observation of female indebtedness to *tama* lies in the practice of giving skirts and bundles in his name at mortuary observances. As Itagoma put it, "Tamagu lesakaigu kagu. Uula basagali yagana" (My *tama* gave me my [staple] food. [That is the] reason why I will give things at mortuary observances [in] his name).

9. Trobriand widows often complain that their children, particularly their sons, do not adequately honor their side of this arrangement. Part of the problem lies in disputes between widow and son as to just how much food the widow needs. Widows have food income from mortuary presentations of skirts and fiber bundles. The widows always tell their sons that this income is low; the sons always claim that their mothers are lying and that, in fact, it is high.

10. When a man marries, his wife must learn the intricacies of his dietary avoidances. Trobrianders use the English loan word, and say that for the first year of the marriage the wife is in *trainini* under her mother-in-law. But after that, the mother-in-law basically drops out of the picture and is replaced by a woman of the wife's own generation, usually a woman who grew up in the same household as did the husband. This woman drops in on the married couple periodically to see that the wife is only cooking and serving appropriate plant foods of the air to the husband. These visits can easily become points of friction if the two women do not get along because, if they do not, the husband's *nuta* is apt to appropriate various of the wife's belongings for her own despite the wife's objections. Then, as a quarrel breaks out, both women appeal to the husband to resolve the matter. Caught in the middle, he loses either way. Numerous men told me that the most important consideration in choosing a spouse is to make sure that one's potential wife and one's *nuta* like each other. As one man put it, "Kidamwa gala bitagwanasi mu kwava numta, momova gaga nani" (If your wife [and] your *nuta* don't get along, life is just bad).

11. *Pokala* is an arrangement whereby a man accepts nonbinding payments from another man or men who want a specific piece of his capital property. The payments are nonbinding in that his acceptance of them does not mandate that he reciprocate with the property. Informants say that the payments are only intended to make the man look favorably on the seeker(s) of his property. Nonetheless, most men do not alienate capital property during their lifetimes unless the amount of *pokala* they have received for it constitutes a good purchase price.

12. More literally, "It is not good that you should think him your *keyawa*." In most speech contexts, the word *doki* parallels the English word "think," but it also is fairly frequently used where English speakers would commonly substitute "make into."

13. Malinowski suggested that, as the Trobriand kinship system is exclusively matrilineal, Trobrianders essentially construe *tama* as an in-law. However, my informants unanimously disagreed, saying that *vevai* are restricted to *yawa, yavata,* and *lubou,* and that *tama* is *tama nani,* "just *tama.*"

14. To my knowledge there is no monolexemic term in the Trobriand language for "sharing." When speaking about it people just say that two people agree that whatever one has the other can have if the first has it to spare.

15. In the nonkinship context, a sales and purchase exchange is called *gimwala.* But

informants say that it is more polite not to use that term for it in the kinship context. The result is that, in the kinship context, they refrain from naming it at all.

16. An interesting consequence of this is that *veyo* very rarely transact with one another. I only stumbled onto this fact when my hostess, Itagoma, said that her husband wanted to send their son to high school on the next island, but there was the problem of where he would live. I said, "Well, you may not have any *veyotatu* residing near the school, but you must have some *veyo*. Wouldn't one of them board your son?" She looked aghast and said, "Susan! The last people who would board my son would be *veyo!*"

17. Weiner characterizes *veyotatu* as same *dala* (Malinowski's "sub-clan") people and insists that a person's *dala* identity is immutable. I too thought that this was the case until, as it happened, one day wailing broke out in the village. Everyone around me started running toward the house from whose porch the sound was coming. I joined in and, as I ran, I asked, "Who died?" The answer was, "No one. Two men have just repudiated their common *dala* identity. Come on!" It turned out that the two men had been quarreling for months and had decided that, as they could not get along, they must have eaten sufficiently different foods that they were no longer the same kind of person. The woman who was out on the porch wailing was announcing the "death" of their status as one another's *veyotatu*. Shared blood is not mutable, but dietary commonality certainly is.

18. One of the ways in which the Trobriand kinship system differs from all of the Western kinship systems of my acquaintance is that it is an entirely postnatal construct. A newborn child is not related to its genetrix as a kinsperson, but rather as property (*guguwa*). The genetrix of a newborn child is termed *toliguadi* "child owner." Informants are explicit that, just as yams are men's property because men do the bulk of the work of growing them, so children are women's property because women do the bulk of the work of growing them. Children only enter into the kinship system when they are orally fed after birth.

Because the neonate is the property of the woman who produced it, she has the right to dispose of it at will. She can refuse to feed it, in which case it dies. She can feed it herself. Or she can give it away to some other woman to feed. In the first instance, the child disappears without ever entering the kinship system. In the second two instances it enters the kinship system. As it does, it ceases to be its genetrix's, or anyone else's, property. This, informants say, is because the moment the neonate consumes food, it becomes a person and people do not own people.

19. Ward Goodenough (personal communication) has pointed out to me that it is not uncommon—indeed it is routine—for matrilineal kinship systems to have somewhat bilateral kinship classifications. However, to my knowledge, none of the others has been claimed to be "*exclusively* matrilineal," the claim that Malinowski advanced for the Trobriand kinship system.

20. Saying what *uligubu* exchanges are about is a bit tricky, because the term *uligubu* is a commodity label rather than an exchange label. *Uligubu* equals the amount of yams grown on a single garden plot. So when someone says that he is giving *uligubu* to someone else, all he is saying is that, for whatever reason and under whatever exchange arrangement, he is giving that person a garden-plot's worth of yams. Nonetheless, my informants were unanimous that no man gives *uligubu* to his (in Malinowski's sense) sister's husband in order to retain rights in his sister's children. Some informants suggested that

perhaps what Malinowski mistook for this sort of thing is the common practice wherein a man gives his sister's husband *uligubu* in exchange for a *kula* shell. A single shell is worth enough in yams that it takes most men several years worth of *uligubu* payments to purchase one. The danger is that if a man contracts to buy one and makes those payments and, at the end, the seller reneges on the shell, the man is out a great deal of irretrievable wealth. To hedge against this eventuality, most men only contract to buy shells from a sister's husband because, if a sister's husband reneges on the shell, the wife's brother can threaten to cancel his sister's and sister's children's death vengeance. If that is cancelled, the wife will leave her husband and take her children with her.

21. My point here parallels Read's assertion (this volume) that all cultures possess a means to calculate relationships among multiple individuals through recursive use of a few basic relationships.

References Cited

Malinowski, Bronislaw. 1929. *The Sexual Life of Savages in Western Melanesia.* New York: Harcourt Brace and World.

Montague, Susan. n.d. "Trobriand Kinship." Ms.

Powell, Harry. 1953. "Trobriand Social Structure." Ph.D. dissertation, London School of Economics.

Schneider, David M. 1968. *American Kinship: A Cultural Account.* Chicago: University of Chicago Press.

Weiner, Annette. 1976. *Women of Value, Men of Renown.* Austin: University of Texas Press.

8. Development and Ancestral Gerrymandering: Schneider in Papua New Guinea

LAURA ZIMMER-TAMAKOSHI

DAVID SCHNEIDER has argued that there is no such thing as kinship, and has described the notion that kinship may be used as an idiom as "sheer nonsense" (1972:59, 1984:vii). According to Schneider, the use of a genealogical grid as an organizing principle may or may not be part of a society's system of symbols and meanings, its culture. And, where kinship does provide a model of relatedness, it is an empirical question whether or not physical reproduction (or engendering) is a primary meaning of kinship, or whether relatedness can be achieved in other equally important or more important ways (1984:200–201). This chapter demonstrates the usefulness of Schneider's arguments against kinship as a necessarily privileged system in non-Western societies by examining the case of Gende claimants to land ownership at the Kurumbukare mining prospect in Papua New Guinea. This case shows the confusions that arise when claimants adopt narrowly defined, Western "descent" principles to back up land compensation claims that might be legally contested.

Ancestral gerrymandering, or the production and maintenance of ancestors through funeral payments (*kwiagi*) and pig feasts, is an old Gende custom. Contributors to a *kwiagi* are often biological descendants of the deceased. Affines and unrelated persons, however, may also contribute with the idea of obtaining the deceased's land rights as well as ancestral protection and other benefits the deceased may bestow upon their new, self-designated and highly generative descendants. Though the rhetoric surrounding these rites uses reciprocal kin terms such as "parent/child," "father/son," and "uncle/nephew," the meanings of the terms are not focused solely on biological relationships. Rather, the meanings stress the caring and exchange that exists between the two reciprocals, without which—biology notwithstanding—there can be no viable or positive relationship. Thus, for compensation to be given on the basis of biological descent alone would be an injustice for the Gende, in whose system a biological child who does not reciprocate the care and investments of his or her parents is "no child at all" and distantly related (or unrelated) persons can legitimately create relationships modeled on ideal, reciprocal kin relations with both living and deceased persons, including relationships with "ancestral" landowners. This system, however, is being challenged as some few Gende and other claimants at Kurumbukare—conscious of Western judgments on such matters and, perhaps, not up to par in their own reciprocal relations—are tinkering with their cultures in efforts to validate their competing claims for compensation in a situation of unusual economic opportunity (and uncertainty) by asserting that biological ties are more relevant in a modern or global context than reciprocity and traditional exchange. This case portends that future studies of kinship development will emphasize kinship's empirical uses, in particular the economic and political contexts in which biological relatedness becomes, contrary to traditional practice, a potentially key factor.

Gende "Kinship"

My long-term fieldwork with a group of Papua New Guinea highlanders known as the Gende (also known as "Bundis") supports David Schneider's contentions that (1) the use of a genealogical grid as an organizing principle may or may not be part of a society's culture, and (2) that even where kinship provides a model of relatedness, it is an empirical question whether physical reproduction is a primary meaning of kinship or whether relatedness can be achieved in other ways (Schneider 1984:200–201). On the surface, the Gende are a typical patrilineal society, with named clan and lineage divisions and bifurcate merging kinship terminology. Descent groups—known as *narawa,* meaning "line" or "rope"—are modeled on lines of male ancestors and their male and female children, all of whom are expected to defend, if not use, jointly and contiguously held lands. During the early years of my fieldwork in the 1980s, Gende clans appeared fairly stable, with long-term genealogies and origin stories telling how they came to settle in their present locations, and only minor shifting of clan alliances among individuals and lineages. One of the lineages of the clan with which I was most closely associated, for example, had joined Tundega clan for political and economic reasons, forging alliances during the last major stint of interclan warfare, just prior to European contact in 1932. In other instances, clans that had become overpopulated simply split by permitting intermarriage between major lineages. Sometimes these changes were accompanied with name changes, but just as often they were not; old lineage names became new clan names, and the set of "new clans" maintained the old clan name for their confederation. In view of my initial reactions to the wholesale name changes and ancestral gerrymandering that I witnessed during recent visits to Kurumbukare, which I will discuss shortly, it is significant that for at least fifty years—from the time of first contact with German missionaries in 1932 to my arrival in 1982 and after—there existed a nearly complete consistency in clan names and village and hamlet locations (see Aufenanger 1979 [1940]). It is also worth noting, however, that this consistency was very likely a postcontact phenomenon; it certainly does not reflect a more distant past in which no one interfered in Gende affairs and the Gende's ancestors migrated into the region from the more densely populated Eastern Highlands. This migration was—according to different Gende accounts—accomplished over a long period of time in many small steps, through sparsely or unpopulated areas, and by many small groups and individuals.

According to the Gende's cultural memory, Gende kin relations have always been enacted within an intricate web of marriage, life course, and other reciprocal exchange ties. The basic model, however, is simple. "Parents"—who may be one's biological parents, members of one's father's, and sometimes mother's, clan, or even persons who claim no biological connection—look after "children," investing pigs and other forms of wealth in their upbringing, in male and female initiations, in marriages, and in their general well-being. Often, the mother's and father's sides compete to invest the most in a child. While this competition is usually friendly, and is often suspended in the case of a couple's younger children, pressure is on the father's side to be the most giving lest the father's *narawa* be seen as stingy, weak, or insulting to the child's mother and her clan. Failure to give enough is taken to indicate lack of respect and may lead the mother's (or some other) clan to claim the child as one of their own. Adult "children" are expected to reciprocate their parents' investments by supporting their parents' political and social ambitions, taking care of them when they are old, and properly mourning their deaths and passage into the afterlife with suitably large feasts and other sacrifices. Again, young men and women are expected to be generous in paying back their mothers' kin for any previous investments in them (such as those made in male and female initiation ceremonies), thereby upholding the honor of their own lineages and patriclans.

While one's biological parents may contribute the most to one's nurturance and upbringing, it is neither uncommon nor unexpected for other

relatives—or persons seeking to establish themselves as one's "relatives"—
to make equal or even bigger contributions. Socially and politically ambitious
men and women make a practice of investing in their own, their siblings',
and other people's children, both in and outside of their patriclans. Kin
groups wax and wane, in part as a result of such Big Men and Women keeping the agnatic cores of their groups strong by affiliating individuals from
weaker *narawa*. Regardless of who an individual's biological parents are, then,
whoever is (or are) significantly more nurturing assumes the role of "true
parent(s)" in an individual's life. The reverse is also true, with a "true child"
being one who does what is expected for his or her "parents" (biological or
otherwise). In the past, in a context of migrations, conflicts over land, and
endemic warfare, efforts to maintain group size and the affiliation of strong
and reliable young men and women were undoubtedly crucial to a group's
success. In today's context of dramatic economic change and inequality, in
which local development is wildly unpredictable and long in coming, and in
which many local entrepreneurs and migrants fail to achieve their economic goals and forfeit on exchange debts to "parents," many children are edged
out of secure kinship positions by more prosperous villagers and migrants
who take their place in the affections and strategies of their parents as "good"
or "better children," receiving village lands and brideprice support once intended for the now dispossessed "bad" or "false" children.

A measure of the seriousness of the situation is the marked bacheloriza-
tion of Gende society, along with an increase in the number of Gende wom-
en marrying wealthier, non-Gende men (Zimmer-Tamakoshi 1993). This is
the reverse of the situation occurring in other areas in Papua New Guinea,
where active mining development and local wealth of often fantastic propor-
tions has lured women from poorer areas, seeking to marry wealthy husbands
(see Jorgensen 1993). While some bachelors live on the periphery of village
society, eking out an existence helping other men's wives in their gardens,
most prefer urban migration with all the risks that entails.

One major risk is failure to find a job lucrative enough to permit continued investment in village affairs, a situation which raises the possibility that
one may lose one's reciprocal kin status entirely and not be welcome back
into the village under any circumstances. Dispossessions and demotions are,
however, rarely so irrevocable. Should fortunes change, one may once again
invest in working kin relationships (Zimmer 1987, 1990). And the Gende,
disturbed by the social turmoil inequality has caused, long ago innovated a
very active card-playing exchange system in which wealthier villagers (and
visiting migrants) encourage other villagers to play, with the outcome that
some money is redistributed throughout the more general population. This

eases some of the inequality and social tension that exists within families, between husbands and wives, and even between groups (Zimmer 1986).

For the most part, at least during the past sixty or so years, these dispossessions, repossessions, and hyperpossessions have occurred within as opposed to between clans.[1] It does happen, however, that some people shift allegiance from one clan to another or that an unusually ambitious individual develops an extensive network of "parents" and "children" involving many clans. Examples include children becoming members of their mothers' clans when their fathers' people do not pay expected bride- and child-wealth payments or fail to give sufficient support to growing children. Sometimes adult males also shift their allegiance and support to other clans in order to get better deals (including land rights) for themselves.

Clan-shifting, and even shifting allegiance from one "father" to another within the same clan, is a serious occurrence, which often leaves bad feelings in its wake. A rejected "father," for example, experiences deep shame for his apparent inability to "father" (i.e., to nurture or support) children of the *narawa*. While Gende do make such choices, they are not "optative" in the same way as for nonunilinear descent systems where "one may claim affiliation with as many descent categories as he has identifiable ancestors" (Feinberg 1990:86) because the ideal of patriliny remains strong among the Gende. This patrilineal ideal is less a matter of strict genealogical reckoning than it is a commitment to the notion of "male strength." Thus, when a man's (or an entire clan's) children are more beholden to another "father" (or clan) than to him (or them), his (or their) sense of maleness is attacked.

When Big Men attract non–clan members into their fold, these newcomers are often from weaker groups. They are sometimes orphans, or the children of sisters whose husbands have died or whose clans do not have sufficient land and other resources to support the families and adult children. Big Men's greater contributions to the exchanges and affairs of other groups assert their power and influence over others at the same time that such contributions and takeovers may stimulate the "losers" to decide to somehow redeem their honor, fortunes, and "children" in the future.

Another illustration of the Gende's continuing fidelity to a patrilineal ideal as well as their willingness to manipulate to their advantage the flexibility inherent in their exchange system is the case of men and women living at the Gende settlement of Okiufa on the outskirts of the Eastern Highlands town of Goroka (see Zimmer-Tamakoshi 1998). The settlement at Okiufa is composed of a core of migrant families related matrilaterally. In existence for several generations, Okiufa is a rare safe haven for Gende migrants to raise children, send them to urban schools, make the most of husbands' small to moderate incomes, and live without constant fear of attack from rascals and other urban ills.

In charge of this settlement and its daily affairs is a core group of women and their brothers from two closely related Gende villages. These leaders siphon carefully saved income back to their clans, thereby strengthening their kin ties, rights to village lands, and rural option. While women play a prominent role in Okiufa's social life, the community is not matrilineal. The men of Okiufa, especially husbands who are from other villages and other clans than the core leaders' groups, work hard to support their own patriclans and are more apt to support and bring clan brothers' children to town for educational purposes than they are sisters' children. Women divide their giving between their own and their husbands' clans because they feel that this strengthens their position in urban settings, which, in Papua New Guinea, are not normally friendly to female interests. By maintaining their clan ties, women may be able to escape bad husbands by turning to their brothers in town or returning to their own patrilineal lands. Like the women in the *wok meri* groups studied by Lorraine Sexton, Gende women at Okiufa are demonstrating how to make the best of modern economic opportunities and pitfalls without at the same time actually changing the structure of their society (see Sexton 1982; 1986).[2]

Ancestral Gerrymandering

I had many times witnessed strategizing similar to that of the women at Okiufa on past visits to the Gende. I was, nonetheless, caught off guard by the wholesale "ancestral gerrymandering" that I found going on at the proposed Kurumbukare mine site in the mountainous rain forest to the north of the Gende's main garden and living areas, when I went there in 1995 to do a landowners-genealogical survey for Highlands Gold (see Zimmer-Tamakoshi 1997a, 1997c) and on a revisit in 2000. On reflection, it appears that being hired by the company biased me, at least initially, toward a relatively rigid, Western biological view of kinship. Still more significant and interesting, the Gende, knowing full well that I understood their traditional mechanisms of land tenure and kin relations nevertheless wanted my genealogical report to reflect a Western view of kinship. Certainly the company would have preferred a solid, familiar ground on which to judge who should or should not receive compensation payments. And, as is obvious now, the Gende wanted to give the company something they could work with. Any amnesia on my part, however, was not to be. Although the company sought to discover who were the "real landowners" of particular parcels of land in the vicinity of the proposed mine and its various operations, and saw my task as collecting "complete and true" genealogical, historical, and origin-myth data to support the claims of discrete *descent* groups, what my Gende informants were telling me jarringly contradicted my earlier genealogical renderings of their social groupings. The new renditions were, for the most part, mutually consistent, however, thus suggesting wholesale cooperation in the re-creation of Gende society.

Kurumbukare is located in a lush, rain-forest area, formerly populated by a few old caretakers (known as *waspapa* in pidgin English) and the occasional group of hunters and male initiates from the surrounding five language groups, of which the Gende are but one. It is the site of a proposed chromite and cobalt-nickel mine and camp that has attracted, in recent years, many hundreds of representatives; and families come to stake their claims to the land with an eye to future compensation payments. Many of these claims are based on assertions that the ancestors of the contemporary claimants had settled the region in and around Kurumbukare long ago, with subsequent generations moving up into the highlands and leaving behind *waspapa* "watchmen" to guard such resources as wild fruits, good fishing and hunting locations, and grave sites. Unfortunately (or fortunately as the case may be), almost all of these *waspapa* have long since died. Muddying the picture considerably, individuals and groups who allegedly stayed behind to guard the lands at Kurumbukare entered into many strategic and often-shifting alliances with different members of the five surrounding language groups. In the process, they allocated land or hunting and collecting rights indiscriminately to increase the size of local settlements or to marry into more powerful clans. As a result, discovering who today's "real landowners" are, even if one could capture the past in movies or in written documents, would prove to be a difficult if not an impossible task, as the company should have known from the experiences of mining and resource development operations elsewhere in Papua New Guinea (see Hyndman 1994; Kirsch 1997; Wesley-Smith 1992).

Realizing that more was going on than was meant to meet the eye, and slowly beginning to think like a Gende again, I saw my own work plans expand to include not only the passive collection of clan genealogies among the claimants (Gende and non-Gende alike) at Kurumbukare, but also to uncover the motivations and principles at work among the different factions as they so obviously strove to legitimate and, to a large extent, coordinate their particular claims. It was expected by all concerned that these claims might eventually be contested in a court of law, and that the principles that would count for the most in the judge's eyes would be biological "kinship" and principles of patrilineal descent and inheritance of land narrowly defined. Such a high degree of flexibility in "kinship" and land tenure as is demonstrated in my work with the Gende is not commonly recognized in other parts of Papua New Guinea, although researchers familiar with the "chaos" of land claims at other development sites are beginning to recognize similarities to the Gende phenomenon. What was becoming obvious to me was the desire on the part of most claimants at Kurumbukare (both Gende and, to a slightly lesser degree, non-Gende) to work out a genealogical picture that would include the largest number of claimants, thereby reducing conflicts over who will receive compensation and giving the company a conceptual system that it could handle. The Gende and others at Kurumbukare are well aware that foreign companies have withdrawn from Papua New Guinea because of landowner conflicts, and they wanted to ensure that they did not drive the company away.

Without going into all the details of my landowners' survey, the most interesting discovery I made was that the Gende's conception of kinship—their model of relatedness—was more fluid and loosely related to physical reproduction (i.e., reproduction as Westerners conceive of it) than even I had suspected in over six years' field research with them. Imagine my surprise—and initial cynicism—when people I had known from the beginning of my research in 1982 and 1983 as belonging to particular clans, now claimed they belonged to entirely different clans—indeed, ones I had never even heard of. There were, for example, many persons at Kurumbukare who came from Yandera village, the site of much of my fieldwork, and home of two major Gende clans, Tundega and Yandima. At Kurumbukare, however, members of Tundega and Yandima clans claimed to be members of entirely different clans. These clans had allegedly settled long ago at Kurumbukare as the Gende's ancestors moved from one part of the Eastern Highlands area near what is now the town of Goroka into the Ramu and Kurumbukare areas and—in the case of all save a few loners and *waspapa*—from thence on up into the main population areas in the highlands above Kurumbukare. When I pressed for details of this transformation in clan membership, my informants were vague or hostile, some suggesting that I had been confused during my earlier fieldwork and misunderstood them. Some claimed that it was their wives who were really members of Tundega or Yandima clans and not they, the men. If that were so, however, a majority of men in Yandera village would have been living uxorilocally, that is, with their wives' people. That, however, was not the case. I knew it. And they knew it.

At first, it seemed I was being asked by my informants at Kurumbukare to participate in a big lie. In fact, the majority of Gende claimants were acting quite reasonably. Many must have shaken their heads with worry and frustration at my obtuseness and the possibility that I would blow everything by suggesting to the company that they did not belong to the clans in which they were now claiming membership. Somewhat ironically, as I learned at the end of my survey from company personnel, it was individuals from Yandera village who had been the strongest supporters for my being asked to do the genealogical survey in the first place, because, as they put it, "she knows our ways."

Working "Kin" Relations

Throughout my study, I was aware that most of the claimants at Kurum-bukare were dealing with one another, negotiating relationships and alliances with one another, in hopes of huge compensation payments but in uneasy anticipation of the possibility of protracted court hearings to prove their claims. After every interview I conducted, the interviewees would be sur-rounded by others who would grill them about my questions and their an-swers. I know this because I was told so by a number of different individu-als, including my local research assistant, and often the people made little effort to hide these negotiations and conferences from me. There were a few oddballs and trouble-makers, of course, including one old man, a former aid-post orderly from the area, who claimed the entire area as his own, having allegedly inherited it from a lone, long dead and allegedly childless *waspapa* who had adopted him when he was a boy. Another was the local assistant the company had assigned to me, who also was in the process of developing a "lone, adopted child" relationship to one of the (conveniently) deceased *waspapa* of the area. At the conclusion of the research, this assistant told company officials that my genealogies were "useless" and full of lies, and that he alone was heir to the vast tracts of rain forest in question. At the time, the company chose to accept my version of events at Kurumbukare, there being little doubt all hell would break loose between the larger community and the company if a sole claimant were taken seriously.

For the most part, however, Gende claimants at Kurumbukare were rely-ing on time-honored mechanisms to create stronger ties to one another and to the land in question. One important mechanism for transferring land rights is known as *kwiagi*, postmortuary ceremonies and exchanges gener-ally hosted by the deceased's closest kin, who pay off the deceased's debts and then acquire "ownership" of the land once used by the deceased. The rela-tionship does not end there, however, because the new landowners must regularly sacrifice pigs in honor of their ancestors at important exchange events in the coming years. While land rights generally pass from fathers to sons, daughters who also contribute to *kwiagi* and other exchanges with their fathers' people may also obtain similar rights for themselves or their children. Indeed, all those interested in obtaining land rights may invest heavily in the *kwiagi*, thereby establishing themselves as the rightful heirs. In other words, one can retrospectively establish and maintain a relationship with the deceased, even a "kinship" relationship.

It soon enough became apparent to me that the claimants at Kurumbukare were doing just that and more: they were holding *kwiagi* in honor of deceased *waspapa* and more desirable clan ancestors; they were also establishing closer relations with one another through artful clan re-creations and marriages with non-Gende clans who were also claiming land. I began to grasp this more clearly when I both observed a *kwiagi* attended by members of different clans and language groups in one of the settlements at Kurumbukare and when I thought back on one *kwiagi* I had attended long before, in 1982, during my first year of fieldwork. That earlier *kwiagi* was then hailed as a "retirement party" for the oldest and most powerful Big Man in Yandera village. The old leader, head of Yandima clan and the father of many prosperous sons, some living in Yandera and others in town, held a party inviting everyone in the village and beyond. The party was held to announce his departure for his wife's village, which was much closer to Kurumbukare. There he planned to retire from political leadership of Yandera and to promote his family's interests in his wife's clan territory. Prospectors had explored the area off and on for years, and there had been several landowner surveys, the initial one carried out by anthropologist Peter Lawrence. In 1983, there was renewed speculation (premature, as it turned out) that a mine was soon to open at Kurumbukare. The old leader's wife's group was much smaller than Yandima clan. Thus, it was easy for the old Big Man to move in and establish, through the first and subsequent *kwiagi* and the continuing economic support of his sons, substantial land claims and kin relations that his sons were now taking full advantage of, presenting themselves to me and to the company as members of the local land-owning clan.

Well, I thought, all of this is legitimate in Gende terms. If they want to burn their bridges behind them and leave Yandera village to their wives' relatives or someone else in order to align themselves more closely to the proposed Kurumbukare mine site, so be it. David Schneider's soulmates walk the Bismarck mountains and Ramu foothills and plains! Old "kin" relations can be exchanged for new as long as the appropriate exchanges are made and there are few or relatively weak contenders for particular ancestral ties. One thing kept niggling at the back of my mind, however: What about Yandera? Yandera, even more than Kurumbukare, had for years been the location of intensive mining interest as one team of geologists after another probed for rich copper and gold deposits. To complicate matters for the Kurumbukare new-comers, word leaked out in the summer of 1995 from company personnel that the Yandera prospect, then owned by the same company, might be an even richer site than Kurumbukare. So, while I was carrying out my survey of the different settlements at Kurumbukare, members of groups I had already can-vassed would head off to the higher mountains behind us, returning home to Yandera or nearby villages to reassert their claims in those areas. Rather perversely, I imagined their consternation should I, after completing my surveys at Kurumbukare, be called to Yandera to do a genealogical/landowner survey there.

It was difficult to imagine what the Gende would do if both mines went into operation and it became necessary to prove their descent, or legitimate relationship with ancestors, in two separate clans to outsiders used to the notion that patrilineal descent is both unilineal and singular. Based on what I had observed at Kurumbukare, however, it seemed that among the Gende, it was possible to belong to more than one "patrilineal clan" at the same time, and that the only people who were likely to be surprised at this are we West-erners who tend to think of kinship and clans in terms of biological repro-duction.[3] Even when we accept the notion that kinship is negotiable—as in adoption or artificial insemination or other reproductive strategies involv-ing several persons—it seems necessary that the child belong to one small family and not several. As I now see it, the most serious problem for the Gende and their neighbors is not so much having to convince a Western-style court of the cultural legitimacy of their claims to land at Kurumbukare and Yan-dera. The court after all can read my report.[4] The Gende's major problem will be how to afford the doubling, or possibly tripling, of "kinship" obliga-tions that they are setting into operation. While they are hoping for big pay-offs from the mining company, the system in which they are operating has a way of expanding outward. There will be many challenges and *kwiagi* as other claimants, those now living further out from the main centers of likely de-velopment, move in to assert their "rights," their "kin" claims to compensa-tion. Such a process has already begun at other mine sites in Papua New Guinea, Porgera being one of the more dramatic examples.

In light of all this, it may be tempting for the company and any future judges to consider the claims of lone persons as less expensive in the long run. But given the Gende's way of settling disputes, this choice would be unten-able if not outright dangerous. Threats have been made against the old claim-ant's life, for example, and he and his sons are afraid to come close to Ku-rumbukare, preferring to press their claims from Port Moresby in interviews with the company and with me as I was preparing to return to America.

Conclusion

That one can create reciprocal "kin" relations with persons long dead, and that one can do so with several different sets of "ancestors" is enough to make one's head spin. It also makes one wonder about the possibility of cross-cultural comparison and the limits of cultural relativism. While their situations are not as dramatic, there are other New Guinea societies like the Gende, whose "kin" relations vary and multiply depending on how many opportunities there are and how persistent and capable individuals are of playing out the possibilities (see, e.g., Cook 1970, 1980; Feil 1984; Sillitoe 1979; Strathern 1971, 1976). It is, for example, a common practice among New Guinea Big Men to expand their networks by acquiring followers and "kin" from other clans. Similarly, Susan P. Montague (this volume) suggests that biogenetic definitions are inadequate to account for Trobriand understandings of "kinship." In what she calls a two-tier kinship system, ego's "mother" (*ina*) is not the "mother" by virtue of being ego's genetrix. Rather, she is ego's "mother" by virtue of providing the child with food. In other words, she is *ina* to a child by virtue of being in an exchange relationship with that child. Should the woman cease to provide food for a child at any time during its minority, the woman ceases to be that child's *ina*.

We do not have to leave the Pacific to locate other, equally interesting comparisons (and contrasts). Although the kinship principles vary, the ambilineal societies of Polynesia afford individuals flexibility of group membership as well as the potential for tracing out and combining different prestigious lines of descent for the politically ambitious. Examples abound where "kinship" is adapted to the economic, social, and political needs of the people, or, if we want to focus on the "politics of culture," at least some of the people in a particular society (Franco 1993; Tiffany 1974). A question for comparison is the degree to which biology does or does not matter in the ideologies and practices of individuals within particular cultures.[5]

Turning to the question of the limits of cultural relativism: The Gende's cultural logic is certainly legitimate to them, and it is possible for outsiders to understand and respect that logic, but can ancestral gerrymandering be carried too far? Even for the Gende? I have already noted the difficulty of being able to support compounding "kin" ties in connection with every profitable land base, such as the Kurumbukare and Yandera mining prospects—the Gende understand the concept of credit! But is there a multinational company in good economic standing in the global economy that can afford to play out the game of compounding relationships as far as the Gende and their neighbors seem prepared to go? Or will the Gende ultimately be forced by foreign companies to modify their conceptions of "kinship" and land ownership principles so as to be more in keeping with the West if they are to develop their lands and derive the income that they very much want— and need, if one considers the net loss of women to wealthier non-Gende groups (see Zimmer-Tamakoshi 1993)? It is significant that the company who hired me to do the landowners survey, Highlands Gold, has since withdrawn from the project and that a new company, required by law to do the usual impact assessments and genealogical surveys, apparently found it useful not to include an anthropologist on their assessment team. Who wants to know about these funky "kinship" systems? On the other hand, most Gende (and, need I suggest, the Gende's ancestors?) seem committed to working out a deal that will benefit the most people. Therein lies an impasse in modern development between local value systems and the values and beliefs of foreign managers of capitalist enterprises.

Does biological kinship even (or ever) matter to the Gende? The answer is yes, biological kinship does matter to a certain extent, and more in certain circumstances than in others. It is recognized among the Gende that biological parents contribute blood, semen, bone, and other physical matter to a growing fetus, while mothers provide milk for growing children. These contributions must be reciprocated. However, it takes many persons and many things and actions to raise a child and contribute to its physical and social well-being, so the Gende's concepts of parenthood and other "kin" relations go beyond simple biological or genetic relationships.

It is striking to me that even in the context of the dizzying ancestral gerrymandering going on at Kurumbukare in recent years, biological kinship appears to matter more to the losers in the Gende's great game of life than to men and women who are able to manage their ever-changing affairs with a reasonable amount of satisfaction for themselves and most of their "kin" and other exchange partners. An illustration of just how biological kinship does matter under certain circumstances, and how even the best of the transactors must consider it to some degree, involves the case of a Gende Big Man who was killed in a fight with an angry and dispossessed kinsman and some of the Big Man's sons and brothers who were all disappointed with the way "development"—or the lack of it—had failed to benefit them (Zimmer-Tamakoshi 1997b). The sense of injustice felt by the dispossessed kinsman very likely had been fueled by the years he spent in town becoming more accustomed to Western concepts of kinship, land tenure, and inheritance rules. The bottom line, however, was that he had never kept up his exchange obligations to village kin, that the Big Man had been a major contributor to the younger man's deceased father's *kwiagi,* and by doing so the Big Man had acquired use of much of the deceased man's garden lands. The younger man's attempt to argue that the land was his birthright, that he was his father's "only son" and, therefore, legitimate heir, left out the important reciprocal nature of all Gende "kin" relations. Put another way: "kinship" is an active process involving work, and for the Gende it is always a reciprocal process.

One final set of questions, to which I have few answers as yet, has to do with women and their access to land rights. *Kwiagi* are traditionally held for women as well as men, particularly in the cases of women who have lived a long time, raised many children and pigs, and invested heavily in the affairs of their husbands' clans. When such a woman dies, her "children," both "sons" and "daughters," as well as her husband's brothers and others of her husband's clan will make sure that her clan is amply repaid for the contributions she has made to their clan. Failure to do so is to insult the deceased's clan and to risk ancestral displeasure, physical combat, and possibly a land takeover. Throughout my landowners' survey, and in contrast to the rest of the extensive fieldwork I have carried out among the Gende, women were very much in the background and were never among the representatives interviewed on clan and group genealogies; they were often left out of the men's accounts as "irrelevant." This omission is strange, since women continue to contribute pigs to *kwiagi* and other transactions, thereby helping to create and maintain ties to land, facts that should include women in the pool of landowners who can expect to receive compensation payments from future mining operations at Kurumbukare.

Since I kept asking about the women, the men eventually began including sisters and mothers in their genealogies as well as brothers, fathers, and other male relatives. Why they left the women out in the first place seems to have something to do with Western concepts of "male head of household" and a Western misunderstanding of patrilineal systems, believing that things only pass down through males. Such models oppose Gende models of gender and kinship relations, in which wives may accumulate ties to their husbands' lands, and sisters may—and often do—assert rights to their own clan lands. Jane Fishburne Collier and Sylvia Junko Yanagisako (1987:29–35) acknowledge David Schneider's insights on kinship and kinship studies, particularly his critique of biological models of kinship, as opening the way for a clearer understanding of systems like those of the Gende. Western assumptions that males are heads of households and owners of land while women are the bearers and caretakers of children and the domestic sphere pervade both Western social science and the thinking of international mining company managers.

Needless to say, women were not happy about being left out, at least initially. They did not say much in front of the male leaders who controlled the interviews, but they did grumble about it in my presence, often hinting darkly that the men were up to something and that they did not like it. The women's discontents bode poorly for any smooth transition to well-compensated "landowners" in the region should the mines begin operating. Gende women have stopped development projects before when those projects failed to include women in the promise of prosperity for all (see Zimmer-Tamakoshi 1996). As at the Bougainville copper mine, chaos and civil war can result when women's rights are not considered in the deals and contracts made between mining companies, the state, and local peoples.

Notes

1. To be dispossessed is to lose ties; to repossess is to regain them, usually through exchange; and by "hyperpossessions" I mean to indicate that there are Big Men and Women today who are unusually wealthy and "come to possess" more relatives than one would normally have, even if ambitious.

2. *Wok meri* (literally, "women's work" in New Guinea pidgin English) are networks of small women's groups that save and invest money the women earn from coffee production and the sale of vegetables and other goods in urban markets in highlands Papua New Guinea. The women's purposes include enhancing their control over their earnings, improving their own and their families' socioeconomic status, and demonstrating to men how money can best be used and invested.

3. The Gende situation differs from a cognatic descent system in which an individual may assume membership in either the mother's or father's group, or even both. By contrast, in putatively unilineal systems like the Gende's, achieving membership in more than one clan, assuming that it is possible at all, entails heavy exchange obligations.

4. Some of my informants, however, expressed the opinion that a Western-educated judge would not accept their form of "kinship," expecting each claimant to be a member of either one clan or another.

5. See Richard Feinberg (1990) for a discussion of this and related issues.

References Cited

Aufenanger, H. 1979. *The Gende of Central New Guinea: Of the Life and Thought of a Tribe in the Bismarck Ranges, Papua New Guinea* (1940). Trans. P. W. Holzknecht. In *Oral History* 7 (8–9).

Collier, J. F., and S. J. Yanagisako. 1987. "Toward a Unified Analysis of Gender and Kinship." In *Gender and Kinship: Essays toward a Unified Analysis.* Ed. J. F. Collier and S. J. Yanagisako. 14–50. Stanford, Calif.: Stanford University Press.

Cook, E. A. 1970. "On the Conversion of Non-Agnates into Agnates among the Manga, Jimi River, Western Highlands District, New Guinea." *Southwestern Journal of Anthropology* 23:190–96.

————. 1980. "Manga Kinship Terminology." In *Blood and Semen: Kinship Systems of Highland New Guinea.* Ed. E. A. Cook and D. O'Brien. 397–422. Ann Arbor: University of Michigan Press.

Feil, D. K. 1984. *Ways of Exchange.* St. Lucia: University of Queensland Press.

Feinberg, R. 1990. "New Guinea Models on a Polynesian Outlier?" *Ethnology* 29 (1): 83–96.

Franco, R. W. 1993. "Movement and Samoan Marriage in Hawaii." In *The Business of Marriage: Transformations in Oceanic Matrimony.* Ed. R. A. Marksbury. 231–44. ASAO Monograph No. 14. Pittsburgh: University of Pittsburgh Press.

Hyndman, D. 1994. *Ancestral Rain Forests and the Mountain of Gold: Indigenous Peoples and Mining in New Guinea.* Boulder, Colo.: Westview Press.

Jorgensen, D. 1993. "Money and Marriage in Telefolmin: From Sister Exchange to Daughter as Trade Store." In *The Business of Marriage: Transformations in Oceanic Matrimony.* Ed. R. A. Marksbury. 57–82. ASAO Monograph No. 14. Pittsburgh: University of Pittsburgh Press.

Kirsch, S. 1997. "Indigenous Response to Environmental Impact Along the Ok Tedi." In *Compensation for Resource Development in Papua New Guinea.* Ed. S. Toft. 143–55. Papua New Guinea Law Reform Commission Monograph No. 6. Port Moresby.

Schneider, D. M. 1972. "What Is Kinship All About?" In *Kinship Studies in the Morgan Centennial Year.* Ed. P. Reining. 32–63. Washington, D.C.: Anthropological Society of Washington.

————. 1984. *A Critique of the Study of Kinship.* Ann Arbor: University of Michigan Press.

Sexton, L. 1982. "Wok Meri: A Woman's Savings and Exchange System in Highland New Guinea." *Oceania* 54:133–50.

————. 1986. *Mothers of Money, Daughters of Coffee: The Wok Meri Movement.* Ann Arbor: University of Michigan Press.

Sillitoe, P. 1979. *Give and Take.* New York: St. Martin's Press.

Strathern, A. 1971. *The Rope of Moka.* Cambridge: Cambridge University Press.

————. 1976. "Transactional Continuity in Mount Hagen." In *Transactions and Meaning.* Ed. B. Kapferer. 277–87. Philadelphia: Institute for the Study of Human Issues.

Tiffany, S. 1974. "The Land and Titles Court and the Regulation of Customary Title Successions and Removals in Western Samoa." *Journal of the Polynesian Society* 83:35–57.

Wesley-Smith, T. 1992. "Development and Crisis in Bougainville: A Bibliographic Essay." *Contemporary Pacific* 4:407–33.

Zimmer, L. J. 1986. "Card Playing among the Gende: A System for Keeping Money and Social Relationships 'Alive.'" *Oceania* 56 (4): 245–63.

————. 1987. "'Who Will Bury Me?': The Plight of Childless Elderly among the Gende." *Journal of Cross-Cultural Gerontology* 2:61–77.

————. 1990. "Conflict and Violence in Gende Society: Older Persons as Victims, Trouble-Makers, and Perpetrators." In *Domestic Violence in Oceania.* Ed. D. A. Counts. 205–24. Special issue of *Pacific Studies* 13 (3).

Zimmer-Tamakoshi, L. 1993. "Bachelors, Spinsters, and Pamuk Meris." In *The Business of Marriage: Transformations in Oceanic Matrimony.* Ed. R. A. Marksbury. 83–104. ASAO Monograph No. 14. Pittsburgh: University of Pittsburgh Press.

———. 1995. "Kurumbukare (Ramu) Landowners and Genealogical Survey." Prepared for Highlands Gold Ltd., Port Moresby, Papua New Guinea.

———. 1996. "The Women at Kobum Spice Company: Tensions in a Local Age Stratification System and the Undermining of Local Development." *Pacific Studies* 19 (4): 71–98.

———. 1997a. "Everyone (or No One) a Winner: Gende Compensation Ethics and Practices." In *Compensation for Resource Development in Papua New Guinea.* Ed. S. Toft. 66–83. Papua New Guinea Law Reform Commission Monograph No. 6. Port Moresby.

———. 1997b. "The Last Big Man: Development and Men's Discontents in the Papua New Guinea Highlands." *Oceania* 68 (2): 107–22.

———. 1997c. "When Land Has a Price: Ancestral Gerrymandering and the Resolution of Land Conflicts at Kurumbukare." In *Rights to Land and Resources in Papua New Guinea: Changing and Conflicting Views.* Ed. P. Brown and A. Ploeg. 649–66. Special issue of *Anthropological Forum* 7 (4).

———. 1998. "Women in Town: Housewives, Homemakers and Household Managers." In *Modern Papua New Guinea.* Ed. L. Zimmer-Tamakoshi. 195–210. Kirksville, Mo.: Thomas Jefferson University Press.

Conclusion: Muddles in Schneider's Model

WARD H. GOODENOUGH

DAVID SCHNEIDER and I were undergraduate classmates at Cornell, where, together with our future wives, we established a life-long friendship. Because David got his Ph.D. after I got mine, our graduate student careers (see Feinberg, this volume) inevitably led to a kind of sibling rivalry between us, David assuming what amounted to the role of younger sibling, though he was in fact a year older than me. At the same time we continued to be friends, so when David took issue with me on kinship in his book *A Critique of the Study of Kinship* (1984), he was concerned that he might anger me and spoil our friendship. He sent me a copy of the manuscript to give me a chance to tell him where he might be doing me an injustice. I pointed out a few matters of fact to correct, but advised him to go ahead and say his piece as he was saying it; we would still be friends. Our disagreement was such that there was no way I could ask him appropriately to revise what he was choosing to attribute to me without its spoiling his whole argument. Floyd Lounsbury and I were Schneider's straw men, especially in regard to how he chose to construe what we and other anthropologists understood by genealogy and kinship as anthropological concepts.

So what do I understand about these matters and other related issues discussed from various perspectives in this volume? These chapters raise a number of important issues. The meaning and uses of "cultural relativism" are explored (Montague, Zimmer-Tamakoshi, Leaf, Ottenheimer). Kinship and genealogy as useful anthropological concepts, which Schneider flatly rejected (1984), are questioned (Montague) or appraised (Read). Componential analysis, which was anathema to Schneider, is frequently discussed as a method for describing the denotative meanings of kinship terms (Fogelson; Read).

The notion that there is a philosophy of kinship which plays a fundamental role in human social values is persuasively argued (McKinley). In what follows I shall try to present my thinking on these issues.

The Natural Basis of Cultural Kinship and Genealogy

The majority of women must bear at least several children if a society is to replenish its population over time, let alone increase it. Given the prolonged dependency of children on adults for their survival, mothers tend to have several dependent young living with them at any one time during their child-bearing years. As a group, a mother and her children constitute a natural isolate in a human community as against other such mother-child groups. As the members of such a group look primarily to one another for mutual support, emotional bonds develop among them.

This, however, is only part of the basic human situation. Human mothers cannot provide adequately for their young without assistance (Hrdy 1999). But who are these helpers most likely to be? Those with whom close emotional in-group ties were established in childhood are likely to continue to lend support to the primary provider, especially the mother's siblings and mother's mother. Given the ubiquitous gendered division of labor, moreover, and differences in adult male and female roles, these others providing assistance need to include at least one adult male as provider, tutor, and role model for male children. Given the virtually universal avoidance of incest, women's sex partners as well as women's brothers become candidates for the role of male provider and tutor. A woman's sex partner may or may not be the genitor of her children. What is important is that he be in a continuing relationship with her. How these matters are handled varies across societies, which have different cultural understandings about them, but all human societies have to handle them in some way.

There are important consequences to this need for a male provider. One is a distinction between a male provider and tutor with whom a woman shares a dwelling and her male sibling with whom she shared a mother (and probably a male provider, as well). Another consequence, important for this discussion, is the development over time of clusters of these mother-children groups. The groups in these clusters, deriving from a common mother and perhaps mother's mother, are likely to feel more closely tied to one another than to members of other such clusters. Here are the natural roots of what we call "kinship," especially collateral kinship, for it is the ramifying numbers of such mother-children units that produce kindreds of one kind or another, as well as descent groups. A corollary of this development is the cultural construction of what Robert McKinley (this volume) labels "the philosophy of kinship."

Mothers' male consorts can also serve as referents for linked family clusters. Unless other factors intervene, those units that have branched off more recently will feel closer to one another than those that have branched off earlier from more distant common ancestry. Obviously, a number of other factors can serve to warp this symmetry, including geographic propinquity and the sharing of territory affected by residence customs, co-membership in larger social units (such as property-holding groups), and soured relations as a result of disputes or violations of social obligations. These considerations will be discussed later.[1] Whatever other factors are involved, the ramifications of nearer and remoter genealogical connection remain.

Genealogy

The genealogical method for studying kinship was developed by W. H. R. Rivers (1900). He found that by asking a society's members how people were connected genealogically, he could construct genealogies and then ask what kinship terms they used for the various people in the genealogies, referring to them by name only. I have myself employed the method with excellent and even surprising results in my research in Chuuk (Goodenough 1951).

When I and most other anthropological students of kinship use genealogy, we do not assume that it is a biological procreative pedigree, as Schneider and his followers, including some contributors to this volume, have chosen to assume. A genealogy does not necessarily show how people are biologically related; it is a ramifying chain of parent-child links and marital ties that are recognized as such by members of a society under study in accordance with their cultural criteria for doing so. Biological pedigrees may be needed for the genetic study of inherited diseases, but they are not the genealogies used in ethnographic practice by cultural anthropologists for getting at principles of family and kinship organization. The *citamangen-fak* (roughly "father-child") relationship in Yap is a recursive one re-created in each generation, producing a genealogical chain. Indeed, one can construct a genealogy out of any relationship that is recursively reproduced through time, such as master-apprentice and teacher-student relationships.

As properly used by anthropologists, then, genealogies are *not* ethnocentric projections of Euro-American folk cultural ideas about kinship and kin relatedness.[2] Unfortunately, anthropologists have made a distinction between kin who are connected by socially recognized parent-child links, which they call consanguineal, and kin to whom a person is connected by one or more

marital ties, which they call affinal. Such a distinction, with the term "consanguinity," reflects the Euro-American use of "blood" as the symbolic totem representing the mystical bond among those who consider themselves
to be kin. But the anthropological meaning of consanguinity should be distinguished from its meaning in Euro-American legal and folk cultural usage.
These meanings are easy to confuse, and anthropologists have consequently
questioned whether the term "consanguinity" (and "kinship" in the Euro-
American sense) should be applied to "father-child" links in societies such
as those in the Trobriand Islands, Yap, and Australia, where socially recognized paternity is not linked to biological procreation.

Along with genealogy, Schneider rejected componential analysis as a method for getting at the denotative meaning in referential usage of kinship terms
because it used so-called kin-type notation or genealogical diagramming (see
Read, this volume). He saw such usage as an ethnocentric projection on other
cultures of a biological model of kinship, but it was not. It was simply a notation for genealogical connections as defined by any particular culture's
construction of parent-child links.

Genealogies, then, and genealogical notations for analytic purposes are
applicable to societies such as the Trobriand Islanders and the Yapese, who
deny that paternity is biological, and to some Balkan societies that deny that
maternity is biological. In each case, members of the society use established
cultural principles to assign to a woman the role of or right to be the primary female nurturer of a neonate child and to assign to a man a role in relation to the child by virtue of his being or having been the recognized husband or sexual consort of the primary female nurturer. There is no society
without such cultural principles. They may involve folk-theories of biological procreation, such as the idea of shared body substance of some kind, or
they may not. Socially significant parenthood is a culturally defined relationship, not a purely biological one. And the jural content of parenthood (the
rights and obligations) is entirely defined by culture.

As I have discussed elsewhere in regard to child adoption (Goodenough
1970b), the rights and duties that constitute jural parenthood are transfer-
able in whole or in part and permanently or temporarily in many societies.
These transactions are again culturally specific. Adoption in the Euro-American sense is not a cultural universal, but transfers of one sort or another in
parental entitlements occur in many societies.

Confronting transfers of parental entitlements leads inevitably to the question of how such entitlements, whatever their content, are socially recognized
and thereby established in the first place. Clearly the process of biological
reproduction is in some way relevant, especially in establishing a claim to

motherhood in the sense of a right to be primary female nurturer. In Chuuk, traditionally, giving birth to a child was in itself sufficient. Being married to the birth-giver provided first claim to fatherhood as primary male provider. A Chuukese friend who had been childless in his first marriage and who had remarried a woman who was pregnant by her deceased husband wrote to me ecstatically about how now, at last, he would have a child of his own. That he was not the biological genitor was irrelevant. He gave land to that child, and the child's paternal genealogical links were through him.[3]

An instructive case is provided by the people of Mota in northern Vanuatu (Rivers 1914; Scheffler 1970). There, jural parenthood was established by the natural mother's husband when he paid the midwife's fee. If he was unable to pay, another man might step in and pay it, thus making himself the jural father and his wife the jural mother. The husband of the woman who bore the child had the right to redeem parental status for himself and his wife later at considerable cost. Even such an extreme case as this allows for the construction of genealogies through chains of socially recognized parent-child links.

Widespread is the cultural practice of recognizing what is technically a person's kindred—either the circle of recognized kin or of closer as distinct from more distant nominal kin. Closeness may be determined by degrees of genealogical distance, but more commonly it involves other considerations as well, such as whether and how well one has honored relationship obligations. In Kiribati, for example, one may maintain kin ties with genealogically more distant persons from whom one may have a chance of inheriting property as the nearest collateral and not maintain such ties with a genealogically closer person from whom one has no chance of inheriting property because there are closer intervening collaterals. Among the Lakalai of New Britain, those whose grandparents were members of the same sibling set (whether uterine siblings or cousins who got together to form a working sibling set) were expected to be members of one another's kindreds (Goodenough 1962, 1970a:49). The sibling set, however put together, was the point of reference for determining who were close kin beyond the nuclear and patrilocal extended families. As these examples indicate, what we are to mean by the term "kindred" in any particular ethnographic case has to be described for that case, the term acquiring a referent in that instance that may differ from its referent in any other. It follows that the anthropological concept of a personal "kindred" as a circle of putative genealogically connected relatives of various kinds, however the local culture may define membership in that circle, may be appropriately applied to societies like that of the Trobriand Islands, Susan P. Montague's argument (this volume) to the contrary not withstanding.

What the foregoing considerations indicate is that there is no disagreement between Schneider and me regarding the need for ethnographers to establish what the particular cultural (emic) system is for reckoning and thinking about kinship in each society studied. My account of social organization in Chuuk (Truk) was just such an undertaking (Goodenough 1951). This approach obviates the attribution of Euro-American folk cultural ideas about kinship to other societies. Schneider failed to face up to the fact that in order to describe customary practices and beliefs in their own terms one must have a system of metaconcepts as a point of departure for describing those terms and for establishing for comparative purposes what customs in one society are the analogs, functionally and structurally, of customs in other societies. This was the problem I undertook to address for kinship and marriage in *Description and Comparison in Cultural Anthropology* (Goodenough 1970a). Schneider refused to confront it and therefore, in effect, threw up his hands at the whole idea of cross-cultural comparability.

Kinship

As observed by all contributors to this volume, kinship involves much more than genealogical links and their analogical extensions. As anthropologists have always recognized and Schneider has emphasized, it consists of social relationships. These relationships are classified into types and different labels, that is, kinship terms, are attached to the most important. In Chuuk, for example, there are, among others, *saam-naaw* (which we may roughly gloss as "father-child"), *iin-naaw* (roughly "mother-child"), and *pwiipwi* (roughly "sibling of same sex") relationships. These relationships involve different rights and duties, as I have described in some detail (Goodenough 1951:11–119, 1965a), and they also have different emotional loading. When people enter into nonkin relationships to which they give the rights and duties of a kin relationship, they may analogically extend kin terms to these relationships. Thus Americans may say, "We are like brothers." In Chuuk, people who are close friends will say publicly, "We are in a *pwiipwi* relationship," and expect others to recognize it. In America and Chuuk alike, people recognize that these relationships are modeled on genealogically based relationships and that they are not "true" in this latter sense.

Kin relationships may also serve as the model for peaceful social relationships generally (DeMallie, this volume; McKinley, this volume). There are societies in which all people who have social dealings with one another do so as nominal rather than close kin and interact in terms of the etiquette, taboos, and licenses of kinship roles. The Moala of Fiji (Sahlins 1962), the

Lakalai of New Britain (Chowning 1966; Chowning and Goodenough 1966), as well as many local castes in South Asia provide examples. Here the way to establish the nominal kin relationship between any two people is to find how each relates to a third party known to both of them. Among the Lakalai, for example, if such a third party is my "maternal uncle" and your "father," then we are cross-cousins. Among the Moala and the Lakalai, people may try out what they are to one another through more than one third party in order to establish the relationship they want, for example, "cross-cousin" or "parallel cousin." In such societies, of course, marriages are necessarily with relatives, at least nominal ones, of some kind. Caution must be observed in interpreting such arrangements in regard to possible preferential marriages. If one may not marry a nominal "sibling" but only a nominal "cross-cousin," it does not necessarily follow that cross-cousin marriage is a preferred form of marriage. It may mean that this is the only large set of nominal kin from which one can take a spouse. In that case, it is not a matter of preference but of eligibility.

Such social uses of kin relationships as models for social organization generally or as models for voluntary contractual relationships rest, of course, on close, genealogically based kin relationships, however these are culturally understood and whatever the ideology of kinship may be.

Kinship and Descent

Rivers (1924:86) and George Peter Murdock (1949:15) have both pointed out that descent as a theory of kinship should not be confused with descent as a principle for allocating membership in a social group or category. They advocated using the term "descent" to refer to principles of allocating membership in ancestor-based kin groups, and so the term has been used by most trained anthropologists, who refer to patrilineal, matrilineal, and cognatic descent as principles of such allocation. Schneider and Kathleen Gough (1961) used the expression "matrilineal kinship" in the title of an outstanding volume they edited, but they used it in reference to how the presence of matrilineal descent groups affected kinship roles and kinship ideology. They did not mean to imply that in the presence of such descent groups kinship, as a set of genealogically based relationships, is reckoned only through women. Indeed, personal kindreds in almost all societies with matrilineal descent groups include kin through fathers as well as through mothers. The Nayar of southwestern India have presented a possible exception (Gough 1961; Goodenough 1970a). Similarly, kindreds in societies with patrilineal descent groups also include kin through the mother. Kinship through the father may be seen as based on different principles than kinship through the mother, a not uncommon cultural construction; but kinship reckoning in any case involves the use of genealogies as chains of socially recognized parent-child links.

As Schneider pointed out (1961), in the presence of matrilineal (and, I should add, patrilineal) descent groups, fellow members of such groups necessarily have a special relationship with one another that differs from their relationship with other kin who are not fellow members. With land-holding matrilineal descent groups, for example, maternal uncles are likely to be allocated authority that they do not have in the absence of such groups. At the same time, fathers, who lack authority roles, may have important nurturing roles, as in the Trobriand Islands (Malinowski 1929; Montague, this volume) and among the Lakalai (Chowning and Goodenough 1966; Chowning 1966).

While we classify descent groups as matrilineal, patrilineal, and cognatic, it is necessary to remember that the cultural principles giving rise to any one of these types are not identical cross-societally. An ethnographer has the responsibility of determining what the cultural principles are in each case. To talk about such groups in ethnographic accounts, we necessarily use such terms as lineage and clan, but we must make clear what these terms are referring to. A matrilineal lineage in Chuuk is not organized on the same principles as a matrilineal lineage in Lakalai. The same consideration holds for kindreds, whose boundaries vary across cultures, as well as for any other social institution.

Do such culturally different specifics mean that everything is relative and noncomparable? Of course not. Comparison is always done with respect to the search for cross-societal regularities and significant differences relating to specific cultural or social variables. Granted that matrilineal lineages differ in some respects cross-culturally, do societies with matrilineal descent groups nevertheless differ significantly in some cultural respects from societies that lack them? Such questions have occupied students of kinship and social organization, including, of course, Schneider and Gough (1961), for well over a hundred years. I have discussed the methodological issues in such comparison at length and need not recapitulate them here (Goodenough 1970a).

Kinship in Theory and Kinship in Practice

In any community, there is a system of kin relationships and expected behavior that serves as a basis for judging what actually goes on in social interaction. Two men are known to be brothers in fact and are expected, therefore, to be mutually supportive, but they are bitter rivals or go their own way independently of one another. Such does not invalidate the system of expectations. Indeed, the brothers are likely to be pointed to as examples of how not to behave. I have described in some detail an incident in Chuuk of behavior among kin that was inappropriate (Goodenough 1965a).

A kinship system is also subject to manipulation, as observed by Zimmer-Tamakoshi (this volume). People may falsely claim descent from a long-deceased property holder in order to acquire rights to that property or, for the same reasons, claim membership in a clan. Indeed, genealogies are falsified for all kinds of reasons. Such falsification requires the existence of something to be falsified; it does not mean that there is no cultural system. When circumstances encourage mass manipulation of a system, a group's common understanding of the system and how it is supposed to work may become sufficiently eroded as to lead to major changes in it or to its complete dissolution.

Componential Analysis

There has been widespread misunderstanding of componential analysis as a method for describing the structure of meaning inherent in the use of kinship terms. Since factors such as social context, who is speaking to whom, and so forth, affect how these terms are used, I have insisted that such analysis be confined, especially for comparative purposes, to denotative use in answer to the question of social fact, what is A to B? A is B's sister in English, for example. A is B's *feefinan* ("his female sibling of opposite sex") in Chuukese. Note that in each case one uses a possessive construction. The answer to the question does not indicate a kind of person, but a kind of relationship of one person to another. Schneider's allegation that componential analysis does not deal with kin relationships but with persons as objects of some kind (Leaf, this volume; Read, this volume) is in error.

As I have described it (Goodenough 1965b, 1968), the method requires identifying clusters of kin terms that are reciprocal in use (i.e., labeling social relationships), with as many as needed for reciprocal closure (e.g., "father," "mother," "son," "daughter" in English), then finding semantic features that will differentiate among these clusters, before getting down to the features that will differentiate one term from another within a cluster (e.g., "sex of alter in the relationship" as with English "father" and "mother," and generation difference and seniority as with "mother" and "daughter"). In some terminologies, moreover, there are sets of terms that take modifiers. The two modifiers "step-" and "-in-law" in English usage, for example, can properly be applied only to the set of terms "father," "mother," "son," "daughter," "brother," sister." The modifier "great" or "grand" can be applied only to the terms "grandfather," "grandmother," "grandson," "granddaughter," "uncle," "aunt," "niece," "nephew," and the modifiers "first, second" and "once, twice removed" can be applied only to "cousin." These make up the first order of complementary, contrasting sets to be semantically differentiated in a componential analysis of English kin terms (Goodenough 1965b). People who have undertaken to do componential analysis on their own without having been trained in how to do it, have, by my standards, usually made a poor job of it.

There are alternative approaches to componential analysis. Floyd G. Lounsbury (1964) has applied rewrite rules to kin-type notation and defined primary meanings in regard to the nearest kin type a term can denote, and then, through the rewrite rules, generated the more distant kin types to which the term can also be applied. Dwight W. Read (this volume) begins with terms for nearest possible kin types and then derives secondary meanings for these terms and for other terms as relative products of the basic set. Thus one's "uncle" in English folk usage is defined as one's "father's brother" or "mother's brother." Read correctly observes that children learn who their kin are and what terms to apply to them arbitrarily with explanations given in terms of relative products. "She is your cousin because she is my father's cousin" is how we are taught. But what we don't get taught this way is why being my father's cousin makes her my cousin rather than my aunt. That is, we are not taught the semantic structure of the terminological system. We are left to infer it. Only after we have grasped that semantic structure can we generate for our children such explanatory statements.

Relative products are used similarly to explain relationships in Chuuk. "He is your *saam* because he is the *pwii* of your *saam*," meaning "he is your male kin in senior generation to you because he is the same-sex, same-generation kin of your (nearest understood) male kin in senior generation to you." (This example shows clearly why one prefers to translate this as "he is your 'father' because he is 'same-sex sibling' of your 'father,'" having first defined what "father" is a gloss of in Chuukese.) Again, one learns this arbitrarily as a child, but in due course one learns the semantic role of same and different generation distinctions in order to be able to generate such an explanation to someone else. Generation distinctions are, of course, genealogical, being based on chains of socially recognized parent-child links, as I have already indicated. To be able to generate reliable and intelligible relative-product statements, one must, in short, be culturally competent in the same way that one must be linguistically competent to generate new grammatically and semantically acceptable and intelligible utterances.

Componential analysis is a method for constructing testable models of the content of such competence, much of which lies below the level of conscious awareness. That such competence, where kinship terms are involved, should include across cultures at least a subjective understanding of generation and hence of genealogy is not surprising, given the universality of social reproduction through the process of bearing and rearing children, who in turn bear and rear children. It is important to note that the different methods for describing the denotative meanings of kinship terms produce results that can all be mapped into one another and that account for usage. It follows that the subjective models people acquire that enable them to generate the appropriate use of kinship terms are not necessarily identical. There is no "true" model for a society as a whole. Any model that enables one to generate the socially acceptable use of the terms is ethnographically valid. It belongs to a population of such valid models. We may judge among different but equally valid models on the basis of such scientific criteria as simplicity and elegance. But the simplest and most elegant may not be what many of the people under study have in mind.

When one compares the results of componential analysis cross-culturally, one finds that the differences in the denotative semantic structures among different kinship terminologies indicate precisely what is to be meant by cultural relativism and the problems of translating from one language into another. Cultural relativism does not make such translation impossible, but what the problems are and what are the bases for cross-linguistic misunderstanding need to be precisely indicated. For the limited cultural domain to which it applies, componential analysis does that. It does not deny cultural relativity, but provides a basis for bridging it.

Relativism

Cultural relativism and cross-cultural commensurability are vigorously debated matters these days (e.g., Leaf and Ottenheimer, both this volume). It should be clear from what I have been saying that for all our cultural differences, there are underlying structural and cultural constants deriving from our psychobiological nature (Goodenough 1980). People must eat to live, and we recognize that all societies have customary activities oriented toward obtaining, distributing, preparing, and consuming food. The customary expectations relating to these things vary considerably. What is a delicacy for one group is abhorrent to another. I was told in Kiribati that eating chicken eggs was disgusting, but people there relished eating fish eyes. Such is cultural relativity in spades. Yet we all engaged in eating. A cross-cultural study of differences and similarities in obtaining and consuming food does not strike us as impossible because cultures are incommensurate. Similarly, different languages have very different phonological systems, but they all have systems that can be described by the same data-gathering and analytical procedures. The underlying functional and structural constants in human existence do not determine the precise content of any culture, but they provide constraints on the range of variation that cultural content can readily take. The universal ramifying process of bearing children and the universal need to allocate responsibility for nurturing, socializing, and educating them are what underlie the universal applicability of the *anthropological* concept of kinship.

Conclusion

Clearly, I fundamentally disagree with Schneider about the utility for anthropology of the concept of kinship. In this I agree with most of the contributors to this volume. If a guiding concern of anthropology is to provide insight into the human condition, a concern to which I subscribe, cross-cultural comparison is essential, and kinship has long provided some of the best data for such comparison. Yet, as Richard Feinberg, Raymond D. Fogelson, Murray J. Leaf, Read, and Martin Ottenheimer (all this volume) point out, Schneider's notion of culture makes such comparison and generalization all but impossible. This limitation of his approach is well exemplified by his abandonment of kinship as a viable topic for cross-cultural analysis. Along with most of this book's contributors, I reject Schneider's version of cultural relativism and its negative implications for anthropological theory.

Accordingly, I have tried to show how Schneider at times distorted his colleagues' and predecessors' positions in order to differentiate his approach from theirs. We can see this in the way he misrepresents "genealogy" and its use in kinship studies. Unfortunately, some of Schneider's students have uncritically accepted his caricature of his adversaries' views. In that respect I hope I have helped to set the record straight.

Although I disagree with the excesses in many of Schneider's theoretical pronouncements, I do consider his paper on "matrilineal kinship" (1961) a major contribution. More importantly, I hold his ethnographic work in high regard. Yap is a complex and ethnographically challenging society. Although Schneider disparaged his fieldwork in his later years, he helped reveal Yap's social organization and courtship practices. His insistence, in which he was far from alone, that ethnographers approach each culture "in its own terms," attempt to learn the meanings of its symbols, and follow those meanings wherever they might lead has stimulated excellent ethnography by many of his students (including Raymond J. DeMallie, Leaf, and Montague, who are contributors to this volume). As noted in several of the preceding chapters, Schneider has inspired innovative research in feminist, gay, and lesbian studies and has generated new ways of looking at Pacific Island cultures. As McKinley (this volume) aptly notes, Schneider often was infuriating. Yet he raised compelling questions and presented them in a way that did not permit their being ignored. The need to respond to his challenges has forced many of us to clarify our positions for the betterment of anthropology.

Notes

1. For examples of asymmetrical kindreds, see Goodenough (1970a).

2. As Rivers (1915:700) said, "Kinship cannot be determined and defined by consanguinity even among ourselves, still less among other peoples" (see Scheffler 1970:372). I agree with Harold Scheffler that all systems of social relationship recognized by anthropologists cross-culturally as kin relationships are rooted in parturition, but I also agree with Rivers that such a state of affairs does not imply the Euro-American concept of consanguinity.

3. In the United States, we should note, an adopted child's significant kin ties follow genealogical links through the adoptive parents, not the biological genitor and genetrix, even though they are considered to be fictive links, as noted by Scheffler (1970:372).

References Cited

Chowning, Ann. 1966. "Lakalai Kinship." *Anthropological Forum* 1:476–501.

Chowning, Ann, and Ward H. Goodenough. 1966. "Lakalai Political Organization." *Anthropological Forum* 1:412–73.

Goodenough, Ward H. 1951. *Property, Kin, and Community on Truk.* Yale University Publications in Anthropology No. 46. New Haven, Conn.

———. 1962. "Kindred and Hamlet in Lakalai, New Britain." *Ethnology* 1:5–12.

———. 1965a. "Rethinking 'Status' and 'Role': Toward a General Model of the Cultural Organization of Social Relationships." In *The Relevance of Models for Social Anthropology.* Ed. Michael Banton. 1–24. ASA Monograph No. 1. London: Tavistock.

———. 1965b. "Yankee Kinship Terminology: A Problem in Componential Analysis." In *Formal Semantic Analysis.* Ed. E. A. Hammel. 259–87. Special issue of *American Anthropologist* 67 (5), pt. 2.

———. 1968. "Componential Analysis." In *International Encyclopedia of the Social Sciences.* 3:186–92. New York: Macmillan and The Free Press.

———. 1970a. *Description and Comparison in Cultural Anthropology.* Chicago: Aldine.

———. 1970b. "Epilogue: Transactions in Parenthood." In *Adoption in Eastern Oceania.* Ed. Vern Carroll. 391–410. Honolulu: University of Hawai'i Press.

———. 1980. "Some Reflections on the Common Denominator of Cultures." *SCCR Newsletter* 8 (1): 10–18

Gough, Kathleen. 1961. "The Nayar: Central Kerala." In *Matrilineal Kinship*. Ed. David M. Schneider and Kathleen Gough. 298–384. Berkeley: University of California Press.

Hrdy, Sarah Blaffer. 1999. *Mother Nature: A History of Mothers, Infants, and Natural Selection*. New York: Pantheon Books.

Lounsbury, Floyd G. 1964. "The Formal Analysis of Crow- and Omaha-Type Kinship Terminologies." In *Explorations in Cultural Anthropology: Essays in Honor of George Peter Murdock*. Ed. Ward H. Goodenough. 351–93. New York: McGraw-Hill.

Malinowski, Bronislaw. 1929. *The Sexual Life of Savages*. London: G. Routledge and Sons.

Murdock, George Peter. 1949. *Social Structure*. New York: Macmillan.

Rivers, W. H. R. 1900. "A Genealogical Method of Collecting Social and Vital Statistics." *Journal of the Royal Anthropological Institute* 30:74–82.

———. 1914. *The History of Melanesian Society*. 2 vols. Cambridge: Cambridge University Press.

———. 1915. "Kin, Kinship." In *Encyclopedia of Religion and Ethics*. Ed. J. Hastings. 8:700–707.

———. 1924. *Social Organization*. New York: Knopf.

Sahlins, Marshall D. 1962. *Moala: Culture and Nature on a Fijian Island*. Ann Arbor: University of Michigan Press.

Scheffler, H. W. 1970. "Kinship and Adoption in the Northern New Hebrides." In *Adoption in Eastern Oceania*. Ed. Vern Carroll. 369–89. Honolulu: University of Hawai'i Press.

Schneider, David M. 1961. "Introduction: The Distinctive Features of Matrilineal Descent Groups." In *Matrilineal Kinship*. Ed. David M. Schneider and Kathleen Gough. 1–29. Berkeley: University of California Press.

———. 1984. *A Critique of the Study of Kinship*. Ann Arbor: University of Michigan Press.

Schneider, David M., and Kathleen Gough, eds. 1961. *Matrilineal Kinship*. Berkeley: University of California Press.

Contributors

Raymond J. DeMallie (Ph.D., Chicago, 1971) is a professor of anthropology and director of the American Indian Studies Research Institute, Indiana University at Bloomington. Among his many publications are *North American Indian Anthropology: Essays in Society and Culture* (1994), coedited with Alfonso Ortiz, and the forthcoming Plains volume of *Handbook of North American Indians,* for which he served as editor. He has worked extensively with the Sioux and Assiniboine in North Dakota, South Dakota, and Montana, and is particularly interested in Plains Indian peoples and the development of cultural approaches to understanding the American Indian past.

Richard Feinberg (Ph.D., Chicago, 1974) is a professor of anthropology at Kent State University. His publications include *Anuta: Social Structure of a Polynesian Island* (1981), *Polynesian Seafaring and Navigation: Ocean Travel in Anutan Culture and Society* (1988), the edited volume *Leadership and Change in the Western Pacific* (1996), and *Oral Traditions of Anuta* (1998). The major focus of his research during three decades of studying Pacific Island peoples has been remote Polynesian communities in the Solomon Islands and Papua New Guinea.

Raymond D. Fogelson (Ph.D., Pennsylvania, 1962) has taught anthropology at the University of Chicago for more than thirty-five years. Among his many publications is the forthcoming Southeast volume of the *Handbook of North American Indians,* for which he serves as editor. His areas of interest include native North America, particularly the Cherokee and Muskogee peoples, as well as psychological anthropology, religion, ethnohistory, deltiology, and cryptozoology.

Ward H. Goodenough (Ph.D., Yale, 1949) is University Professor Emeritus of Anthropology at the University of Pennsylvania. His publications include *Property, Kin, and Community on Truk* (1951), *Description and Comparison in Cultural Anthropology* (1970), and *Culture, Language, and Society* (1971; rpt., 1981). He has conducted extensive ethnographic research in Micronesia and Papua New Guinea. The American Anthropological Association honored him with its Distinguished Service Award in 1986.

Murray J. Leaf (Ph.D., Chicago, 1966) is a professor of anthropology and political economy at the University of Texas at Dallas. His publications include *Information and Behavior in a Sikh Village: Social Organization Reconsidered* (1972), *Man, Mind, and Science: A History of Anthropology* (1978), and *Pragmatism and Development: The Prospect for Pluralist Transformation in the Third World* (1998). His research interests have consistently focused on the relationship between social organization and thought and on the problem of developing formal techniques by which the internal order of cultural systems can be found rather than imposed.

Robert McKinley (Ph.D., Michigan, 1975) is an associate professor of religious studies at Michigan State University. He has published on Malay kinship and religion, headhunting rituals in Southeast Asia, ideological aspects of the famous Crow and Omaha kinship terminologies, and theoretical understandings of the phenomenon of culture in the journal *Man* and various edited collections. His current work focuses on Malay notions of intersubjectivity, contemporary religious pluralism, prestate regional interactions, and the uniqueness of anthropology as a way of knowing.

Susan P. Montague (Ph.D., Chicago, 1974), a cultural anthropologist who specializes in cosmology, teaches at Northern Illinois University. She is the coeditor of *The American Dimension: Cultural Myths and Social Realities* (2d ed., 1981) and has published articles on Trobriand Island mortuary rituals, attitudes toward education and alcohol, interisland trade, and uses of Christianity in *The Journal of Anthropology, Mankind,* and several edited collections. She has conducted extensive fieldwork in the Trobriand Islands and also works in the area of American culture, primarily focusing on success models.

Martin Ottenheimer (Ph.D., Tulane, 1971) is a professor of anthropology at Kansas State University. His publications include *Marriage in Domoni* (1985; rpt., 1994), *Modeling Systems of Kinship and Marriage* (1992), and *Forbidden Relatives: The American Myth of Cousin Marriage* (1996). He has conducted extensive ethnographic research in the western Indian Ocean and in the area of kinship analysis.

Dwight W. Read (Ph.D., UCLA, 1970) is a professor of anthropology and statistics at the University of California at Los Angeles. He has edited two special issues of the *Journal of Quantitative Anthropology,* one on "Computer-Based Solutions to Anthropological Problems" (1990) and another on "Formal Methods in Anthropology: Past Successes and New Directions" (1993). As part of his current research on the interrelationship between the material and the ideational domains in human societies, he has developed a major computer program, Kinship Algebraic Expert System (KAES), that constructs a formal (algebraic) model of the logic underlying the structure of a kinship terminology.

Laura Zimmer-Tamakoshi (Ph.D., Bryn Mawr, 1985) is an associate professor of anthropology at Truman State University and the media review editor for *Pacific Studies.* She has published many articles on her work in Papua New Guinea, constructed an award-winning fieldwork Web site <http://www.truman.edu/academics/ss/faculty/tamakoshil/index.html>, and edited the collection *Modern Papua New Guinea* (1998). Since 1982 her work in Papua New Guinea has focused on social and economic change, gender, nationalism and sexuality, domestic violence and rape, and land compensation issues relating to inequality and unequal development.

Index

Composed in 10.5/13 Minion
with Minion display
by Jim Proefrock
at the University of Illinois Press
Manufactured by Cushing-Malloy, Inc.

University of Illinois Press
1325 South Oak Street
Champaign, IL 61820-6903
www.press.uillinois.edu